Fabulous Female Firsts

Because of Them We Can

ALSO BY
MARLENE WAGMAN-GELLER

Women of Means: Fascinating Biographies of Royals, Heiresses, Eccentrics, and Other Poor Little Rich Girls

Great Second Acts: In Praise of Older Women

Women Who Launch: Women Who Shattered Glass Ceilings

Still I Rise: The Persistence of Phenomenal Women

Behind Every Great Man: The Forgotten Women Behind the World's Famous and Infamous

And the Rest is History: The Famous (and Infamous) First Meetings of the World's Most Passionate Couples Eureka! The Surprising Stories Behind the Ideas That Shaped the World

Once Again to Zelda: The Stories Behind Literature's Most Intriguing Dedications

Fabulous Female Firsts

Because of Them We Can

Marlene Wagman-Geller

mango
PUBLISHING
CORAL GABLES

Cover Design: Jayoung Hong
Cover Photo: Shutterstock/Janet Reno, Sandra Day O'Connor, Sally
Ride, Kathryn Bigelow, Aretha Franklin, Madeleine Albright
Layout & Design: Jayoung Hong

For permission requests, please contact the publisher at:
Mango Publishing Group
2850 S Douglas Road, 2nd Floor
Coral Gables, FL 33134 USA
info@mango.bz

For special orders, quantity sales, course adoptions and corporate
sales, please email the publisher at sales@mango.bz. For trade
and wholesale sales, please contact Ingram Publisher Services at
customer.service@ingramcontent.com or +1.800.509.4887.

Fabulous Female Firsts: Because of Them We Can

Library of Congress Cataloging-in-Publication number: 2019948835
ISBN: (p) 978-1-64250-180-3 (e) 978-1-64250-181-0
BISAC category code BIO022000—BIOGRAPHY &
AUTOBIOGRAPHY / Women

Printed in the United States of America

To my Female Firsts: My mother, Gilda Wagman
My daughter, Jordanna Geller

"We can do it!"

—Rosie the Riveter

Table of Contents

Prologue

Let's Hear It
for the Girls!

No matter how near we are to our biblically allotted
three score years and ten, we always remember
our milestone firsts: first kiss, first car, first horizontal
episode. Mothers are likewise big on firsts: the first word
their child speaks, first step, first lost tooth. These events
constitute the magical moments, forever tucked away in
the tissue paper of the heart.

While these firsts serve as the Proustian madeleine that
summons remembrance of things past, trailblazing
women opened doors that affected the world, thereby
allowing entry to those who followed. Because of these
pioneers, generations of women have felt empowered to
reach for their own brass rings. The runner-ups make the
hole wider and the edges duller until the ceiling starts to
disappear, leaving behind the oasis of opportunity.

Of course, behind their monumental achievements lies an unfortunate truth: had gender discrimination not been entrenched since Eve caused the exit from Eden, women's entry into erstwhile all-male domains would have raised nary an eyebrow. The fact that intrepid females used their variations of battering rams to muscle their way into the realm of equality is all the more remarkable as they did so against a prevailing zeitgeist that dictated they were not welcome in the polling stations, pinnacles of power, or boardrooms. Rather, the bedroom and the kitchen were their domains. The triumph of female accomplishments is enhanced by their having succeeded despite biblical and societal sexism.

When I was coming of age in my Torontonian hometown, the boys took shop class; the girls attended home economics classes—the other type of economics was never in our purview. And why would it be? After all, we were going to be wives, and our husbands would worry about all matters financial. Similarly, at recess, while the guys raced by on the school's skating rink, dreaming of becoming the next Bobby Orr, gals congregated on the non-icy patches of the playground. Our accomplishment was mastering the intricacies of Double Dutch on our skipping-ropes while belting out the equally difficult task of correctly spelling M-I-S-S-I-S-S-I-P-P-I, the rhyme that accompanied our jumps. We did not aspire to more athletic pursuits because no sports scholarships existed for our gender, and thus, there was a lack of parental nudging. Inside our school, the teachers were predominantly female; the principals were men. At home, our mothers greeted us with cookies and milk and the admonishment to be on our best behavior so as not to tax our fathers after a hard day at the office. Given such a non-fertile environment, my friends and I only competed to be the first to be married, the first to own a house, the first to procreate. Perhaps in some future utopian clime, our daughters will look at the concept of glass ceilings as baby boomers do bobby socks, saddle shoes, and poodle skirts—as a nod to a bygone milieu.

Hope is on the horizon. Language is a litmus test of societal mores, and the sexist diction of my youth has gone the way of the dodo: postman, policeman, fireman; the titles Mrs. and Miss have evolved to Ms. In 2017, Merriam-Webster chose their word of the year, one that speaks to possibilities rather than limitations. Their decision was based on the avalanche of online hits after three events from that year: the Women's March, the movie *Wonder Woman*, and the hashtag #MeToo; the word was "feminism."

Currently, on a similar wave of optimism, a number of female advancements in key leadership roles in business, higher education, and government are a sign that the winds of change are blowing. For example, the College of William & Mary, the second oldest institution of higher education in the United States, recently named Katherine Rowe its first-ever female president. The 2018 midterm election witnessed a record number of women elected to Congress, including several firsts: the first Native American woman, Muslim woman, and Somali-

American woman, the first openly LGBT woman, and the youngest woman.

Hillary Clinton took her best shot to strike a hammer blow at the glass ceiling in the political arena when she became the first female major party presidential nominee in United States history. She acknowledged this momentous occasion in a video played at the Democratic National Convention where her face appeared among shards of glass after a montage of previous all-male presidents. She had planned to hold her election night celebration in Manhattan's Jacob K. Jarvis Convention Center, which has a literal glass ceiling. In her concession speech, she metaphorically crossed her fingers, saying, "I know we have still not shattered that highest and hardest glass ceiling, but someday, someone will." Indeed, that will be a monumental first.

The concept of female firsts is a shout-out to those who have refused to view anatomy as an impediment to success. As Susan B. Anthony so eloquently expressed in her writings on the need for gender equality, "Men their rights and nothing more / Women their rights and nothing less." Because ladies were able to rise above chastity belts, bound feet, and corseted bodies, they deserve the shout-out, "Let's hear it for the girls!"

Chapter 1

Quite Contrary
(1865)

I n the film *Forrest Gump,* Lieutenant Dan snarls at
Forrest, saying, "They gave you, an imbecile and
a moron, the Congressional Medal of Honor." While
President Johnson conferred the award for Gump's valor
in Vietnam, an earlier President Johnson conferred the
award for a lady's valor in the Civil War. Dr. Mary Edward
Walker was the first and the only woman to have received
the Medal of Honor.

In 1862, Abraham Lincoln signed a bill introducing the
Medal of Honor for the bravest of the brave in the field of
battle. The original design depicted Minerva, the Roman
goddess of War and Wisdom (though the two traits seem
paradoxical), banishing the allegorical figure of Discord.
Ironically, although a female figure was emblazoned

on the award, in the nineteenth-century zeitgeist, it belonged in the domain of men.

While there is a Miss Congeniality pageant title, if there were one for Ms. Unconventionality, it could well have gone to a woman born in 1832 in Oswego, New York, the youngest of the seven children of Alvah and Vesta Walker. They gave their youngest daughter, Mary, the middle name of Edward, and christened her sisters Vesta, Aurora Borealis, and Luna. The Walkers were freethinkers and abolitionists whose home was a stop on the Underground Railroad. They embraced a radical philosophy for their era and raised their offspring devoid of traditional gender roles. The Walkers eschewed dresses as they considered corsets and tight lacing an impediment to circulation and long skirts a magnet for germs. Because of Mary's clothes, boys pelted her with rocks; as an adult, her unorthodox manner of dress resulted in an arrest. She said that nobody would ever know what she had to go through just to step out of the door each morning. On one occasion, criticized for wearing pants, she insisted, "I don't wear men's clothes. I wear my own clothes."

Because of their different drummer values, Alvah and Vesta founded their own elementary school, and they taught their pupils to be independent thinkers. During her free time, Mary pored over her father's medical journals—he was a self-taught physician—and eagerly read newspaper accounts of the first Women's Rights Convention held in nearby Seneca Falls. Mary enrolled in the progressive Falley Seminary in Fulton, New

York, and as with most educated women of her time, became a teacher; she then obtained a position in Minetto. She earned enough money to attend Syracuse Medical College (the first institute for physicians in the United States to admit both sexes on an equal basis) and graduated with honors in 1858, the only female in her class and the second in the country to earn a medical degree.

In 1856, Mary married fellow physician and freethinker Albert Miller; both bride and groom wore a suit and top hat. Other nontraditional twists were Mary did not take her husband's last name and refused to repeat the vow "promise to obey." The couple established a private practice in Rome, New York, but neither it nor their relationship proved a success. Patients did not care to visit the cross-dressing Dr. Walker, and Albert's "freethinking" extended to adultery. Mary left them both behind in 1859 and petitioned for a divorce that the court took ten years to grant.

As news of the devastating number of casualties at the Battle of Chickamauga in 1863—the second bloodiest battle of the Civil War—spread through the country, Mary tried desperately to obtain a commission in the Army's Medical Department. Since the beginning of the conflict, she had worked as a volunteer at a makeshift hospital set up in the Patent Office in Washington and had treated wounded troops on the battlefields in Warrenton and Fredericksburg, Virginia. But what she really wanted, and what she was repeatedly denied because of her gender, was a surgeon's commission that would have allowed her to use her skills to save more lives. Dr. Walker could have served disguised as a man, something nearly four hundred women resorted to in the Civil War, but she never considered that option. Mary wanted women to receive public acknowledgement for their efforts, and obscuring her sex would have negated her goal.

Undeterred, Mary went to the Secretary of War, Edwin M. Stanton, and presented herself as a dedicated physician. He found Walker's attire reprehensible and held firm in his refusal to commission a woman for any rank other than nurse. Unwilling to accept his decision, in 1864, Mary wrote a letter to President Lincoln stating that she had been denied a commission "solely on the ground of sex" and requested "a surgeon's commission with orders to go whenever and wherever there is a battle." Lincoln replied that he could not interfere with the Army's Medical Department.

In contrast, Dr. J.N. Green, the lone doctor of the Indiana Hospital, was grateful for her assistance and gladly took her on as a volunteer. In addition, he petitioned Attorney General Clement A. Finley to formally grant Dr. Walker a position so she could receive a salary, a request Finley denied. Nevertheless, Mary designed a blue uniform, replete with a green sash, the sign of a battlefield physician. Proud of her service, Walker wrote, "I let my curls grow while I was in the army so that everybody would know I was a woman."

The Indiana Hospital soon received more doctors who immediately conflicted with the sole female surgeon. They regarded practicing next to a female as "a medical monstrosity." A further source of animosity arose when the Sanitary Commission recommended amputations whenever a limb had sustained a serious injury, a practice Dr. Walker described as "wickedly cruel." She surreptitiously told the wounded to refuse the operation, and after the War, many wrote letters of appreciation for saving both their extremities and their lives. As news of her medical prowess spread, there was an outcry to grant her an official post. The Board of Medical Officers agreed to review her case, but their representative, Dr. G. Perin, without watching her operate, dismissed her skills as "not greater than most housewives possess."

Dr. Walker proved to be an intrepid soldier and was not afraid to cross enemy lines. Confederate soldiers became accustomed to the sight of the unconventional woman, who one described as "a thing that nothing but the debased and depraved Yankee nation could produce... She was not good-looking, and of course had tongue enough for a regiment of men." For once, the Union soldiers concurred with the Confederacy.

While on these missions, Walker collected information on the enemy, and during an assignation, she gleaned information that led Major General William T. Sherman to modify his war operations, thus staving off defeat. Despite her success, the days of the doctor-turned-spy came with a short expiration date. A Confederate sentry captured her, and the South sent her by train as a prisoner of war to the brutal, filthy, and overcrowded Castle Thunder in Richmond, Virginia. Her captors reported the new prisoner's arrival, describing her odd appearance and her unladylike defiance, "We must not admit to add that she is ugly and skinny, and apparently above thirty years of age." The maltreatment and starvation she endured at Castle Thunder haunted her for the rest of her life. Four months later, the South released her in exchange for a Confederate officer. Her health and eyesight suffered from captivity, but her fiery spirit remained undaunted.

Dr. Walker returned to Washington, and steadfast in her desire for official army status, she wrote to ask General Sherman to assign her the rank of a major and to send her to care for female prisoners in Louisville, Kentucky, most of whom were held on suspicion of spying. He complied, and she received a salary of $100.00 a month in addition to $434.66 in back pay. After six months, Mary was worn down by officials who felt she was too lenient, and her patients who were distrustful of one of their sex in a man's role. She asked for a transfer that would allow her to once again treat wounded soldiers, but instead the authorities placed her in charge of a refugee home in Clarksville, Tennessee. Her military career concluded in 1865, a month after General Robert E. Lee surrendered at Appomattox Court House.

In 1865, Mary experienced the apogee of her life when President Andrew Johnson signed a bill awarding her the Medal of Honor for Meritorious Service, making Mary its first female recipient. The bill said Walker had "devoted herself with patriotic zeal to the sick and wounded soldiers, both in the field and hospital, to the detriment of her own health, and has also endured hardships as a prisoner of war four months in a Southern prison." Thrilled with her medal, she wore it every day and affixed it to her left lapel when she delivered feminist lectures, always clad in formal male garments.

Throughout the 1870s, Marie worked in the suffrage headquarters in Washington alongside Susan B. Anthony, Lucy Stone, and Belva Lockwood. However, Dr. Walker soon ran afoul of her fellow suffragettes, who felt her wardrobe made them a target of ridicule that detracted from their great cause. A *New York Times* reporter described Mary as "that curious anthropoid."

A further source of contention was that Susan B. Anthony and Cady Stanton were engaged in the struggle to add an amendment that would enfranchise women, while Mary argued that they already had the right to vote as the phrase "We the people" was not gender based. There was no need to change the Constitution for a right it already promised.

In 1917, the Medal of Honor Board rescinded Dr. Walker's prized possession, an act that must have elicited some choice words she had picked up at Castle Thunder. She reportedly told the government, "You will receive it over my dead body." The Board members argued that the award could be only given to those who had served "in actual combat with the enemy, by gallantry or intrepidly,

at risk of life, above and beyond the call of duty." Mary
was vociferous in her complaints, refused to hand it over,
and displayed the medal until her passing in 1917.

Fifty years after Mary's death, her descendant, Anne
Walker, led a campaign—one she likened to a full-time
job—to right the historic wrong. She took her plea to
Presidents Nixon and Ford before President Jimmy Carter
reinstated Dr. Walker's medal. Of the 3,500 Medals of
Honor awarded, only one has been bestowed to a woman.
The award with the unique history resides at the Oswego
Historical Society.

At the top of the Medal of Honor is the word *VALOR*,
which aptly embodies the spirit of Dr. Walker. The words
of a nursery rhyme describe her as well, "Mary, Mary,
quite contrary..."

Chapter 2

Victoria's Secret (1872)

Now and again, as ladies bowl over the remaining barricades, there emerges the specter that one day there may be a triumphant outcome for a female aspiring to the Oval Office. Victoria Woodhull made a prescient statement when she became the first female candidate to run for president, proclaiming, "What may appear absurd today will assume a serious aspect tomorrow."

One hundred and forty years later, when Hillary Rodham Clinton dropped out of the 2008 presidential race, she made the stirring remark, "Although we weren't able to shatter that highest, hardest glass ceiling this time, thanks to you, it's got about 18 million cracks in it." Few know, however, the name of the woman who put the first crack in that elusive glass ceiling.

The lady whose life would not have been out of place in a nineteenth-century novel, Victoria California Claflin, was born in 1838, the seventh of ten children, and lived in Dickensian squalor in a wooden shack in Homer, Ohio, a whistle-stop town in Licking County. Her mother, Roxanna or "Roxie," was an illiterate German immigrant and a follower of the Austrian mystic Franz Mesmer (from whose name the word mesmerize derives). The alcoholic patriarch, Ruben, known as "Buck," peddled moonshine and opium as a cure for cancer. In one instance, it resulted in murder charges. At age fourteen, Buck marketed his daughter as a medium in his traveling medical show; she was to state her father "made her a woman before her time." Her sister Celeste, known as Tennessee or "Tennie," was obliged to hustle potions— and her body. In all likelihood, their shack went up in flames so Buck could collect the insurance money. Victoria married at age fifteen, pushed by her pyromaniac parent into the arms of the far older "Dr." Canning Woodhull, who loved wine, women, and morphine. Eventually, despite the stigma of divorce, Victoria took her departure, along with her married name, her daughter, Zula Maud, and her son, Byron, who suffered from brain damage. Victoria claimed Byron came by his disability when his father dropped him on his head.

Her second marriage was to Colonel James Blood, a Union Civil War hero and spiritualist. He did not believe in freedom just for slaves; as an adherent of "free love," he insisted on an open relationship, a proposition that struck a respondent note in his wife. She later declared,

"I have an inalienable, constitutional right to change that love every day if I please." Blood brought the beautiful and brilliant sisters, Victoria and Tennie, to New York, where they became the most notorious ladies in Manhattan. They treated the social norms of the 1870s as no more substantial than the spirits with which they professed they communicated.

The siblings made their first big splash in 1868 when they astounded a male-dominated metropolis by becoming the first women to open a brokerage firm on Wall Street. The press went berserk, and *Harper's Weekly* dubbed them "the bewitching brokers." The enterprise was all the more remarkable given the era's mores, where females were not welcome to pass through Wall Street even in covered carriages. Their office bore a sign: "All gentlemen will state their business and retire at once." The official opening on February 14 was besieged by so many throngs of the curious that one hundred police officers had to maintain order. A great proportion of their clientele were ladies who preferred to work with members of their own sex: widows, high-class prostitutes, and actresses. Suffragette superstar Susan B. Anthony heralded the arrival of the sisters on Wall Street as "a new phase in the women's rights question." The irony—one not lost on the siblings' legion of detractors—was that Cornelius Vanderbilt had bankrolled their business. His investment was logical, as Tennie was the mistress of the multimillionaire railroad baron, whose term of endearment for his paramour was "little sparrow."

On the flip side, Roxie and Buck had followed their daughters to Manhattan when the money had started to roll in, and Woodhull felt duty bound to take them in. Victoria's household included her two children, her sister, both her past and present husbands, and Roxie and Buck. To make matters worse, Roxie forged Tennie's signature on a blackmail letter to Vanderbilt that led him to sever ties with his "little sparrow."

Wall Street was just the beginning for the scandalous sisters of the Victorian era. With the funds earned from the brokerage, in 1870, Victoria and Tennie founded the radical newspaper, *Woodhull & Claflin's Weekly*. Their periodical's battle cry was, "We advocate the rights of the Lower Million against the Upper Ten!" In the mainly feminist press, they printed installments of Karl Marx's *The Communist Manifesto*. Marx considered them a little too radical for his taste and found their interest in his economic doctrine confusing given their Wall Street wealth. Increasingly political, Victoria testified on suffrage for women to a congressional committee—the first female ever to address Congress. She argued that women already had the right to vote as all citizens born in the United States had been granted that right under the Fourteenth Amendment. She also cited the Fifteenth Amendment (that had abolished slavery in 1870) as pertinent to women, who had long been in servitude. In response, the Ohio Representative, John Bingham, cried out, "Madam, you are no citizen...you are a woman!"

In May 1872, when the Equal Rights Party congregated in Apollo Hall, New York, it nominated Woodhull to run against the incumbent Republican president, General Ulysses S. Grant. Woodhull stood before 668 delegates in New York and vowed to fight "despotism, inequality, and injustice." She also campaigned to raise the hemlines on women's skirts to alleviate the burden of dragging them through muddy streets. Perhaps even she could not have imagined a presidential candidate campaigning in pastel pants suits. Woodhull chose as her running mate escaped slave-turned-abolitionist Frederick Douglass, who may not even have been aware he was on the ticket. Woodhull spoke to packed houses across the country, espousing the view that women needed to be freed from subservience in marriage just as the slaves had needed to be freed from slavery. *The New York Herald* endorsed the nonconventional candidate, and their headline declared: "Victory for Victoria in 1872." Immediately, her checkered personal life was held under the spotlight, and the public had fertile grounds for attack—starting with her sharing her marital home with two husbands. Victoria defended herself by explaining she had taken in her alcoholic, disabled ex as an act of charity, not bigamy. Other poison barbs were directed at her ties to spiritualism and free love. The scandal was so great she had to withdraw eleven-year-old Maud from school. As a result of Victoria's pioneering protest, cartoonist Thomas Nast drew her caricature dressed in black with bat wings sprouting from her shoulder blades, snarl upon her face, clutching a placard: "Be Saved by Free Love." In the background, a woman struggled up a steep path, carrying a baby and an alcoholic husband, with the caption, "I'd rather travel the hardest path of matrimony than follow in your footsteps." The full-page cartoon was entitled, "Get Thee Behind Me, (Mrs.) Satan!"

Hillary Clinton supporters sporting yellow roses visited Susan B. Anthony's grave, where they placed "I voted" stickers on her tombstone. A far different scenario played out with this nineteenth-century female presidential hopeful. On Election Day 1892, the candidate and her sister were in Ludlow Street Jail. Two deputy marshals who had appeared at the door of their brokerage house noticed their carriage speeding down Wall Street and gave chase. They apprehended the sisters and produced a warrant charging them with sending obscene publications through the mail. The vice crusader Anthony Comstock, who referred to himself as a "weeder in God's garden," had conspired to have them arrested on a charge of obscenity after they printed articles exposing the alleged affair of the city's most eminent preacher, the Reverend Henry Ward Beecher, the brother of the author of *Uncle Tom's Cabin*, Harriet Beecher Stowe. Victoria had accused him of an adulterous affair with a female parishioner, Elizabeth Tilton. Victoria had not been incensed by his sidestepping of his marital vow; rather, she was upset by the hypocrisy of his threatening brimstone from his pulpit for those who broke the Seventh Commandment. In her paper, she had vowed to make it, "hotter on earth for Henry Ward Beecher than Hell is below." What hurt her further was the United States District Attorney was a member of the Reverend's

Plymouth Church congregation. The arrest for sending the libelous periodical through the US post office led to the passage of the Comstock Act; it sought to uphold a strict moral code by barring the circulation of "obscene literature and articles of immoral use." Victoria and Tennie secured their release after posting $16,000 in bail. Spoiler alert: the female presidential candidate and her black running mate did not garner a single electoral vote. Her percentage of the popular vote is undocumented (possibly because some of the polling stations discarded any ballots that favored her). Not only was her liberal platform far beyond her times, there was also the matter of her age; at thirty-four, she did not meet the thirty-five-year minimum. The authorities released the sisters a month after their arrest and exonerated them after a judge ruled that existing obscenity legislation did not apply to the press.

On that Election Day morning, Susan B. Anthony went to a polling station in Rochester, New York, and became the first woman in America to successfully insist on exercising her right to vote. She cast her ballot for President Grant, whose Republican party had announced its willingness to listen to the ladies in the run-up to the election. Two weeks later, Anthony was also behind bars for attempting to cast a vote. Woodhull closed her campaign with a prophetic letter to the editor of *the New York Herald*, "To the public I would say in conclusion they may succeed in crushing me out, even to the loss of my life: but let me warn them and you that from the ashes of my body a thousand Victorias will spring to avenge my death by seizing the work laid down by me and carrying it forward to victory."

Post-prison life took her on a downward spiral, and Victoria and Tennie left for London, where they "decided to use draconian measures to sanitize their images." And sanitize them they did. As with their other outlandish schemes, their desire at reinvention worked. Within a few years, Victoria had taken her third husband, John Biddulph Martin, a wealthy banker; Claflin wed Sir Francis Cook and became Lady Cook. The newly minted Mrs. Martin—one of the first women in England to own a car—lived in a manor house on a 1,200-acre estate in the Cotswolds. She was a generous contributor and fundraiser for the restoration and purchase of Sulgrave Manor, the home of George Washington's ancestors. As did Mrs. Banks in *Mary Poppins*, she worked for British suffrage. She died in 1927, age eighty-eight, a year before English women won the right to vote.

Mrs. Woodhull-Blood-Martin was a woman of contradictions: a stockbroker who embraced Marxism, and a denouncer of traditional marriage who spent her final years as the wife of a member of the British landed gentry. How a rebel woman—in today's parlance a nasty woman—traversed such an extraordinary road remains Victoria's secret.

Chapter 3

Fear Less
(1903)

In 1888, Alfred Nobel read his obituary, "*Le Marchand de la mort est mort*" ("The Merchant of Death is Dead"). The article stated that the dynamite king, who had "become rich by finding ways to kill more people faster than ever before, died yesterday." The journalist had erred; it had been Ludwig, Alfred's brother, who had passed away. The headline served as Nobel's clarion call; to alter his legacy, he bequeathed his staggering fortune to those who had conferred the "greatest benefit on mankind." The most revered people in history have journeyed to Sweden; among them was the first woman to win the Nobel Prize, a lady of many firsts: Marie Curie.

Curie, one of the world's most eminent mathematicians, was born in Warsaw in 1867, the daughter of Dr. Sklodowski, a teacher at the Lycee of Warsaw, and

Bronsitawa Sklodowska, a principal of a girls' school. Their daughter Marya was a serious child whose favorite pastime was playing with test tubes. The family were members of the Polish intelligentsia fighting against occupation by Czarist Russia, and several extended family members were in exile in Siberia for acts of resistance.

Marya Sklodowska became Marie Curie as a result of Warsaw University's ban on female students. As hungry for knowledge as Dr. Faustus, she participated in her city's Flying University, an underground women's school whose members met clandestinely. A chance at the Holy Grail of education presented itself when Bronya, her older sister, suggested she work to support Bronya, who would study medicine at the Sorbonne first, and then upon graduation would return the favor to Manya, as her family called Marya. Accordingly, Marya took a job as a governess, and in her spare time, she worked on solving mathematical problems received by post from her father. The "homework" helped distract Marya from the severe depression she had suffered since she was ten and had lost her mother to tuberculosis. What also proved a distraction was the older son of her well-to-do employers; they vetoed marriage due to her low social status.

After five dismal years, Marya's prospects changed when Bronya sent her a one-way ticket from Poland to Paris. In 1891, at age twenty-three, she traveled forty hours in fourth class; that entailed bringing her own food and a stool on which to sit. The young woman displayed fortitude by traveling alone, an activity associated with prostitutes. The obsessive workaholic rented a sixth-floor garret in the Latin Quarter, studied French, and earned money cleaning glassware in labs. Begrudging every penny, she rationed her intake of food; on more than one occasion, she collapsed from weakness. She enrolled in the Sorbonne as one of only twenty-three women out of the two thousand science students and only one of two women to work for a degree in science. Marie—as she chose to be called in her adopted country—came in first in her examinations and berated herself for coming in second in mathematics. She was the first woman to graduate from the Sorbonne.

After four years in Paris, Marie met Pierre Curie, and they bonded over his invention, the quadrant electrometer—what woman could resist? Marie was not husband-hunting, and the older Pierre was a committed bachelor who had once written, "Women of genius are rare." However, as no one was more brilliant than Marie, he wrote in a letter, "It would...be a beautiful thing to pass through life together hypnotized in our dreams: your dream for your country; our dream for humanity; our dream for science." They were married in 1895 in a civil service attended by family and a few friends. For the occasion, Marie wore a blue cotton dress, one practical enough to wear in the laboratory post-ceremony. Their unofficial vow, as Marie put it, was to forge a life, "consecrated entirely to scientific research." In the day, Pierre worked as a physics professor, and Madame Curie taught physics at a girls' school in Sevres. The evenings were dedicated to research. Consumed by their experiments, they frequently forgot to eat, and meals consisted of bread washed down with coffee in a shed that served as a makeshift laboratory. After the birth of her first child, Marie took breaks to breastfeed and eventually hired a wet-nurse; her recently widowed father-in-law, Eugene, a retired physician, helped with child-rearing. Colleagues viewed putting work before maternal nurturing and child-rearing as reprehensible.

Madame Curie needed to come up with names for two daughters—Eve and Irene—as well as the two substances she discovered: radium, named for the rays it emitted, and polonium, named in tribute to Poland. Working as always until the small hours of the night, she once collapsed in front of Eve from exhaustion. Neither she nor her husband suspected—nor wished to—that radioactivity carried harmful side effects. Radium, as with fire and water, proved a two-edged sword.

In 1903, the year Madame Curie defended her doctoral position, she and Pierre received the Nobel Prize in physics, thereby making her the first woman to be so honored. In an era when the male-dominated scientific establishment made it clear that females were not welcome, Marie was at the vanguard of her field and changed the world's perceptions about the nature of atoms, cancer treatments, and nuclear power; her theories also aided in the birth of the atomic bomb. The President of the Swedish Academy introduced the laureates with a biblical quotation, "It is not good that man should be alone. I will make a helpmeet for him."

Only Monsieur Curie delivered the acceptance speech (as the podium was the province of males alone), and thus he garnered the glory. Pierre was generous with spousal credit and took the opportunity to praise his wife and to clarify she was far more than his "helpmeet."

The most successful collaboration and love affair in the history of science ended in 1906 when Pierre died as he crossed a rain-slicked street and a horse-drawn wagon ran into him on the Pont Neuf. The thirty-eight-year old widow wrote, "I lost my beloved Pierre, and with him all hope and all support for the rest of my life." The single mother took over her husband's Sorbonne faculty position, an act that made headlines in the Paris newspapers. Artists, journalists, and society ladies joined students to hear the first woman on the Sorbonne faculty deliver a lecture.

In 1913, Albert Einstein and his son joined Marie Curie and her daughters in a hike in the Swiss Alps. Although he held his colleague in the utmost esteem, he wrote Elsa Lowenthal, his cousin who became his second wife, "Madame Curie is very intelligent, but has the soul of a herring ['haringseele'] meaning that she is lacking in all feelings of joy and sorrow. Almost the only way in which she expresses her feeling is to rail at things she doesn't like. And Irene is even worse—like a Grenadier [an infantryman]. The daughter is also very gifted..."

Einstein was also with Marie when they attended a conference in Brussels focused on "The Theory of Radiation and Quanta." At forty-three years of age, she was the only woman among twenty-three men when informed she had won a second Nobel Prize, making her the only person to have achieved such an accomplishment. The news should have been a glorious moment, but it came when her personal and professional life was in shambles. She had recently been denied a seat in the French Academy of Sciences, as much for being born a Pole as for being a woman. Einstein stood in her corner and called her detractors reptiles.

In addition to the sexist slight, she had another hydra head to slay—apparently Madame liked sex as well as science. Einstein erred when he called Marie "cold as a herring." Marie fell for a married scientist, Paul Langevin, and they rendezvoused in their apartment near the Sorbonne. The obvious drawback was his wife, the mother of his four young children. She was incensed when she discovered their love letters, ones in which Marie demanded he marry her—and the Mrs. Scorned dished the dirt to the press. While an eminent *man* with a mistress may have been given a pass, society branded Marie with the letter A and labelled her a home-wrecking Polish adulteress. Langevin felt honor-bound to fight a duel against the journalist of the exposé; neither was hurt. France was scandalized by the affair, and Sweden was likewise not impressed. From Stockholm arrived the polite suggestion that Madame Curie not receive the Nobel Prize in person as they did not want an adulteress to shake hands with King Gustaf V. She responded in a letter, "I believe that there is no connection between my scientific work and my private life." Madame Curie attended the ceremony and shook hands with King Gustaf; shortly afterward, she suffered a nervous breakdown.

Redemption arrived with the outbreak of World War I when Marie closed the Institut Curie to establish the first military field radiological centers utilizing mobile units to x-ray soldiers to locate bullets and shrapnel. She worked alongside her seventeen-year-old daughter Irene, who contributed to another of Madame Curie's firsts. In 1934, Irene became the second woman to win a Nobel Prize, along with her husband, Frederic Joliot-Curie, for their discovery of artificial radioactivity. The award made Marie and Irene the first parent and child to win the gold standard of prizes. A quip Eve gave an interviewer showed she possessed the humor her mother and sister lacked, "You are not mixing me up with my sister by any chance? You see, I am the only one of my family not to have won a Nobel Prize."

Marie was proud of her two accomplished daughters, but it was her third child, radium—which she kept by her bed to watch its glow—that had contaminated her body for more than thirty years. At age sixty-six, her fingers were blackened and cracked, she was nearly blind, and lesions covered her body. The martyr to science died from the substance that had conferred upon her immortality, a price Madame willingly paid as she felt science took ascendancy over all else. Although her life was one filled with high honors, the self-effacing genius summed up her biography in twenty-one words, "I was born in Poland.

I married Pierre Curie, and I have two daughters. I have done my work in France."

In 1995, Marie achieved another first when President Francois Mitterrand ordered the ashes of the Curies to be transferred from a small-town cemetery to the Pantheon. The memorial is dedicated to the "great men of France" and serves as the final resting place of historical figures such as Victor Hugo, Emile Zola, and Voltaire. The interment made the celebrity scientist the first woman enshrined in the august mausoleum based on her own achievements. In attendance at the ceremony was President Lech Walesa of Poland.

Part of understanding the secret of the soul of Marie Curie lies in her own words, "Nothing in life is to be feared, it is only to be understood. Now is the time to understand more, so that we may fear less."

Chapter 4

Redecorating Heaven (1905)

The décor of the nineteenth century can be described as more is more: windows covered with heavy damask draperies, velvet ensconced furniture, gilt frames, obscured walls. Then came a woman who brought in the light and vanquished Victorian gloom. Elsie de Wolfe left her impeccable mark as America's first female interior decorator.

The girl who was to be a pioneer of the non-rugged variety was born as Ella Anderson de Wolfe in 1865 to a physician father and Scottish mother in a New York City brownstone, now the site of Macy's department store. She was the only daughter of attractive parents who bemoaned her homely shoe-button eyes, long narrow face, and frizzy hair. Elsie, as she preferred to be called, described herself as "an ugly child," an especially horrible assessment for someone forever enamored with aestheticism. In her 1935 biography, *After All*, she recounted how she once arrived home to discover the new drawing room wallpaper struck her as so repulsive she felt physically assaulted, like "something terrible that cut like a knife." She fell on the floor in a tantrum, kicking and screaming.

A love affair with Europe began when Elsie was sixteen and left for Edinburgh "for finishing" in the household of her mother's cousin, a distinguished clergyman, who arranged for her presentation to Queen Victoria. She later described the monarch as "a little fat queen in a black dress and a load of jewels." Half a century later, Elsie would teach a wishful queen, Lady Wallis Windsor, "how to make a home fit for a king." In the interval between her introduction to royalty and her friendship with the great queen's great-granddaughter-in-law, de Wolfe led many lives, even including one that entailed flying with Wilbur Wright.

Her father's death left little other than debt, and Elsie returned to New York to become an actress, thereby challenging the opinion of high society that the stage was a disreputable profession for a respectable lady. As it transpired, it was her onstage style and wardrobe-couture ensembles from Paris that garnered attention more than her acting ability.

Fortunately, Elsie had better luck on the romantic front when she met Elisabeth (Bessy) Marbury, with whom she entered into a "Boston Marriage" (a term for two single women living together, attributed to Henry James' *The Bostonians*); they were romantically linked for the next forty years. Bessy was a scion of old Manhattan money and was the first woman literary agent; her clientele included Oscar Wilde, George Bernard Shaw, and Somerset Maugham. Elsie decorated their stately home in Irving Place with brightly flowered curtains and championed chintz (and so became known as "the chintz lady"). Her preferred color was made manifest when she first viewed the Parthenon in Athens and exclaimed, "It's beige—just my color!" The couple threw parties that made them the hostesses with the mostest; their guest list included Sarah Bernhardt, Mrs. J. P. Morgan, and Mrs. Astor. The designing lady launched her fabulous career when Bessie suggested her new stage should be the dressing of interiors.

With all the drama of the theater she had left behind, de Wolfe swept into the male-dominated upholstery and furniture business and transformed it into an exciting profession; in the process, she made it a domain for women. Soon Elsie was proudly handing out business cards embellished with her trademark wolf-with nosegay-crest in its mouth. The quintessential woman-about-town was readily recognized as the tiny lady with the short white gloves, triple strand pearl necklace, and little dog in her arms.

De Wolfe and Marbury refused to let their era's prejudice against their lesbian lifestyle dampen their professional and social ambitions. Bessie, at age sixty-two, was an active member of the Democratic Party who campaigned for Franklin Delano Roosevelt; she also served as his personal advisor. Elsie was never apologetic about her unorthodox choices, and her motto "never complain never explain" appeared in embroidery on one of her signature pillows.

De Wolfe's decorating took off when a group of wealthy ladies, including Mrs. Borden (Daisy) Harriman, later to become the first woman ambassador, and Anne Morgan, daughter of the famous banker, embarked on a radical undertaking—the creation of a club for women based on the model of an English men's club. By 1905, 550 members had enrolled, and Stanford White, the acclaimed architect, erected a building on Madison Avenue. He convinced its members to take a chance on de Wolfe, saying, "Give it to Elsie and let her alone. She knows more than any of us." The elegance she lent to the Colony Club made her to design what her contemporary, Emily Post, was to manners. Elsie furnished fabulous interiors from Manhattan to Paris, Saint-Tropez to Beverly Hills. In a nod to noblesse oblige, she wrote columns for *The Delineator* that later evolved into the genre known as ladies' magazines. She published her articles in her book *The House in Good Taste*; it became a bestseller.

The dream of accruing her own fortune arrived in one afternoon. Henry Clay Frick, the multi-millionaire steel magnate, asked Elsie to decorate the private quarters of his Fifth Avenue mansion/museum. Their business arrangement stipulated de Wolfe would receive ten percent of everything she purchased on his behalf. While in Paris, Elsie persuaded Frick, who grudgingly postponed his golf date for half an hour, to visit a warehouse to examine its treasures. In that half an hour, they obtained what is estimated to have cost between two and three million dollars and provided de Wolfe with one of the highest incomes for that year in America. De Wolfe was in charge of fourteen rooms, including Mrs. Frick's boudoir—complete with eight panels painted by Francois Boucher for Madame de Pompadour. The future Edward VIII invited the celebrated designing lady to decorate sections of Buckingham Palace, but his abdication nixed the project. The debt-ridden doctor's daughter became the queen of international chic and the arbitrator of taste. Elsie also donned an activist hat in 1912 when she carried a banner in a suffrage parade. However, most felt her participation was more economic than political—the act was good for business, the altar on which de Wolfe worshipped.

It is hardly a tossup which was Elsie's greater love, Bessie Marbury or her home, the Villa Trianon in Versailles, a deserted Louis XV pavilion on the grounds of Palace of Versailles. The pavilion became a showplace and the crown jewel of de Wolfe's legendary entertainments. The decadent decorator created mirror-paved galleries; walls held gilt-framed Old Master drawings that surrounded leopard-upholstered furniture. There was even a painted ceiling in the library showing the mistress of the manor as a cloche-hatted, short-skirted flapper leaping across the Atlantic to France with a small dog at her heels.

Mirrors were also de rigueur in the dressing room because, "Know the worst before you go out!"

De Wolfe's days as a businesswoman and hostess continued until 1914; the outbreak of World War I transformed the Villa Trianon from a pleasure dome to a hospital when Elsie offered her home to the Red Cross. She served as a dedicated nurse to burn victims (accompanied by her French maid) and received the Légion d' Honneur. For two years, never far from the risk of German shells, she put the soldiers' needs above her own. With the advent of the Armistice, the best-dressed actress on Broadway and the highest paid decorator in the world embarked on her third career as the most feted American hostess in Europe. Her parties were known for their skimpy menus—she was a dedicated dieter—profusion of flowers, and guest lists that included Coco Chanel, Douglas Fairbanks, and a spattering of deposed monarchs. Wallis Simpson observed, "She mixes people like a cocktail—and the result is sheer genius."

The era's most celebrated interior decorator was an unforgettable character: she stood on her head at the slightest provocation, posed as Mata Hari, and when Cartier delivered an aquamarine and diamond tiara, an elderly Elsie dyed her snow-white locks pale blue in color-coordinated homage. But nothing the design diva did topped what she orchestrated in 1926 when she became a bride. Figuring money and a title belonged together, she wed Sir Charles Ferdinand Mendl at the British Embassy in Paris and embarked on a month-long honeymoon in Egypt. Their odd union produced the dropping of many jaws. The groom was fifty-five years old and the bride was at least a decade older than the fifty-seven years she claimed as her age. Moreover, her only previous relationship had been with a woman. The nuptial made sense to the couple as Elsie was rich, and Sir Charles gave her the title she used for the remainder of her days: Lady Mendl. The marriage was one of social convenience as was evidenced when, ten years later, Elsie published her autobiography and hubby hardly merited a mention.

Exquisite when it came to decorating, Elsie fell short in other arenas; she chose paintings based on whether they matched a sofa. Upon a visit to Gertrude Stein's home, she was horrified by the work of Salvador Dali. Her political actions also did not bear too much scrutiny, something not surprising for someone who harbored sympathy for Marie Antoinette. In 1933, in Rome, while watching an Easter parade, she praised the extravaganza, saying, "only Mussolini and Jesus Christ could stage a spectacle like this" and posed for a picture giving the Fascist salute.

In addition to being the Grande Dame of well-appointed interiors, de Wolfe was the winner of the best-dressed woman award in her seventieth year, the originator of blue-dyed hair, and an exhibitionist who, even in her old age, enjoyed her ability to stand on her head. In 1940, with the Nazis goose-stepping into her beloved Paris, Sir Charles and Elsie fled in their Rolls-Royce.

Their final destination was California, where de Wolfe commandeered a Beverly Hills mansion that she christened After All (her favorite expression, which was also the title of her autobiography) and transformed it into a palace of mirrors and palm trees. The estate also contained one of her most cherished possessions, a stool from her Versailles home that had once belonged to Marie Antoinette. As was her lifelong pattern, interiors, rather than people, remained her passion. She recognized this character trait when she wrote another book, *The House of Good Taste*, "Probably when another woman would be dreaming of love affairs, I dream of the delightful houses I have lived in. I think that is why some people like my rooms—they feel, without quite knowing why, that I have loved them while making them."

In addition to a decapitated queen's stool, Elsie kept her scrapbooks, time capsules of a bygone era. They record her jewelry, parties, and telegrams from Wallis Simpson. Another memento was a dog tag, estimated at $1,000 to $1,500, that recalls the French poodle that she dyed the perfect shade of blue. A *House & Garden* cover preserves the living room of the Beverly Hills home where she waited out the Second World War.

With the Nazi defeat, De Wolfe returned to Versailles, where she spent her final years. Her remark illustrated the true love of her life, "If I have done anything really fine, it is the Villa Trianon." In 1950, Elsie received her final commission: redecorating heaven.

Chapter 5

It Took a Yankee
(1926)

Urban legend has it that the word *golf* is an acronym
for "gentlemen only ladies forbidden." Although
the etymology is incorrect, what is true is that women
and sports have often seemed incompatible. If a lady
attempted to sneak in during the ancient Olympic Games,
the men would throw her off Mount Typaeon. Fortunately,
Gertrude Ederle merited a kinder fate, and she became
the first woman to conquer the English Channel.

The Jazz Age mermaid proved what could happen
when women were freed from corsets, long skirts, and
stockings. Gertrude Caroline, nicknamed Trudy, was born
in 1905, one of four daughters and two sons of German
immigrants Henry Ederle, owner of a successful New
York City butcher shop, and his wife, Anna. At the age of
eight, Gertrude had her first encounter with deep water,

and the result was she almost drowned. The experience encouraged her to learn to swim; her father taught her by tying a rope around her waist and throwing her into a river. She later recalled of her summers at her family cottage in Highlands, located in Monmouth County on the Jersey Shore, "I just went out the back door and jumped in the Shrewsbury River." At age five, she had developed a hearing problem after a bout of measles, and though the doctor cautioned exposure to water would worsen her disability, she never heeded his advice.

At age twelve, Gertrude joined the famed Women's Swimming Association in Manhattan and made her mark in amateur competitions. Word of her aquatic prowess spread, and she found herself representing America in the 1924 Paris Olympics. Away from home, she had the time of her life; she said of her sojourn in France, "We used to get a taxi and go around Paris. We'd stand up and go screaming around the streets. People would say, 'There go the crazy Americans.' We sure did have a lot of fun." Gertrude won gold and bronze medals, an accomplishment more impressive as she had performed with an injured knee. Moreover, along with the other female American athletes from the United States, she had the handicap of fatigue. The girls were staying in hotels far from the center of Paris because American officials did not want them contaminated with what they viewed as the city's bohemian morals, and they traveled five to six hours each day to practice in the Olympic pool.

Gertrude's rendezvous with history began when Helen Wainright, an Olympic teammate, had been the Women's Swimming Association's candidate to attempt what no other woman had done before: swim the English Channel. After Helen sustained an injury when she stepped off a New York City trolley, the club pinned its hopes—and funding—on Ederle.

Her 1925 bid to accomplish the feat terminated in failure. Her coach, a Scot named Jabez Wolffe, had grabbed her arm after he felt she was in jeopardy, a move that had immediately disqualified Ederle. Gertrude was furious at the unwanted—and what she claimed was unmerited— aid. She felt he had acted out of envy as he had tried and failed to make the crossing twenty-two times. She was also less than impressed when he told reporters, "The torments of seasickness, inflammation of the eyes, great cold, and other disagreeable features may prove too much for any woman swimmer." At the time she worried, "All I could wonder was, 'What will they think of me back in the States?'"

She embarked on the same mission the following year with a new coach, Englishman Bill Burgess, who, in 1911, had been the second person to swim the Channel. Rather than ask the Association to back her yet again, she raised the requisite $9,000. With the help of her sister Margaret (Meg), she designed a red two-piece bathing suit—something considered scandalous in the era—one that would not drag in the waves yet would be "decent in case I failed and they had to drag me out." Ederle also created her wraparound goggles; ones kept watertight with molten candle wax. On August 6th, shortly after 7 a.m., Meg smeared her with lanolin, petroleum jelly, olive oil, and lard to protect her from both the cold and the poisonous jellyfish before she waded into the water at Cape Gris-Nez, France. She saw a red ball on the French shore, a warning to small craft to avoid a sea that promised to be very choppy. "Please, God, help me," she prayed. She made her way toward England using the basic crawl, and at times, sang "Let Me Call You Sweetheart" to the rhythm of her stroke. Concerned about her well-being, the crew constantly asked, "Do you want to come out, Trudy?" Her invariable response was, "What for?" The exchange led to her nickname of "What For?" The reporters on board sang "Yes! We Have No Bananas" until the weather turned nasty and they were sick over the side of their boat. Gertrude's determination was helped by tantalizing bait. In the boat, her father and Meg held up signs which held messages such as "one wheel" and "two wheels," references to the red roadster she had been promised if she proved successful.

As Gertrude approached her destination, thousands of spectators who crowded the shores of a beach near the white cliffs of Dover could make out her red-capped head. They realized Gertrude was on the brink of becoming a historic first, but what they did not realize was the final few hundred yards of a Channel swim are always the hardest. Dozens of hopefuls, cold and disorientated, had been driven back by the unforgiving tides and currents within the sight of shore; like aquatic incarnations of

Moses, they were able to see the Promised Land only to be denied entry. The previous year, Bernard Freyberg had succumbed three hundred yards away from success, and he had won a Victoria Cross at the Battle of the Somme. If a World War I hero had met defeat, what was the likelihood this female teenager could beat the odds? Bookies estimated her chances of failure at six to one. In the 1926 issue of the *London Daily Sketch*, journalist John Hayward advised women to stop chasing an absurd dream as "no woman has ever yet been anywhere near success and wasn't likely to be." The male doom-mongers had admired the ladies' pluck but patronizingly had pointed out that if only five men had ever swum the Channel, what hope was there for the fairer sex?

With nightfall descending, Gertrude approached the British coast; she recalled that when her foot touched the sand, it "was a wonderful moment." Not only was Ederle the first woman to conquer the Channel, she also bested the previous record set by Sebastian Tirabocchi, an Italian who lived in Argentina. The statistic marked the first time in sporting history that a woman had completed an event in a shorter time than a man. If she had been able to clip along in a straight line, it would have been a twenty-one-mile trip. Because the sea had proven so rough, she had, in actuality, swum thirty-five miles.

For a brief, shining moment, the endless argument over whether the female sex could compete physically against men was suspended. A week later, Gertrude boarded the Cunard steamship Berengaria for the voyage home. As the vessel approached New York, she received a request, "Miss Ederle, would you please go to the upper deck? The planes want to welcome you. They want to drop flowers down." Her response, "You're kidding, aren't you?" They were not. "So I went up there. The planes circled around and swooped down and dropped those bouquets. They were just gorgeous. I never felt anything like that. I was proud, very, very proud, so proud." When Ederle returned to the States, an estimated two million New Yorkers lined the sidewalks chanting, "Trudy! Trudy!" and showered her with applause—and hills of confetti. Officials ushered her into Mayor Jimmy Walker's office in City Hall as exuberant crowds stormed the doors. The mayor compared Ederle's achievement to Moses parting the Red Sea. News of her success pushed the stories of Rudolph Valentino's funeral and Jack Dempsey's training for the Gene Tunney fight off the front pages.

Years later, when others had successfully swum the Channel, Grover A. Whalen, New York City's official greeter, said that of all the celebrities he had welcomed, not one made the impact of the girl from the Jersey Shore. *The New York Times*' description of the historic first was, "the biggest thing in athletics ever done by a woman, or a man for that matter." France's *Le Figaro* described her as "the most glorious of nymphs" while Germany's *Nachtausgabe* heralded her swim as "one of the greatest athletic achievements of all time." Heywood Broun in *The World* newspaper forecasted, "When Gertrude Ederle struck out from France, she left behind her a world which has believed for a great many centuries that women is the weaker vessel. Much of government, most of law, and practically all of morality is based upon this assumption. It may be that she will turn out to be an even greater discoverer than Columbus. It was only a continent which he found." President Calvin Coolidge invited her to the White House and pronounced her "America's best girl." Paraded before surging crowds, the shy, hearing-impaired young woman became the toast of many towns. A song written about her, "Tell Me, Trudy, Who Is Going to Be the Lucky One?" referred to the cascade of marriage proposals that came her way; she accepted none. Gertrude appeared in the movie *Swim Girl, Swim* in 1927 for a fee of $8,000 and toured America's vaudeville stages for a reported $2,000 to $3,000 a week demonstrating her Channel-beating stroke in a specially built swimming tank. She later made cameo appearances at Billy Rose's Aquacade at the New York World's Fair in 1939.

While others might have milked fame and fortune, Gertrude never felt comfortable in the spotlight and willingly faded into the shadow while aviator Charles Lindbergh and baseball great Babe Ruth astonished the world with new feats. In 1928, on the eve of a European tour, Gertrude had a nervous breakdown and retreated from public view. Five years later, she suffered a debilitating spinal injury when she tripped on an apartment stairway. She spent more than four years in a cast, and her legs wasted away from inactivity. Her hearing worsened, and her fiancé abandoned her. When reporters discovered her on the anniversary of her achievement, their columns reported her fall from fame and headlines read, "Trudy Has Swum Sea of Troubles."

Although Ederle had proved the fickleness of fate, she had paved the watery way for others such as the second woman to swim the Channel, American Mille Gade, and the third, Englishwoman Mercedes Gleitze, and a host of others.

Gertrude's final years before her death in 2003 from cardiac arrest were spent far afield from her glory days, in a nursing home in Wyckoff, New Jersey. The ninety-eight-year-old mostly watched television, legs wrapped in a red plaid blanket, unable to walk. She said she missed her adored Meg, who had predeceased her. However, she retained her "What For?" pluck as evidenced when she reminisced about the day she had her rendezvous with history, "It was just that everybody was saying it couldn't be done. Well, every time somebody said that, I wanted to prove it could be done. It took a Yankee to show them how."

Chapter 6

Steel Gardenia (1940)

The Civil Rights timeline has witnessed significant African American firsts, each a step closer to Dr. King's "We Shall Overcome." In sports, Althea Gibson competed at Wimbledon in 1951; in music, Marion Anderson sang at the Metropolitan in 1955; in literature, Toni Morrison received the Nobel Prize in 1993. Another trailblazer was Hattie McDaniel, the first African American woman to win an Academy Award.

In her acceptance speech for her 2010 Oscar for Best Supporting Actress for *Precious*, Mo'nique stated she was wearing a royal blue dress, along with a gardenia in her hair, because Hattie McDaniel had dressed in that fashion seventy years earlier when she had broken Hollywood's color barrier. Hattie's nomination resulted in a collective shock as everyone felt her *Gone with the Wind* co-star

Olivia de Havilland was a shoo-in. Mo'nique thanked her predecessor, "for enduring all that she had to, so that I would not have to." Mo'nique's praise was unequivocal; however, while the modern-day star's triumph did not raise eyebrows, Hattie caused jaws to drop when she became a card-carrying member of the be-careful-of-what-you-wish-for club.

The woman who created a tempest in a celluloid teacup was the youngest of thirteen, born to former slaves in 1895 in Wichita, Kansas. Her father, Henry, had fought for the Union in the Civil War and later became a Baptist minister who moonlighted as a banjo player in minstrel shows. Her mother, Susan, was a gospel singer. As a child, Hattie sang so often Susan sometimes bribed her with spare change to buy a moment of silence.

In 1901, the family moved to Colorado, where Hattie was one of only two black children in her elementary school; she ended her education in her early teens to join her father's troupe. A natural entertainer, she became popular in the African American theater scene in Denver, and her gift of pantomime led to her reputation as the black Sophie Tucker. Acclaim likewise followed for her sexually suggestive renditions of the blues, many of which she penned. However, even after a nationwide tour of vaudeville houses, McDaniel was often forced to supplement her income with work as a domestic. By age twenty, she was also a widow. Her marriage abruptly ended in 1922 when her husband of three months, George Langford, was reportedly killed by gunfire. Her father died the same year, and devastated by the back-to-back losses, Hattie took solace in performing. In 1925, she appeared on Denver's radio station, an appearance that garnered her the distinction of being the first African American woman to perform in this medium.

In 1929, her booking organization went bankrupt as a result of the Great Depression, and Hattie found herself stranded in Chicago with no job and meager savings. On a tip from a friend, she departed for Milwaukee and obtained a position as a bathroom attendant at Sam Pick's Club Madrid. The club only engaged white performers, but Hattie, an irrepressible singer, belted out tunes from the restroom. Patrons took notice of her voice and good nature, which led the owner to allow her onstage. After her rendition of "St. Louis Blues," she became a wildly popular attraction. She remained in the club for a year until her siblings, Stan and Etta, invited her to join them in Los Angeles. In Tinseltown, she had dreams of becoming what twinkled in the firmament; however, black actors' role choices consisted of African savage, singing slave, or obsequious employee. Stan threw her a life preserver, and she found work in the radio show "The Optimistic Do-Nuts." She earned the nickname Hi-Hat Hattie after showing up in evening attire for her initial broadcast.

Hattie's long dreamed of screen debut occurred in 1931 when she played a bit part as a maid, for which she was able to draw on firsthand experience. Her breakthrough was as Marlene Dietrich's domestic in *Blonde Venus*;

three years later, she appeared as Mom Beck in *The Little Colonel*, starring Shirley Temple and Lionel Barrymore. With her perfect comic timing, she appeared alongside the biggest stars of the silver screen: Clark Gable, Jean Harlow, and Henry Fonda. She was so successful that MGM did not allow her to play any role other than as a domestic or to lose an ounce, though she tipped the scale at three hundred pounds. Mammy had to be fat. Typecast as the woman with the apron, she was one of the logical candidates to secure the coveted role of Mammy in David O. Selnick's 1939 production, *Gone with the Wind.* The competition for the part was as fierce among black hopefuls as for the part of Miss Scarlett was among whites. First Lady Eleanor Roosevelt had recommended her own maid for the role, but Hattie had her own patron—the King of Hollywood, Clark Gable. She nailed the audition when she appeared in a plantation maid uniform and so impressed Selznick he called off other tryouts, "Save your overhead, boys. We can start shooting tomorrow." What further helped was she fit the stereotypical perception of the Southern servant as she was the doppelganger of Aunt Jemima, whose image proliferated on Quaker Oats boxes. During the epic film, clad in trademark apron and bandanna, she delivered lines in antebellum lingo: "What gentlemen says and what they thinks is two different things," and "I ain't noticed Mr. Ashley askin' for to marry you." Although cast as the servant, she told Selznick she would not utter a racial epithet or employ the caricature phrase "de Lawd."

The premiere of *Gone with the Wind* at the Loew's Grand Theater in Atlanta was the apogee celebration of 1939, and women arrived in hoop skirts, men showed up clad in breeches, and Confederate flags flapped in the Southern breeze the night of its premier. Absent from the revels were the black performers, as Jim Crow held sway. Clark Gable threatened to boycott the gala unless Hattie was of its number; he relented after she insisted that he not create a scene. A second salve was a telegram from Margaret Mitchell, the celebrated author of *Gone with the Wind*, who said of Hattie's absence from the premier's festivities, "I wish you could have heard the cheers when the Mayor of Atlanta called for a hand for our Hattie McDaniel."

If McDaniel's exclusion from opening night was not pain enough, blacks heaped criticism on her as they viewed the epic film as a valentine to the slave-owning South. Walter White, head of the National Association for the Advancement of Colored People, sneered she was an 'Aunt Tom.' She lashed back by asking, "What do you expect me to play? Rhett Butler's wife?" However, her most memorable comeback was, "I'd rather play a maid and make $700 a week than be a maid and make $7." One can only wonder how she would have reacted to the fact that seventy-two years later, Octavia Spencer won an Academy Award for Best Supporting Actress for her role in *The Help*—as a maid. On top of the back-to-back backlash from whites and blacks, Hattie had to deal with the demise of her second marriage to Howard Hickman, which both began and ended in 1938.

In 1940, *Gone with the Wind* garnered ten Academy Awards. Predictably, Best Actress went to Vivien Leigh; unpredictably, Best Supporting Actress went to Hattie McDaniel, the first time an African-American had been honored and an event that did not repeat itself for another fifty years, when Whoopi Goldberg received the tribute for *Ghosts*. Although the more liberal North allowed her to attend the Hollywood gala at the Ambassador Hotel and personally receive her award, she and her African American escort were seated at a segregated table. In her sixty-seven-second emotional acceptance speech, she stated she "hoped to be a credit to her race." Gossip columnist Louella Parsons for once put down her poisoned pen: "If you had seen her face when she walked up to the platform and took the gold trophy, you would have had the choke in your voice that all of us had when Hattie, hair trimmed with gardenias, face alight, and dressed up to the queen's taste, accepted the honor in one of the finest speeches ever given on the Academy floor." Hattie, overcome with emotion, returned to her seat by the kitchen to thunderous applause.

After *Gone with the Wind*, Hattie suffered a reversal of fortune, partially due to the demise of stereotypical roles. With the advent of World War II, Hollywood came under pressure to portray blacks in a more positive light to encourage their patriotism. As a result, a new black star emerged, Lena Horne, who was everything Hattie McDaniel was not: young, sexy, and not a maid (as stipulated in her contract). Turning once more to love to fill the gaping career hole, she married her third husband, Lloyd Crawford, in 1941. She was ecstatic when she confided to gossip columnist Hedda Hopper she was expecting a long-awaited baby. With nesting instinct in full gear and funds saved from acting, Hattie purchased her dream house in a wealthy enclave in Los Angeles. The white, two-story estate boasted seventeen rooms decorated in a Chinese theme. She celebrated the purchase with a huge party, where one of the guests was Clark Gable. The joy of first-time homeownership came with an expiration date. Her neighbors launched a campaign to evict her based on a white-only ordinance. Hattie fought back, and the result was a Supreme Court decision that eliminated "restrictive covenants" that kept African- Americans from residing in certain areas. Joy at the victory ended when Hattie discovered the pregnancy was a hysterical (false) one, born of desperation to have a child. The truth threw her into a tsunami of depression. On top of that, her marriage ended in 1945, and Hattie cited the reason was her husband had threatened to kill her. Her fourth and final walk to the altar was with Larry Williams, in Yuma, Arizona, but that union was only of a few months' duration.

Shakespeare's Hamlet said, "When sorrows come, they come not in single spies but in battalions," and Hattie had weathered hers: white and black slings, aborted marriages, imaginary pregnancy, and a curtailed career. Bloody but unbowed, she returned to radio, a medium which knew no color, the one where she had reigned as Hi-Hat-Hattie. However, after taping several episodes of *The Beulah Show*, she met the one foe she was not able to overcome. By 1952, she was too ill from breast cancer to work and died in the hospital situated on the grounds of the Motion Picture House in Woodland Hills. At the church service, she received a variation of her Academy ovation when thousands of mourners turned out to celebrate her life and its singular achievement of breaking the color barrier in film.

Through her bequest, she directed her Oscar be presented to the predominantly black Howard University for their drama department in remembrance of its having honored her with a luncheon after her historic win. Mysteriously, the trophy vanished during the 1960s racial unrest, and to this date, its whereabouts remain unknown. One theory claims rioting students tossed it into the Potomac in protest against racist stereotyping.

Even in death, Ms. McDaniel could not escape the long shadow cast by Jim Crow. In her will, she had stated, "I desire a white casket and a white shroud; white gardenias in my hair and in my hands, together with a white gardenia blanket and a pillow of red roses. I also wish to be buried in the Hollywood Cemetery." She had always loved being among the stars, and the cemetery held the remains of Rudolph Valentino, Douglas Fairbanks, and other silver screen immortals. Though the floral, clothing, and casket requests were respected, her desired final resting place did not come to pass because of its segregationist policy.

Posthumously, the Old South did become a civilization gone with the wind. In 1999, the new owner of the cemetery offered to have Hattie's remains transferred, though her family declined the offer. In a posthumous mea culpa, he placed a monument on its grounds. A further acknowledgement was two stars on Hollywood's Walk of Fame and her image on a 2006 postage stamp. The latter was fitting as she had left her stamp on American history. Hattie McDaniel had proved not just a credit to her race, but to the human race, the embodiment of a steel gardenia.

Chapter 7

A Bumpy Ride
(1941)

U pon hearing the word "president," the image that is conjured is of a man wearing a dark suit and tie standing in the Oval Office. In sharp juxtaposition, during World War II, Bette Davis assumed the same mantle as the Chief Executive when she held the position of the first female President of the Academy of Motion Picture Arts and Sciences.

This august body had its origin in 1927 during a dinner at the home of MGM head honcho Louis B. Mayer. A week later, thirty-six members dined at Los Angeles's Ambassador Hotel (later the tragic site of the assassination of Robert Kennedy); the International Academy of Motion Picture Arts and Sciences was born. Douglas Fairbanks served as its first president.

The Academy Awards ceremony debuted in 1929 at The Roosevelt Hotel's Blossom Room with 270 attendees. The 13.5-inch gold-plated statuette issued to the winners served as the most coveted of prizes. The official name of the ultimate trophy is the Academy Award of Merit, but it goes by the vernacular: Oscar.

A theory as to the origin of the moniker links it to Oscar Wilde, who while on a US lecture tour, was asked if he had won the Newdigate Prize for Poetry. The wit replied, "Yes, but while many people have won the Newdigate, it is seldom that the Newdigate gets an Oscar." Another legend has it that the Academy librarian, Margaret Herrick, saw a sketch of the prototype and remarked, "He looks a lot like my Uncle Oscar." Bette claimed that after she had won the award in 1935, she nicknamed it after her husband's middle name because the statue shared the same flat derriere.

A road less traveled began in Lowell, Massachusetts, with the birth of Ruth Elizabeth in 1908. The driving force of her youth was her mother, Ruth; her father, Harlow Morrell Davis, was a Harvard Law School graduate who worked as a government patent attorney. Harlow divorced his wife when the young Ms. Davis was seven, and her younger, mentally challenged sister, Barbara, was five. The future star went by Betty until a friend of her mother, who was reading Balzac's *La Cousine Bette,* suggested the spelling change, with the words it would "set you apart, my dear."

In her teens, Bette returned to New England where, desperate for money, she waited on tables at school and once posed nude for a woman making a sculpture. She was determined to become an actress, and Ruth took her to Manhattan in 1928 where she unsuccessfully auditioned for a role in the prestigious Civic Reparatory Theater. Her first professional acting job was with a winter stock company in Rochester run by director George Cukor, who dismissed her after a few months. To offset the back-to-back rejections, after her New York acting debut in 1929 at the Provincetown Playhouse in Greenwich Village, *The New York Times* stated she was "an entrancing creature."

The movies had learned to talk a few years before, and Hollywood was keen on luring Broadway actors and actresses who had commanding voices to take screen tests. Ruth and Bette, with $57 between them, took the train to the coast on a lark they never expected to last a lifetime. Universal Studios gave Ms. Davis a $300-a-week contract. However, by 1932, her career had consisted of lackluster films, and the studio moguls agreed she had "the sex appeal of a string bean." At five feet, three inches and 112 pounds, she was not the Hollywood ideal of the long-limbed blonde bombshell beauty. At a later date, she would smugly state that over the years, she drew more people into theaters "than all the sexpots put together."

Discouraged, mother and daughter decided to return to New York. That was when George Arliss, the English actor, hired her as his leading lady in *The Man Who Played God*, her breakthrough movie role. The film proved a success, and Warner Brothers signed her, beginning a love-hate relationship with the studio characterized by Bette storming off sets. The burgeoning diva's suspension for refusing to act in what she considered inferior parts culminated in a lawsuit by the star.

Unlike leading ladies of the day, Ms. Davis had no qualms about playing unsympathetic roles and was thrilled in 1934 when Warner Brothers lent her to RKO Studios to play the cruel waitress Mildred in W. Somerset Maugham's *Of Human Bondage* opposite Leslie Howard as Philip, the crippled hero. She observed, "villains always had the best-written parts." Bette was always proud of her two Oscars, one for *Dangerous* in 1935, the second for *Jezebel* in 1938. She said, "I'm not a bit modest about them. I don't use those boys for doorstops." A lingering regret was when she turned down the chance to play one of the greatest roles in cinematic history—Scarlett O'Hara in *Gone With the Wind*. Ultimately, as queen of the red carpet, Ms. Davis became the first person to receive ten Oscar nominations.

Ms. Davis, the possessor of a prickly personality, was dreaded off-screen as much as she was adulated onscreen. The consensus was working on a Bette production proved traumatic for all. Those of a charitable nature referred to her as "a real piece of work." Co-star Brian Aherne pronounced, "Nobody but a mother" could have loved her. Another colleague reported that on the set, Davis needed to be the entire band and all the instruments, "including the bazooka." *The New York Times'* journalist Jeanine Basinger recalled she had the unenviable task of informing the star that she could not smoke her ever-present cigarette at a dinner honoring Frank Capra, whose asthmatic wife, Lu, had stored her oxygen tank under the table. Bette's rejoinder was, "Well, get her out of here!" She made an art out of lighting up; cigarettes were to her what swords were to Errol Flynn. Nevertheless, Bette, the giver of no f***s, did not care about ingratiating herself either in her personal or private life. She remarked, "Until you're known in my profession as a monster, you're not a star."

A serial bride, her husbands were likewise not in Camp Bette. Her first trip down the aisle was with Harmon (Ham) Oscar Nelson, Jr. (as in Oscar's backside), a prep school sweetheart. She proudly proclaimed he took her virginity on their wedding night—"and it was hell waiting!" He began hitting her and insisted she have an abortion as motherhood would hinder her moneymaking career. Davis turned for solace to multimillionaire Howard Hughes; she revealed the tycoon told her she was the first woman who had brought him to a climax. Rather than be flattered, she assumed that was just his customary postcoital line. She added, "Huge he was not." Ham found out and threatened Hughes with blackmail; Hughes responded by hiring a hit man. At the end, Hughes paid Ham $70,000, which, as a point of honor, Bette repaid. Another lover was actor Ronald Reagan, of whom she reminisced, "I used to think of him as 'little Ronnie Reagan'—not because he was short, he wasn't, he was tall and well-built. The 'little' was for his acting talent." Undaunted, Bette wed Arthur Franworth; he died from a head injury when his colleague found Franworth in bed with his wife and struck him on the back of his head. She described her third marriage as a reign of masculine terror; hubby described it as a failed attempt at castration. William Grant Sherry, a former prize-fighter-turned-Laguna-Beach-artist tossed a trunk at her and threw her out of the car—and that was on their honeymoon. She had three children from her marriages, including Barbara, so christened after her mentally handicapped sister; however, detesting the name, she called her B. D. She also adopted children, Michael and Margot. Margot suffered from brain damage; at age three, Bette placed her in an institution. Divorce arrived when William fell in love with their baby's nanny. Bette's final marriage, to actor Gary Merrill, ended after ten miserable years in their home, aptly called "Witch Way." She said of her unholy matrimonial forays, "All my marriages were charades, and I was equally responsible. But I always fell in love. That was the original sin." She opined she had confused "muscle with strength."

In the 1940s, Bette was the highest paid woman in the country, known as "the first lady of the screen" and as "the fourth Warner brother." At the pinnacle of her profession, the thirty-three-year-old assumed Hollywood's top job when the Academy of Motion Picture Arts and Sciences elected her as the fourteenth, and the first female, president of the five hundred-member body.

Her tenure was brief: she "resigned in fury" after eight weeks because the board wanted her to "be a figurehead only. Because I was a woman, I had to be controlled." Fox studio head Daryl F. Zanuck had nominated her, and Tinseltown approved. Columnist Hedda Hopper put down her customary poisoned pen: "If any woman here deserves that job, it's Bette." Davis later wrote, "I never imagined that I would hold its most exalted post. As the only woman so honored, I was frankly proud." The position did not prove a love connection, and Bette commented, "I was not supposed to preside intelligently." When she tendered her resignation, Zanuck informed her she would never work in Hollywood again, but she did not fade away.

The egomaniac who made everything "all about me" awed in *All About Eve* (1950), her perfect portrait of an aging actress. Claudette Colbert was originally slated for the role, but in the words of Bette, "she hurt her back, thank God." In her most frightening role, *Whatever Happened to Baby Jane?* (1962), Davis, in pancake makeup and a wig of blonde ringlets, played a demented, elderly woman clinging to her glory days as a child star.

In tribute to the first lady of the movies, at age sixty-nine, she became the first woman to receive the Life Achievement Award of the American Film Institute. Upon acceptance of the tribute she stated, "I suppose...they decided 'Let's give it to a dame.'" Even old archenemy Jack Warner showed up at the gala for "the explosive little broad with the straight left."

Preferring vinegar and venom to sugar and spice, the dame's final role echoed the embroidered words on her pillow, "Old Age Ain't No Place for Sissies." In her mid-seventies, fate dealt Bette four hammer blows. She underwent a mastectomy, suffered a stroke, broke her hip, and underwent acute alcoholic withdrawal. Nevertheless, in Dylan Thomas fashion, she raged against the dying of the light, even though she had a lot to rage against.

Someone once described Hollywood as the place where "they eat their young." In Bette's case, the young bit back. B. D. published *My Mother's Keeper*, a diatribe in which she portrayed her own Mommy Dearest as a human wrecking ball. Bette said of the book, "I will remember every hate-filled sentence, branded on my soul, as long as I live." Mother and daughter never spoke again; B.D. was summarily disinherited.

Upon Bette's death in Paris at age eighty-one, worldwide tributes poured in, but perhaps the most poignant came from a statement her maid had made years before, "It's nice and peaceful when Miss Davis isn't around. But I kind of miss her disturbances." Her epitaph could well have come from her classic line in *All About Eve*, "Fasten your seatbelts: It's going to be a bumpy night."

Chapter 8

Tomorrow to Be Brave (1945)

La Légion Étrangère, the French Foreign Legion, one of the world's most unique military forces, had its origin in 1831 with King Louis Philippe to ensure the successful conquest of Algeria by France as a colonial power. Their soldiers, once referred to as crusaders, mounted campaigns in such far-flung countries as Morocco, Madagascar, and Indochina. Currently, more than one hundred nationalities are represented in the 8,500-man fighting force (women need not apply). But in a surreal former era, the extraordinary Susan Travers became the only female legionnaire.

A World War I poster depicted a little girl asking, "Daddy, what did you do in the Great War?" If Susan's sons had asked her the same question, what a tale she could have told. And her stranger-than-fiction life stemmed from a desire to be wicked.

Ms. Travers spent her twilight years at a French nursing home, where the ninety-plus-year-old with the papery-skin appearance was unremarkable. What set her apart was her posh English accent, her penchant for champagne, and two unique pieces of furniture from a vine-entwined desert home where she had lived with the love of her life: a chest of drawers inlaid with mother-of-pearl and an ornate trunk, both from Damascus. A further defining characteristic was she displayed ribbons on her habitual tweed outfits. One defined her as the recipient of the Légion d'Honneur, a French honor established by Napoleon; the others were the Médaille Militaire and the Croix de Guerre. But the ribbon that was the *pièce de résistance* bore the colors red and white, identifying Travers as having served in the French Foreign Legion.

Now a forgotten footnote in French history, Susan Travers was born in London in 1909. Her father, a Royal Navy officer, had married her mother for her money, and their union was not made in heaven. Susan's best times were spent visiting her grandmother in Devon. She attended a school that she regarded as Jane Eyre did Lowood. During World War I, her father was in charge of marine transport at Marseilles (where her grandfather had once served as the British Consul), and in 1921, he brought his family to Cannes as it was beneficial for his rheumatism. The Riviera was on the cusp of becoming the Mecca of the international jet set, and Susan, with her spirit, beauty, and charm enjoyed their privileged playground. Inspired by her neighbor, Suzanne Lenglen, she also became an accomplished tennis player. Financially afloat with a generous monthly allowance from an aged aunt, Susan nonetheless suffered from her father's neglect as he preferred his only son. By her late teens, Susan had developed a craving for male companionship. "Most of all," she later wrote, "I wanted to be wicked." Her well-heeled parents sent her to a finishing school in Florence; on a trip to Rome, the seventeen-year-old succumbed to the sexual advances of a middle-aged hotel manager named Hannibal. With her slender body, chiseled features, and blue eyes, she was a magnet for male attention; she brushed off her father's reproach that she was "*une fille facile.*"

Susan spent the next decade at skiing and tennis parties all over Europe, enjoying a heady cocktail of champagne, the Charleston, and rushing off to Vienna, Budapest, or Belgrade for a week's entertainment. Susan recalled, "I had lots and lots of friends. Lots and lots of young men. Well, lovers, really." She explained her years of "wining and dining and several affairs with wholly unsuitable men" was a means of escape as her family and native England were "very dull." The idylls of the socialite ended while she was staying in the luxurious retreat of an American divorcee at the time Britain declared war on Germany. Travers, tired of her anchorless lifestyle, joined the Croix-Rouge, the French Red Cross. Her dislike of blood and sickness made her fall short of a Florence

Nightingale, and she became an ambulance driver. Her reason for choosing that route was because, "I wanted adventure. I wanted more action." In 1940, Susan joined the French expedition whose mission was to help the Finns in the Winter War against the Russians.

While she was in Scandinavia, the Nazis overran France, and Susan made her way to Britain. Hungry for purpose and further action, she contacted General de Gaulle's London headquarters. "There followed what must have been the fastest job interview in the world," and the government in exile recruited her as a nurse with the Free French forces. In 1940, the English woman was on a ship filled with legionnaires on a convoy heading for Africa. The next few months were spent in Cameroon and the Congo. Chafing at working as a nurse, she found a way to be reassigned to North Africa with a battalion of the 13th Demi-Brigade of the French Foreign Legion. Half the Legion had sided with de Gaulle; the other had thrown in their lot with the collaborationist Vichy government.

After a stint in Sudan and Eritrea, Susan arrived at what was then called Palestine and worked as an ambulance driver, a challenging occupation as the desert roads were riddled with mines and subject to attack. She had been an army doctor's driver; that ended when he died after a truck he was riding in hit a mine. Travers managed to survive a number of car crashes, but she suffered a wound from shellfire. Her Hemingwayesque "grace under pressure" endeared her to the legionnaires, who nicknamed her "La Miss." The feeling was reciprocal as she admired the Legion's code of "Honneur et Fidélité." She formed close bonds with many of her comrades, including Pierre Mesmer, who was slated to become Prime Minister of France.

Susan also dabbled in several liaisons, including one with the White Russian Prince, Colonel Dimitri Amilakvari, who later died in a skirmish. Unfortunately, love proved as elusive as clutching the desert sand until 1941 when the thirty-one-year-old became the driver for the forty-two-year-old General Marie-Pierre Joseph François Koenig after a gunshot ended the life of his chauffeur while he was picking fruit in a garden. They developed feelings for one another; however, one fly in the romantic ointment was he was her commanding officer; the other was Marie-Jeanne Klein Koenig, his Penelope in France awaiting his return. Given the romantic entanglements, they initially exercised restraint. The turning point was when Susan was in the hospital with jaundice and Koenig brought her a bouquet of roses. Upon her recovery, he came into her room one night, and she later related that unlike Madame Koenig, she did "everything he wanted." Although they had to refrain from all telltale PDA, the Beirut nights were spent in one another's arms. They kept up a façade that the reason they were always together was because the general needed his driver to be at his constant call. He refused to let Susan live with him due to discretion and because, as he put it, "What the men can't have, I can't have."

The blissful honeymoon came to a halt in 1942 when the military ordered Koenig to defend Bir Hakeim in the Western Desert with the objective of preventing the Axis powers from capturing the Suez Canal. "In for a penny, in for a pound," thought Travers, and she followed her lover, who she always called "general." Travers told him, "Wherever you will go, I will go too," acting upon her vow to stay by his side. In order to protect her from enemy fire, the soldiers placed her in a coffin-sized hole in the desert sands, where, for two weeks, she heard the cries of the dying. The 4,000 French troops and the lone woman spent two weeks encircled by Ernst Rommel's Panzer Division, pounded by their guns and raked by shells from their Stukas. During the Battle of Bir Hakeim in Libya, when their French desert camp came under intense bombardment from German and Italian forces, Rommel told his men that it would take them all of fifteen minutes to crush any opposition. The army hoped they could last a week. Under Koenig's command the 1,000 legionnaires and 1,500 Allied troops held out for fifteen days, and Bir Hakeim became a symbol of resistance. With ammunition and water depleted, and in 128-degree temperatures, Koenig resolved to lead a breakout at night through the minefields and cordons of Nazi panzers that encircled Bir Hakeim. Ms. Travers was the driver for Koenig and the Russian prince on a perilous flight. She pressed the pedal of the Ford to the floor and burst through the German lines, blazing a trail for the other Allied vehicles to follow. Eleven bullets hit the vehicle, and despite crashing into some parked panzers, she, along with her present and past lover, reached the British lines. Of the 3,700 troops,

2,400 escaped, including 650 legionnaires. Koenig became the hero of France; Susan Travers received the Croix de Guerre. Her award referred to her "bravery in the face of several barrages of intense artillery fire, and numerous bullet strikes of her vehicle."

The couple's amorous celebration ended with the arrival of Madame Koenig. In 1943, the army assigned the general to join de Gaulle in Tunisia. He had his eyes on the prize of military advancement, and to avoid a potentially damaging scandal, he abandoned his mistress. Susan showed more bravery in war than in love, and she contemplated suicide. Recalling her family motto, "Neither Afraid Nor Timid," she put down her pistol.

Proud of her efforts, in 1945, she wrote, "I had become the person I'd always wanted to be." At the end of the war, she faced the prospect of returning to civilian life and told the Legion's recruiting officer, who happened to be her friend, "I shall leave all my old friends—I shall go back and live with my family (who had returned to England), and it will be dull." Astoundingly, he invited her to sign up as an official Legionnaire. The woman with the nickname "La Miss" did not need to give her sex on the application as it was a male-only establishment, and there was no medical exam. All she stated was that she was a warrant officer in logistics. In the chaotic postwar months, her request slipped through amid the hundreds of thousands of forms. Ms. Travers, the only woman ever to serve in the Legion, had to, of course, make her own uniform. She departed for Tunisia, where her job was to buy a barrel of red wine and deliver it on the back of a mule. Later, she departed for Vietnam during the first Indochina War. She later said of her wartime exploits, "I just happen to be a person who is not frightened. I am not afraid."

In Southeast Asia, Susan met and married a fellow legionnaire, Nicholas Schlegelmilch, who had also been in Bir Hakeim. In 1947, she resigned her commission, destroyed her wartime diaries, and went on to raise her two sons and live a non-wicked life on the outskirts of Paris. A decade later, the legion invited her to a ceremony at Les Invalides. Standing at attention, she froze as General Koenig, who she had not seen since the war, approached and pinned the Médaille Militaire on her tweed coat. He told her, "I hope this will remind you of many things. Well done, La Miss." He saluted her and turned away; the meeting was to be their last.

In her final years, Ms. Travers agreed to a biography on her life so that her grandchildren would know how wicked granny had been. She named it *Tomorrow to be Brave: A Memoir of the Only Woman Ever to Serve in the French Foreign Legion*. She had chosen the title after a line from a poem her general had read to her under the desert stars, "Distrust yourself, and sleep before you fight. 'Tis not too late tomorrow to be brave."

Chapter 9

Let No Man Drag Me Down (1948)

One of the most iconoclastic moments in Olympic history occurred in 1936 Berlin, where, in a stadium draped with red and black swastika banners, Jesse Owens' historic victory signified the triumph of sportsmanship over tyranny. Adolph Hitler did not appreciate an African American sharecropper's son from Alabama, the grandson of slaves, besting his Aryan athletes. In contrast to Owens' immortal chapter, Alice Coachman, the first African American woman to compete and win a gold medal, became a forgotten footnote in Olympic lore.

The fifth of ten children, Alice Marie Coachman grew up in Albany, Georgia; she was born in 1923, the daughter of strict Baptist parents, Fred, a plasterer, and Evelyn, a maid. As a girl, Alice picked cotton to help her family's finances during the Great Depression. She did not have female friends because they were too ladylike; instead, she played baseball with the boys. Fred insisted his daughters should act dainty, sit on the porch, and drink tea. Nevertheless, any chance Alice could get, she slipped away to the playground. At age eleven, her mother caught Alice jitterbugging at a local dance hall; this was after having been warned that if she was ever found dancing, her mother would give her a whipping. The memory of the corporal punishment remained, and later in life, Alice recalled, "Lord, have mercy, she wasn't lying. 'WHUP! WHUP!' Y' know what? I could run, but she was fast enough to run after me and whup my tail... Shoot, I'm almost seventy-four years old and I still think of that. I still feel it."

Initial training consisted of running barefoot on dirt roads despite sweltering Southern temperatures. She especially enjoyed defying gravity, using ropes and sticks for makeshift high jumps. A family acquaintance who saw Alice's potential told her mother that one day the girl was going to jump over the moon. Mrs. Coachman responded, "She's going to break her neck, that's what she's going to do." Because of segregation, Alice could not train at athletic fields with whites. Alice said of her first training grounds, "You had to run up and down the red roads and the dirt roads. You went out there in the fields, where there was a lot of grass and no track—no nothing." Despite her prowess, Alice never envisioned an athletic career and dreamed of becoming a musician or a dancer, having been enthralled by saxophonist Coleman Hawkins and by actress Shirley Temple.

By the end of seventh grade at Madison High School, Alice was such an outstanding runner (who had also succeeded in clearing a hurdle of more than five feet) that Cleve Abbott, a coach at Tuskegee Institute, asked her parents to let her train with its high school team during the summer. During those months, Alice shattered so many records Coachman invited her to attend as a full-time student. Although her working scholarship entailed cleaning the gym and the swimming pool, sewing football uniforms, and maintaining the tennis courts, she still found time to compete in sports. The school gave her a gift of store-bought shoes, and when asked what they felt like, the teen, who had only participated in athletics barefoot, replied, "They hurt." Coachman also played basketball, and Tuskegee won three consecutive titles and went on to compete at increasingly advanced levels. Three years later, she enrolled at its university and became a pillar of its outstanding track team. Alice's successes were startling: from 1939 to 1948, she garnered ten consecutive wins in the Amateur Athletic Union high jump championships, the first at age sixteen. Alice told the Associated Press, "My dad did not want me to travel to Tuskegee and then up north to the Nationals. He felt it was too dangerous. Life was very different for African-Americans at that time. But I came back and showed him my medal and talked about all the things I saw. He and my mom were very proud of me."

In 1948, the year after Jackie Robinson broke the color barrier in major league baseball, the London Games offered Ms. Coachman her first—and ultimately, her only—opportunity to compete in the Olympics. During the years when she had been at the peak of her ability, World War II had resulted in the cancelling of the 1940 and the 1944 Games. Initially, she was reluctant to accept because of a back injury, but she underwent a change of heart. As Alice explained, "I didn't want to let my country down, or my family and school. Everyone was pushing me." Upon her arrival, she found herself staying for the first time in integrated housing. She said, "It was a beautiful thing to be around that camp. All those people from different countries doing their thing, singing and dancing." Before Coachman's event, the Games had gone badly for the United States women's track and field team. Coachman recalled of the disappointing news, "All the fast girls we had, they would come in last. It was kind of sad." On a rainy afternoon, wearing a tracksuit top, Coachman cleared five feet six inches on her first attempt and thus defeated Dorothy Tyler of Britain (who won silver) and Micheline Ostermeyer of France (who won the bronze). Ms. Coachman became the only American that year to garner the gold. She also earned the distinction of becoming the first black woman to take Olympic gold home. She reminisced of that magic moment, "I didn't know I had won. I glanced over into the stands where my coach was, and she was clapping her hands. I saw it on the board, 'A. Coachman, USA, Number One.' I went on, stood up there, and they started playing the national anthem. It was wonderful to hear."

After Owen's victory, there was no invitation to the Fuhrer's box. When Baldur von Schirach tried to persuade Hitler to at least be photographed alongside Owens, Hitler retorted, "These Americans should be ashamed of themselves for letting their medals be won by a Neger. I would never shake the hand of one." Twelve years later, in England, Coachman experienced a far different reception in Wembley Stadium. The young woman who grew up running barefoot on the dirt roads of rural Georgia received a gold medal from King George VI, Queen Elizabeth II's father. Post award, Alice had an invitation to cruise on a British royal yacht and met French President Charles de Gaulle in Paris on a post-Olympic tour of Western Europe.

What Owens experienced after he had scaled the Olympic heights was that Jim Crow still recoiled from his dark pigmentation. His slight from the Fuhrer in Berlin was matched by the one from Franklin D. Roosevelt in the capital. There was no White House reception for the US runner; the President was scared if he invited the track star, there would be a backlash from southern voters.

Upon Coachman's return, she was the guest of honor at a party thrown by Count Basie, and President Harry S. Truman invited her to the White House, where former First Lady Eleanor Roosevelt gave her a warm reception. Alice enjoyed a 175-mile motorcade ride that wound its way through Georgia from Atlanta to her hometown. Albany welcomed her with a ceremony—one where whites and blacks were seated separately. Although

King George VI had given Alice a gracious greeting, her hometown mayor—although he appeared with her on the auditorium stage—refused to shake her hand. As an additional affront, Alice had to enter and exit through a side door. Although many white supporters, grateful for Alice bringing victory to America, sent gifts to her at a party at her godfather's home, they sent them without a card; they were afraid of a negative reaction from white neighbors. Bitterness, however, held no place in Coachman's DNA. She philosophically observed, "We had segregation, but it wasn't any problem for me because I had won. That was up to them, whether they accepted it or not." Fortunately, there were many on the acceptance side. Alice became the first black woman to endorse an international product, Coca-Cola, and she appeared on billboards with Jesse Owens. Not one to rest on her laurels, she received a bachelor's degree from Tuskegee and another in home economics from Albany State College. Moreover, she created the Alice Coachman Track and Field Foundation to help young Olympic hopefuls and veteran Games participants who were in straitened financial circumstances. After riding the wave of fame, she encountered a series of hard knocks: a breakup with her fiancée and a series of dead-end jobs, including a stint as a maid.

Coachman explained her retirement from track and field by declaring she had accomplished what she had set out to do and now there was a new arena on which to set her sights. "It was time for me to start looking for a husband. That was the climax. I won the gold medal. I proved to my mother, my father, my coach and everybody else that I had gone to the end of my rope." Alice married Dr. N. F. Davis with whom she had a son, Richmond, and a daughter, Evelyn. She never showed them her gold medal, "I figured that sooner or later, if I hold on to it, when they got interested, they would sit down and look at it." After her divorce, she married another Davis, Frank—her former fiancée—and went by the name Alice Coachman Davis.

Despite her trailblazing accomplishment, Coachman faded into obscurity. A popularly held belief was that Wilma Rudolph, a triple-gold medalist in sprints at the 1960 Rome Olympics, was the first African American woman to bring home the top prize. Alice attributed the misconception to the fact that Italy's Games were televised while earlier competitions depended on photographs. Another reason for Coachman's fading from view can be attributed to modesty. As Alice put it, "From the very first medal I won in 1939, my mama used to stress being humble. You're no better than anyone else. The people you pass on the ladder will be the same people you'll be with when the ladder comes down." Self-effacement is indeed a feat for one inducted into both the USA Track and Field Hall of Fame and the US Olympic Hall of Fame—of which honor she said it "was as good as it gets," and a school and a street were named after her in Albany.

During an Atlanta press conference that showcased several of one hundred American Olympic greats in conjunction with the Centennial Games, among them media darlings such as Mark Spitz and Mary Lou Retton, a virtually unknown Olympian attracted the greatest number of reporters. Alice Coachman sat in a corner of the Hyatt hotel ballroom, charming the media. Alice was tickled pink at the lens directed at Olympic history and its Southern connections.

At a time when there were few high profile black athletes beyond Jesse Owens, Jackie Robinson, and Joe Louis, Coachman served as a pioneer. She was aware she was a role model for other black women athletes and stated, "If I had gone to the Games and failed, there wouldn't be anyone to follow in my footsteps." Those who followed in her steps were track stars such as Wilma Rudolph, Florence Griffith Joyner, and Jackie Joyner-Kersee; since her Olympic triumph, black women have comprised a majority of the US women's track and field team.

A quotation Alice borrowed from Booker T. Washington proves it was not only on the field where she aimed high: "I let no man drag me down so low as to make me hate him."

Chapter 10

Pick Up Your Feet (1955)

Geoffrey Chaucer's fourteenth-century work *The Canterbury Tales* revolves around a motley crew of pilgrims who share salacious stories to pass the time on their pilgrimage. One of their number, the Wife of Bath, had outlived five husbands, though she had managed to elude motherhood. Emma "Grandma" Gatewood served as her diametric opposite: the only commonality is that she was also a pilgrim on a journey that made her the first woman to conquer—unaccompanied—the Appalachian Trail.

The idiom "a walk in the park"—denoting something easy—never applied to Emma on either a figurative or literal level. She took to the trail to escape the shadow of her past. Her life up to her historic journey had been

so rife with hardship she knew she could take anything
Mother Nature could dish out.

The Caldwell family was from the socioeconomic level
that some refer to as "the wrong side of the tracks" while
others refer to as "white trash." Emma Rowena was born
in 1887 on a farm in Gallia County, Ohio, near the Ohio
River, one of fifteen children—ten girls and five boys—
who slept four to a bed. In the winter, the snow on the
clapboard roof blew inside the house, and the children
would shake their covers before the snow would melt.
Her father, Hugh, had lost a leg, along with his moral
compass, in the Civil War and had consecrated his life to
whiskey and gambling. Her mother, Evelyn, raised her
large brood in their log cabin. She sent her children to a
one-room schoolhouse when they did not have chores at
the farm, a rare occurrence. Emma's formal education
ended in the eighth grade—the highest level offered; as
she loved learning, she repeated it as often as possible.

Hugh fell at work and broke his remaining leg,
necessitating his hospitalization for two months. While
her mother remained at his side, seventeen-year-old
Emma kept the home fires burning. Upon their return,
Emma worked in Virginia as a maid, and when it proved
intolerable, she took another job that paid seventy-five
cents a week. At that time, she met Perry Clayton (P. C.)
Gatewood, considered the great bachelor catch of Gallia
County as he had a college degree; she wedded him in
1907, at age nineteen. He was eight years her senior, a
teacher, and Emma hoped marriage would provide an

exit from her hard-knock life. She raised eleven children, built fences, burned tobacco beds, and mixed cement, in addition to her household chores. Her haven was the woods, where she learned about wildlife, the medicinal properties of plants, and which plants were edible.

Emma's life transformed to Robert Frost's "The Road Less Traveled" because of a 1949 *National Geographic* magazine she had been flipping through while waiting for her doctor's appointment. She was captivated when she saw photographs of the Appalachian Trail, one she viewed as a window to a wonderful new world. She devoured the article that stated, "The Appalachian Trail is a public pathway that rates as one of the seven wonders of the outdoorsman's world." At the time, just one man, a twenty-nine-year-old soldier, Earl V. Shaffer, had hiked the trail in its entirety. After him, five others had done likewise; all had been men. She determined, "If those men can do it, I can do it." One response to the future question of "Why?" was "I thought it would be a lark;" it was not.

Emma's first attempt in 1954 ended badly. Starting out in Maine, she broke her glasses and got lost; rangers came to her rescue. Their stern advice was, "Grandma, go home." Undaunted, the next year she told her children she was going for a walk—which was not a lie. She just omitted the walk would entail hiking 2,051 miles of mountain footpaths, would begin in Georgia, and would end in Maine. Her omission was based on the certainty her kids would attempt to dissuade their sixty-seven-year-old mother.

Not many women would leave for a lengthy trip with just one change of clothing, but Gatewood was not like many women. Her main outfit was worn jeans and Keds canvas shoes, with a hand-sewn sack slung over her shoulder. Her supplies consisted of a shower curtain as protection against the elements, a Swiss Army knife, a flashlight, an umbrella—which she used to ward off a black bear, a pen, and a small notebook. Dark memories were the only heavy baggage. In terms of food, she brought along Vienna sausages, raisins, peanuts, and bouillon cubes. She felt no need to lug along a tent; like Blanche DuBois, she would depend on the kindness of strangers—in her case, for lodging. On the occasions that did not pan out, Emma slept under a bed of leaves, under picnic tables, and once on a porch swing. Gatewood was resolve and determination bundled into a 5'2" body. She wrote in her notebook, "I did not worry if it was to be the end of me. It was as good a place as any." She determined when she arrived atop Mount Katahdin, her final destination, she would sing "America the Beautiful."

On her pilgrimage, Emma experienced the best and the worst of nature and humanity—as well as danger. On numerous occasions, she encountered back-to-back hurricanes on the east coast, a rattle-snake, and bears. Despite the hardship on the trail, she found peace and wrote in her notebook, "the petty entanglements of life are brushed aside like cobwebs." Word of the elderly woman walking the Appalachian Trail on her own spread like the proverbial wildfire and news of Grandma Gatewood, who the press dubbed "the widow," proved to be catnip to reporters from magazines such as *Sports Illustrated.* In response to those who asked why, she provided varying answers, "Just for the heck of it," "The forest is a quiet place and nature is beautiful. I don't want to sit and rock. I want to do something," "I want to see what's on the other side of the hill, then what's beyond that." One article made its way to her hometown, which is how her children learned what she meant when she said she was going for a walk.

Emma completed her journey in 146 days, an average of fourteen miles a day. She would start out at sunrise and not stop until exhaustion took over. As she stood at her final destination, the peak of Mount Katahdin in Maine, she sang. She said, "I told myself I could do it. And I did it." Throughout her adventure, the public watched her traipse across the evening news on television, wondering whether the older woman, on her own, traversing inhospitable terrain, would survive. Little did they know what Emma had already endured.

What people knew about Mrs. Gatewood was remarkable: she was the first woman to hike the entire Appalachian Trail by herself in one season. However, as with an iceberg, for the one quarter visible, there are three quarters that are invisible. The real reason as to *why* would remain a secret for over half a century.

Gatewood was Ben Montgomery's great-aunt, and his variation of a bedtime story was listening to tales about the family's adventurous granny. As a journalist for *The Tampa Bay Times* in Florida, he decided to investigate the reason why, at an advanced age, his relative walked 2,000 miles through fourteen states, risking exposure to rattlesnakes, bears, flooded creeks—she could not swim—and slippery mountain slopes. In a quest to uncover the truth, he contacted Emma's surviving children, who gave him access to her notebook, journals, and letters. In those sources, he discovered what Emma had withheld from news interviews: P.C. had almost pummeled her to death on several occasions. During one beating, he broke a broom over her head. Her children revealed that their father's sexual appetite had been insatiable, and he forced himself on their mother several times a day. When Emma complained of his sadism, he claimed she was crazy and asked her to what asylum she wanted to be committed. In 1937, she fled to relatives in California, leaving behind two daughters, ages nine and eleven. In a letter to her girls—with no return address—she wrote, "I have suffered enough at his hands to last me for the next hundred years." However, missing her children, she returned home. P.C. had mismanaged their farm, and lacking sufficient funds for the mortgage, they were forced to move to a cabin in West Virginia. A few months later, P.C. beat her "beyond recognition" several times. In 1939, P.C. broke her teeth, cracked one of her ribs, and bloodied her face. Their fifteen-year-old son, Nelson, restrained his father, which provided Emma the opportunity to escape. Infuriated, P.C. left the house and returned in the company of a deputy sheriff. When her husband flung open the front door, his wife was lying in wait with a five-pound sack of flour which she hurtled in his face. The sheriff arrested Emma; she spent a night in jail until the mayor of the small West Virginia town noticed her blackened eyes and bloodied face and arranged for her release. Her son called her to say his dad was gone, and when Emma returned, she saw P.C. had emptied her home of all the furniture. Freedom arrived after thirty-five years when Emma obtained a divorce in 1941, a great stigma in that era—and went on to raise her youngest children without alimony. To avoid the scarlet letter—D—Emma claimed she was a widow. In her notebook, Emma wrote that she had been "happy ever since." In 1968, P.C. told Nelson his dying request was he wanted to see Emma walk through his door once more. It was one walk "his widow" refused to take.

Emma's walking did not end with her first hike. Gatewood returned to the thru-hike (hiking straight through in less than twelve months) in 1957, making her the first person, male or female, to twice tackle the Appalachian Trail. Gatewood said the second time was so she could enjoy it. She completed the trail again in 1964, at age seventy-five, in sections, becoming the first person to hike it three times. In addition to tenacity, Emma had a sense of humor. When Groucho Marx interviewed her on his television show, *You Bet Your Life,* he asked, "What did your folks raise on your farm in addition to you?" Emma replied, "Tobacco, corn, wheat, and a little Cain."

In 1959, she headed west, walking from Independence, Montana, to Portland, Oregon, as part of the Oregon Centennial celebration. She left two weeks after a wagon train but passed it in Idaho. The trip covered nearly 2,000 miles and took ninety-five days. The odyssey of Grandma Gatewood resonated with many women who felt that if someone nearing seventy could hike it in one season, they could follow in her footsteps. The publicity the hiking grandmother garnered brought the Appalachian Trail into the spotlight. Sections of the trail had been poorly maintained, but after her odyssey, conservation efforts concentrated on its upkeep. Grandma Gatewood Memorial Trail, a six-mile hike located in Hocking Hills State Park in Ohio, serves as a tribute to her legacy. Every January, thousands gather in her honor and take part in her favorite pastime—walking. When a fellow hiker asked her which part of the trail she liked best, she responded, "Going downhill, Sonny."

In 1973, Emma awakened from a coma, hummed a few bars of "The Battle Hymn of the Republic" and closed her eyes. On her epic trek, Emma followed the advice her father had given her as a child: "Pick up your feet."

Chapter 11

A Perfect Match (1956)

The color white is de rigueur for participants in Wimbledon; however, on a metaphorical level, the color is emblematic of the fact that for most of its history, the elite club has been a white Anglo-Saxon enclave. Two blows were struck against elitism when Angela Buxton became the first Jewish woman and Althea Gibson became the first black woman to play at Wimbledon.

In William Shakespeare's *The Tempest,* Trinculo states, "Misery acquaints a man with strange bedfellows." In the tennis world, a tale of two friends showed the truth of the Bard's words. Although the women hailed from different worlds, their outsider status united them in a lifelong bond, and in the process, they lobbed a ball over the net of prejudice.

Angela's family had fled the Russian pogroms at the turn of the century; in their adopted homeland, they anglicized Bakstansky to Buxton. She was born in Liverpool, England, in 1934; her father, Harry, started off as a cash-strapped street trader in Leeds who developed a gambling system that enabled him to purchase a string of cinemas. During the Blitz, he sent his wife, Violet, and their two children to South Africa while he remained behind to look after the business.

Under apartheid, it was not long before Angela saw the face of anti-Semitism. Violet was in the common bathroom of their apartment building and was working on her hair. When a man became impatient waiting his turn, he told her, "You Jews are all the same. You think you own the world!" Violet struck him twice with her brush.

Upon their return to England, Violet and Harry divorced, and Angela left for boarding school in North Wales. A junior tournament victory convinced Violet to concentrate on her daughter's career. Angela transferred to a school in Hampstead for children with special talent; its headmistress put her in contact with London's exclusive Cumberland Club. When she asked Bill Blake, the club's director, if she had not been offered a membership because she was not good enough, he responded, "We don't take Jews here." The next slight occurred when the Cumberland staged the Middlesex junior championships. The father of Angela's chief competitor called to inform her they had disqualified Angela; Mrs. Buxton refused to accept the rejection, and her daughter beat her competitor and won the title. As Angela rose in the ranks, the other girls on the circuit gave her the cold shoulder. To offset the discrimination, Simon Marks, the Jewish owner of Marks & Spencer, allowed her to practice on his private tennis court.

Harry financed an extended trip to California so his daughter could further her training. A highlight of her stay was a visit to a movie studio where she had her picture taken with Doris Day. In contrast, at the Los Angeles Tennis Club, she recalled, "After two weeks, and after my application for membership was accepted, they gave me my money back!" Once again, she had been ostracized due to anti-Semitism.

In 1955, the British government selected Angela to represent her country in a tennis exhibition in India. President Eisenhower also sent Althea to the same goodwill tour of the United States Lawn Tennis Association event, and a lifelong friendship began.

Born in 1927, Althea's saga began in a sharecropper's shack when her parents Daniel and Annie relocated from Silver, South Carolina, to Harlem, New York, in a bid to outrun Jim Crow. She struggled academically and often skipped school for bowling alleys and pool halls. Her father, a strict disciplinarian, beat her, and she ran away to a Catholic girls' home, then lived in welfare apartments, taking menial jobs to survive. Buddy Walker, a musician, was so impressed by her athleticism he gave her two rackets from a second-hand store for five dollars each and introduced her to Fred Johnson, the famed one-armed pro at the nearby Cosmopolitan Tennis Club. Sugar Ray Robinson also took the promising athlete under his wing; when she graduated high school, the boxer paid for her class ring. Although there were no actual rules against blacks in tennis, segregation was perpetuated through the barriers of money and social class. Nevertheless, she made a meteoric rise in her sport, and in 1950, Althea played at the West Side Tennis Club in Forest Hills, Queens. Fans shouted from the stands for Althea's opponent to, "Beat the nigger." Gibson, the Jackie Robinson of her sport, achieved a number of firsts: the first black player to be ranked No. 1 in the world, the first African American to win a Grand Slam title, and in 1957, the first black champion at Wimbledon in singles. She accepted the trophy from Queen Elizabeth II. In her autobiography, *I Always Wanted to be Somebody*, she wrote, "Shaking hands with the Queen of England was a long way from being forced to sit in the colored section of the bus." The star appeared on the covers of *Sports Illustrated* and *Time*, the first black woman to be so honored. Gibson had vanquished the odds stacked against her race, gender, and class. Footage depicts a beaming Althea seated in a convertible during her ticker tape parade on Broadway in Manhattan as fans lined the streets to cheer.

In India, during the 1956 French Open, Angela noticed Althea sitting on the sidelines and thought to herself, "What the hell is she sitting there for? One of the best players in the world and she wasn't chosen." The pair

took to one another; Buxton was dawn to Gibson's dry
sense of humor and admired her fine singing voice (she
later became the only Wimbledon champion to sing
at the Wimbledon Ball). They likewise bonded over a
shared love of movies, and when in Manchester, Gibson
sometimes watched three films a day at the Buxton
owned cinemas. Althea called her friend "Angie baby."

The pair won the 1955 French doubles title, and when
Buxton reached the Wimbledon singles final, the first
Brit to do so in seventeen years, Violet decided to attend
its Ball to see her daughter dancing. However, when
Mrs. Buxton went to obtain her ticket, a lady informed
her there were no tickets left. Violet drew herself up
to her full five feet, two inches, and stated that if that
were the case, her daughter would be home with her
and unable to compete at the scheduled event. The
ticket was forthcoming. After their historic doubles win
at Wimbledon, a brave British newspaper headlined,
"Minorities Win."

Their professional partnership came to an abrupt end
when Buxton injured her wrist at a 1956 tournament
in New Jersey. Undaunted, she went on to win the
Maccabiah title in 1957 but soon after retired. Her
post-tennis life was fulfilling as she became a coach,
started the Buxton Tennis center in north London, and
volunteered on a kibbutz during the Six-Day War. Asked
why she went to Israel during a danger fraught time, she
explained her husband was Donald Silk, the president of
the Zionist organization of Great Britain and Ireland. She

took along her three children, ages six, four, and eighteen months, to volunteer on Kibbutz Amiad and assisted in the dining room, the orchards, and the laundry room. Despite her divorce, her allegiance to Israel remained, and she became one of the six founders of the Israel Tennis Centers. In 1981, the Jewish Sports Hall of Fame made her a member. The active, forever-on-the-go Buxton splits her time between England and Florida and is a proud great-grandmother. She is grateful for her storied career but remains irked that although she applied for membership in the All England Lawn Tennis Club in 1958, she is still awaiting a reply. She finds this affront offensive as she had reached the singles quarterfinals of the French Open and the finals of Wimbledon. The Fates did not weave such a kind pattern for her former partner.

It was nothing short of a miracle that a daughter of Harlem broke tennis' color barrier three years after major league baseball had begun to be integrated since tennis, with its added hurdles of money and class, proved more resistant to change. However, as a Wimbledon winner, Gibson appeared at the All England Club's 1984 women's centenary. And in the early 1990s, spectators saw her alone, regal, sitting in the champion's box during the US Open at Flushing Meadows. Her aloof personality did not endear her to others, but her attitude was one of self-defense, a way of shielding herself from the plantation mentality that permeated the time's tennis world. She played on the lawns of Wimbledon and Forest Hills, but it turned into a dual-edged miracle. In the era before corporate sponsors and product endorsement deals, Gibson's triumphs did not translate into financial security. To generate income, she recorded a record album and played a slave in John Ford's *The Horse Soldiers*. She also signed a contract with the Harlem Globetrotters to participate in exhibition tennis during half-time breaks. From 1963, she became the first African American woman to participate on the Ladies PGA golf circuit. One of her supporters was Billie Jean King, a promoter of her sport's illustrious foremothers; King and her then-husband, Larry, invited the forty-one-year-old Althea to play in a pro event. In her later years, she went into a decline and subsisted on social security benefits. Her travails provided a poignant twist to the closing paragraph of her autobiography, "I'm Althea Gibson, tennis champion. I hope it makes me happy."

As Althea sat in a small apartment in New Jersey, she saw the largest tennis stadium in the country named after Arthur Ashe; she watched as baseball retired Jackie Robinson's number in his honor. She grew bitter as history consigned her to a forgotten footnote. The indomitable spirit that had led her to overcome penury and the country-club crowd still survived, and she did not want the world to see her old and feeble. Nevertheless, she made an exception for 'Angie baby.' Her British chum put her in touch with Venus Williams, then an up-and-coming phenomenon. In a phone call, Althea counseled the younger woman before her first US Open final, "Be who you are and let your racket do the talking."

In 1995, Angela was in her kitchen cooking onions when she received a call from the sixty-seven-year-old Althea. Gibson had suffered several strokes and was living in East Orange, New Jersey. Her old friend said, "Angie baby, I can't last much longer. I'm going to commit suicide. I've got no money, I'm very ill, I've got no medication..." Buxton sent her money and placed an ad in *Tennis Week* asking for contributions. Those who remembered Gibson's glory days sent cash; Althea pulled out of her slump and with the windfall bought a silver Cadillac convertible.

In 2003, Althea passed away at age seventy-six. It could not have been easy to be a Robinson, an Ashe, or a Gibson, who blazed a path for others at a considerable cost to themselves. In a white tennis outfit, Althea shone in a white world.

To celebrate the five-time Grand Slam winner, the US Postal Service issued a stamp that showcases Gibson, whose lean, five foot eleven inch body is poised to deliver a low volley. Similarly, the US Tennis Association erected a granite statue to immortalize the tennis great in the US Open. At its unveiling, they also recognized the then eighty-five-year-old Buxton; neck adorned with a pearl choker, she addressed the crowd from her wheelchair. Together, Angie and Althea had proved a perfect match.

Chapter 12

Fearless 261
(1967)

The act of running weaves throughout the film *Forrest Gump*: when the bullies chase Forrest, he runs; when the Viet Cong fire at Forrest, he runs; when Jenny breaks his heart, he runs. The same phenomena dominated the days of Kathrine Switzer, the first woman to complete the all-male Boston Marathon as an official entrant.

The Boston Athletic Association (BAA) founded the famous race in 1897, the year after the revival of the Olympic Games in Greece. The legendary event has its precedent in the legend that in 490 BC, Pheidippides ran from Marathon to his native Athens (a distance of approximately twenty-five miles) to announce his city had won the Battle of Marathon, then died from exhaustion on the floor of the Greek Assembly. In the modern era, the BAA scheduled its event to coincide with

Patriots' Day, a New England holiday celebrated on the anniversary of the Battles of Lexington and Concord. Since the first Marathon commemorated the historic run of a messenger, the Boston Marathon commemorated the historic midnight ride of Paul Revere.

Kathrine Virginia Switzer was born in 1946 in Amberg, Germany, when her pregnant mother, Virginia, went overseas to join her husband, Homer, a US Army major. What marred their reunion were scenes from a devastated postwar Germany. In the hospital, the anxious new father filled out the birth certificate and omitted the "e" in the middle of Katherine. Little did he imagine the error would impact his daughter's life and alter an American athletic institution.

Three years later, the Switzers returned to Fairfax County, Virginia, where Kathrine attended Madison High School. After informing her father she wanted to be a cheerleader, he responded, "You shouldn't be on the sidelines cheering for other people. People should cheer for *you*." Heeding his advice, Kathrine became a member of the girls' field hockey team. To get in shape, she took daily runs despite warnings it would result in big legs and a moustache. Smitten, to borrow Forrest's words, "From that day on, if she was goin' somewhere, she was running!" She also worked on the school newspaper because of the dearth of coverage of girls' sports, a fact Switzer sought to change. Because her name was always misspelled, she decided to use the byline K.V. Switzer, an idea she patterned on idols J.D. Salinger, T. S. Eliot, and e.e. cummings.

As a journalism major at Syracuse University, Kathrine bypassed the sorority route and trained on the men's cross-country team as there was no women's equivalent; her roommates snidely referred to her as Road Runner. A perk of membership was football player Big Tom Miller, a 235-pound nationally ranked hammer thrower and Olympic hopeful with whom she began to go steady. The twenty-year-old was likewise enthralled with Coach Arnie Briggs, who had participated fifteen times in the Mecca for runners: the Boston Marathon. One afternoon, Arnie and Kathrine were running—despite blizzard conditions—as he regaled her with his racing adventures. He was taken aback when she told him something—the physical equivalent of an avalanche: she wanted to do more than *hear* about the race. His response was, "No dame ever ran the Boston Marathon." He repeated the zeitgeist that if they did something that arduous, it would turn a female's features into a man's; a doctor had previously informed her that if she were to undertake such a feat, her uterus would fall out. Unable to dissuade her, Arnie grudgingly agreed that if she managed to run 26 miles, he would escort her to Boston. Weeks before the event, Kathrine completed a 31-mile practice run while an overly exerted Arnie fainted in her arms. A damper on the big day was Tom's reaction; he said he would be joining her because if a girl could do it, he could do it as well.

Because of the frigid temperature on the day of the race, Kathrine had to forego wearing her burgundy top and shorts and donned a bulky men's gray sweatshirt that Arnie had salvaged from the locker room at Syracuse University. Four miles later, no longer cold, she tossed her sweatshirt, a fact that alerted reporters there was a woman participant—something that did not sit well with official Jock Semple. He jumped off the press truck, screamed at Switzer, and ripped the corner of her bib. Tom threw a block that knocked Semple out of the way; photojournalists snapped pictures of the incident, and it became the equivalent of theAmerican Revolutionary shot heard around the world. As the truck carrying the journalists followed, the reporters shouted, "What are you trying to prove?" and "When are you going to quit?" A random man shouted, "You should be back in the kitchen making dinner for your husband." Then Semple went by on another vehicle, yelling in his Scottish brogue, "You are ere een beeeeeggg trouble!" Over the next twenty-four miles, Switzer feared officials had contacted the police to drag her off the course. By Heartbreak Hill, the infamous incline that tortuously signifies the final six miles of the Marathon, Switzer had become an accidental activist, determined to cross the finish line, even if she did so on hands and knees.

Switzer completed the race in four hours and twenty minutes, having left Tom behind. At the finish line, a journalist sneered, "Are you a suffragette?" Retribution was swift: Semple disqualified Kathrine and expelled her from the AAU. She received hate mail and negative press reports. Journalist Jack McCarthy wrote she had posed an unnecessary problem for the race organization and that if he "didn't abhor women golfers so much, woman marathoners would be number one on his list." Will Cloney stated in the Sunday *New York Times,* "If that were my daughter, I'd spank her." She ignored the negativity and realized her real race lay ahead: the fight for female acceptance.

Flak flew at Switzer on the romantic front as well. Tom fumed that her "jogging" had resulted in his attack, an action that would shadow his future. After their wedding, he explained that as he was the serious athlete, their focus had to be his entry in the 1968 Mexico City Olympics. As it transpired, Tom actually helped his wife become a better runner; she was so anxious to avoid him she sprang out of bed every morning at 5:30 a.m. to train. One evening, after returning from marriage counseling alone—hubby having refused to attend—when Tom did not look up from his show, Kathrine, not having an Olympic hammer in hand, used her high-heeled leather boot to smash the television screen. Although she never reconciled with Tom, in 1973 she reunited with a mellowed Jock, who told her, "Come on, lass. Let's get ourselves a wee bit of publicity," and planted a kiss on her cheek.

In order to distance herself from a marriage that could not make it to the finish line, Kathrine headed to Munich for its Olympic Games as a sports journalist for the *New York Daily News.* What began as a dream working vacation morphed into a waking nightmare when members of Black September, a group of Palestinian terrorists, released their homicidal hatred by murdering six Israeli athletes and six coaches.

During the ancient Olympics, wars were suspended to concentrate on the art of athleticism. Pierre de Coubertin reinstituted the Games to foster a spirit of international brotherhood and created the Olympic flag of five interlocking rings to represent the five populated continents. Four decades after the devastation at Munich, Kathrine was a broadcaster at the Boston Marathon and had just returned to her hotel room when she heard a bomb detonate. She believed it was a gas explosion until a second blast went off. She wanted to help the victims, but her third husband, Roger Robinson, a British-born world-class runner, informed her the hotel was on lockdown. A pressure cooker packed with nails had been planted at the race's finish line; its explosion resulted in three deaths and injured 260.

Fifty years after her first Boston Marathon, the seventy-year-young Kathrine ran the route once more, finishing the race just under twenty-five minutes slower than her earlier time of four hours and forty-four minutes. In the vein of Bob Dylan's "The Times They Are A-Changin'," approximately one million fans cheered her on and photographers and television cameras captured her victory at the finish line. Rather than having her bib torn off, officials chose her to fire the starting gun. Switzer wore her original bib number of half a century before—which the organizers retired as a mark of honor. In her memoir, *Marathon Woman,* Kathrine stated that her experience had paralleled the social revolution of the sixties and that she was proud of her activism. Women were officially allowed to compete in the Boston Marathon in 1972, a watershed event Kathrine felt was the equivalent of the suffragettes obtaining the vote. Of that landmark decision, she stated, "In 1967, few would have believed that marathon running would someday attract millions of women, become a glamor event in the Olympics and on the streets of major cities, help transform views of women's physical ability, and help redefine their economic roles in traditional cultures." Currently, 58 percent of marathon runners in the United States are women. Kathrine is thankful to Jock for one of the most galvanizing photos in women's rights history.

To date, Kathrine has entered more than thirty marathons, winning in New York in 1974, and has worked as a television commentator and as a contributor to *Runner's World* magazine. She founded a women's running club, threw out the first pitch at a Boston Red Sox game, and arranged for the Golden Gate to be closed in the San Francisco Marathon. In 2011, the National Women's Hall of Fame inducted her as a member. Of her legacy, Switzer said that it came as no surprise that females continued to embrace the "sense of empowerment" that came with the territory. "We have come a light-year, really. But we have a long way to go." Kathrine was referring to the fact that female sports figures still encounter gender discrimination as it relates to pay and publicity.

In tribute to the one who had done so much, her bib number is often worn by women on their arms when they race; others have it emblazoned as a tattoo. The most endearing gesture for Switzer was four young girls who had her number written on their cheeks or foreheads who held up signs that read, "Go Kathrine Switzer! Equality for all of us!"

Great events hinge on minor ones; had it not been for the freezing temperature in 1967, Switzer would not have become one of the historic figures in America's most famous race. Had she not needed a thick sweatshirt, there might not have been a marathon for women at the 1984 Olympics. Because of the convergence of the chill of a Boston afternoon and the overzealous Jock Semple, thousands of women realized they could run twenty-six miles—without growing a moustache, without losing their reproductive abilities.

The Renaissance woman founded a nonprofit organization that uses running to empower women around the world. She christened it after women's indomitable spirit and the number on her bib on the fateful day that altered the course of her life: Fearless 261.

Chapter 13

The Fearless Girl
(1967)

Wall Street is named after an actual wooden stockade built by the Dutch when New York was Nieuw Amsterdam, erected to protect their trading post from the British. Wall Street became synonymous with finance in 1792 after twenty-four prominent merchants in powdered wigs and waistcoats founded the New York Stock Exchange to bet on foreign battles, elections, and cockfights. One hundred seventy-five years later, Muriel Siebert scaled the rampart when she became the first woman securities trader.

As a child, Stacey Cunningham thought her father was a sock trader. In actuality, he was a stock trader, the reason he hung a LeRoy Neiman painting of the Exchange in his den. After Stacey became the first female president of Wall Street, he presented her with the painting. Ms.

Cunningham takes guests on tours of the Exchange that include the jumbo Faberge urn that Nicholas II gave for a bond issue, one on which he defaulted owing to his execution. The last stop is Siebert Hall, where a display case holds Siebert's rainbow-striped fur coat.

The lady known as Mickie was born in Cleveland in 1928, the daughter of Irwin Siebert, a dentist, and his wife, Margaret. In the early 1950s, doctors diagnosed her father with cancer and a Cain and Abel situation arose when his physician brother, who held the lease on Irwin's office, had him evicted. In her biography, *Changing the Rules: Adventures of a Wall Street Maverick*, Muriel describes the experience at her first hostile takeover. She denounced her relative's cutthroat behavior as typical for a man who charged his mother for medical treatment when he visited her in her nursing home and was too busy receiving an award from his Masonic lodge to be at his dying father's bedside. The Borgia family drama played out when Muriel was at Flora Stone Mather College, a women's school that became part of Case Western Reserve University in Cleveland. Ms. Siebel had the distinction of being the only woman in her money and banking course. To distance herself from family dynamics, Muriel took respite in bridge, a pastime she quipped became so consuming she did not bother to graduate. The real reason for her departure was because of the Siebert family's reversal of fortune that necessitated her obtaining a full-time job.

Horatio Alger, the nineteenth-century author, famously advised, "Go west, young man. Go west." In contrast, a young Muriel headed east to the financial Mecca of Manhattan. What convinced her to do so was a trip she had taken with two friends that entailed a visit to the New York Stock Exchange. The teen tourists received a piece of ticker tape printed with their names as a souvenir. The paper bearing the words, "Welcome to the NYSE, Muriel Siebert" became Muriel's cherished lifelong memento. As it transpired, she was not given a welcome mat.

In 1954, Muriel left Cleveland with five hundred dollars, a used Studebaker, and a dream of breaking into the financial sector. Her older, divorced sister offered her a room in her apartment, but Muriel faced grim job prospects due to anatomy. She finally obtained a position at Bache & Co. as a security analyst trainee; in actuality, she was a glorified gopher with a $65 weekly salary. However, she followed her creed that one creates opportunity by performing, not complaining, and she forged ahead. She derived comfort from the fact that while in college she aced her accounting exams because she could look at a page of numbers and they "would light up like a Broadway marquee." Eventually, she impressed "the men in dark suits" with her ability of "turning junk into gold," and they gave her a position that entailed working in the then-undesirable field of aerospace. In this capacity, she met the celebrated pilot of World War I, Captain Eddie Rickenbacker, who was in charge of Eastern Airlines. She shocked her colleagues during a meeting when she grilled the demigod of aviation with a series of questions. Timidity was never a part of Ms. Siebert's DNA. Rather than taking offense, Rickenbacker was so taken with her tenacity and intelligence he offered her a job, one Muriel declined. Finance, not flying, set her pulse racing.

In two years, Siebert doubled her salary, but what tempered her joy was the knowledge she was still far behind her male colleagues on the pay and power scale, and as such, she decided to resign. The captain gallantly introduced Muriel to two of his bankers; neither had ever hired a woman, and they were unwilling to forego tradition.

Passing her résumé around the Street did not produce a single response. However, when the placement bureau of the New York Society of Security Analysts sent out her same résumé using her initials rather than her first name, M. F. Siebert, potential employers called. In 1958, she received an interview, and a position, in the research department of Shields & Co. for $9,500 a year. Although it was more than she had previously earned, due to the fact that men in the same position were making $20,000, she voiced her concern. The partners tried to placate her by explaining that men, who had families to support, needed to be on a different pay scale. Injustice gave her the gumption to set her sights elsewhere.

Siebert later stated in her memoir that in 1965, the year after Title VII of the Civil Rights Act prohibited job discrimination based on sex, race, color, religion, or national origin, she felt the glass ceiling was just inches above her head, frustratingly near, yet unattainable. She was earning more than a quarter of a million dollars a year and had accumulated three times that amount, but she felt stymied as, barred from being a broker, she was restricted to a paycheck. In her book, she wrote that she had consigned her used Studebaker to the junk heap, but it served as an inspiration: "As the car got older, the driver's side door would stick, and when talking to it didn't help, I just had to resort to kicking it. That became a metaphor for life: When you hit a closed door and it doesn't budge, just rear back and kick it in—but hold it open so others can follow you."

In a nod to Lady Macbeth's admonition to her husband, "screw your courage to the sticking place," Muriel lobbied for a position on the New York Stock Exchange. The first gauntlet Wall Street threw down was the stipulation she had to obtain a member to sponsor her application. The first nine men she approached "ran screaming in the other direction." One claimed he did not know her well enough—though she had met him five years prior; another responded, "Holy s***, Mickie. I won't have a friend left." Ed Merkle expressed an interested in coming to her aid, and his friend Gustave A. Levy, the senior partner at Goldman Sachs, mentioned the Exchange did not have a ladies' room. Merkle responded, "She can pee in her pants for all I care." The Exchange then informed her if they admitted her, she would have to purchase a seat for the sum of $445,000, and furthermore, that a bank had to lend her $300,000 of the total price, something never required of any previous applicants.

Muriel, enmeshed in the crosshairs of a Catch-22, stated, "There would be no loan until I was accepted, and I couldn't be accepted without the loan." Siebert employed her characteristic strategy for dealing with obstacles, "I put my head down and charge."

After nearly two years, Chase Manhattan came through. Victorious, Muriel went to the exchange and handed over a check for the balance of her loan, and as she did so, she recalled the power of the almighty dollar embodied in the old proverb, "With money in your pocket, you are wise and you are handsome, and you sing well too." As the first woman on the New York Stock Exchange, Muriel launched a thousand headlines: *The Independent Record of Montana*: "Skirt Invades Exchange;" from the *Salina (Kansas) Journal*: "Powderpuff On Wall Street," from the *State Journal*: "Wall Street Slipped A Mickie." A Baltimore paper stated, "When it comes to picking good investments, management is most important. Women spend an awful lot of time trying to manage their husbands, so they have a natural advantage." A New Jersey columnist mentioned her achievement alongside a lament about New York becoming another Gomorrah as an appeals court had sanctioned homosexuals dancing together in public. A New Zealand paper reported, "Muriel Siebert is unmarried, cannot cook, lives in the untidiest apartment on Manhattan's swank Upper East Side, and admits to being at least ten pounds overweight. But she does have her good points." Her mother's take on her daughter's trailblazing achievement was she would have much rather boasted about a grandchild. The advent of the first woman broker was a historical day, one not readily repeated. Muriel said, "For ten years, it was 1,365 men and me." On the romantic front, after her entry, she received three marriage proposals, all from men in gated communities, also known as federal prison. She declined and never married or had children.

The news met with resistance. In her memoir, she recounted, "There was all manner of concern for my delicate ears—with several articles postulating that a woman couldn't handle the rough language of Wall Street." In addition to the sexism, she had to combat anti-Semitism, often in the form of inappropriate jokes or slurs. In response to off-colored remarks, she mailed her offending colleagues a message, "Roses are red, violets are bluish, in case you didn't know it, I'm Jewish. Mickie." Other historic firsts for the woman with chutzpah to spare was she became the first female to own and run her own brokerage company, Siebert Financial Corporation. She donated millions of dollars from her firm to help women get their start in business and finance. In 1977, she was the first of her gender to serve as New York state's superintendent of banking. Throughout her storied career, she retained her interest in aviation, leading *The Washington Post* to report, "Muriel Siebert is probably the only member of the New York Stock Exchange who reads *Aerospace Daily* under the hair dryer in a beauty shop." The doyenne of Wall Street claimed it was a source of pride that she could match any male colleague, "Scotch for Scotch." She spoke out against clubs that denied membership to women, claiming it barred her gender from the place where business deals were brokered. She lobbied for a ladies' room at the Stock Exchange and said if she did not receive one, she would provide a portable toilet. Management complied. Ms. Siebert often appeared in public-sporting red cowboy boots, designer pantsuits in red and purple—with Monster Girl, her long-haired Chihuahua, and its successor, Monster Girl 2, as accessories. She claimed affinities with her pets, noting that they were "not intimidated by the big dogs."

In 1992, colleagues arranged for a luncheon to honor Muriel at which she stated it was not yet time for women to declare victory in the battle for equality on Wall Street. Her argument was that though many women were entering its domain, they still were not making partner. She remarked in conclusion, "There's still an old-boy network, and we just have to keep fighting." And fight Muriel did, until she passed away at age eighty-four from cancer.

The bronze sculpture of a four-foot girl, hands on hips in a defiant stance, stands in front of the New York Stock Exchange, and her name echoes the spirit of the flamboyant woman who infiltrated the realm of the men in dark suits: the Fearless Girl.

Chapter 14

Live Long
and Prosper
(1968)

A half-century ago, when the United States was embroiled in race riots triggered by the assassination of Dr. Martin Luther King, Jr., in an era that had experienced the illegality of black and white marriage, Nichelle Nichols became the first black woman to embrace a white man on American television. It was the kiss heard around the galaxy.

The woman destined to boldly go where no one had gone before was born in Robbins, Illinois, near Chicago, as Grace Dell. Even as a fetus, she had an extraordinary life. Her mother, Lishia, was pregnant when Al Capone's brother paid a less than cordial visit to her father, Samuel Nichols, the town's mayor. The mobster's agenda entailed a hit on Samuel for destroying Capone's alcohol mill, although the mob had been paying for Nichols to turn a blind eye. The henchman spared Sam's life when he discovered the truth: Sam had not received a cent because he would never have allowed booze in his town. The mobster even let him live when he saw Lishia had placed a pillow over her bulging belly to hide the gun she would have used had the mob killed her husband. The family's second brush with infamy occurred in 1997 when their son, Thomas, became one of the thirty-nine members of Heaven's Gate who committed mass suicide in San Diego, in the wake of the Hale-Bopp comet. In an emotional interview on *Larry King Live,* Grace, later known as Nichelle, said her family had lost contact with her brother twenty years earlier.

The performing bug bit Grace at an early age, and after a day in high school, she danced at the Sherman House Hotel. One astounding perk was meeting some of the great names of the entertainment world such as Lena Horne, Ella Fitzgerald, and Josephine Baker. At this time, she also decided she did not care for the name Grace and took her mother's suggestion to change it to Nichelle as it was alliterative with Nichols and for its derivation from an ancient name meaning Victorious Maiden.

At age seventeen, Nichelle, hungry for autonomy, believed she had found it with dancer Foster Johnson, fifteen years her senior. Infatuated, she said that on stage he could make Fred Astaire look like he was standing still and felt he was so charming he could talk flowers off the wallpaper. In reality, he was a narcissist, a character trait the teenaged Nichelle mistakenly chalked up to artistic temperament. Aware her parents would veto the relationship, she purposefully became pregnant, and after their wedding, Nichelle and Foster moved to Ohio. The bloom of romance withered as Nichelle did not approve of his alcohol and drug use. Although the marriage collapsed, it produced Nichelle's only child, Kyle, whom she referred to as her greatest accomplishment. When her mother called to say Duke Ellington wanted to hire Nichelle, she flew back to Chicago and performed with his band.

In 1962, Nichelle fell for Gene Roddenberry; the fly in the romantic ointment was his marital status, though he offered the cliché he was only staying for the sake of his children. She felt even if he did divorce, another impediment would be condemnation as an inter-racial couple. The situation came to a head when Gene introduced Nichelle to Majel Barrett, his other girlfriend. Nichelle refused to be the other woman to the other woman and left to work in Paris. There she received a telegram from her agent telling her to fly home immediately; there was a promising role for her in a new television series.

In a move light-years ahead of its time, Roddenberry's vision for his program was a twenty-third-century world that satirized his contemporary one, and he wanted to make a key member of the starship *Enterprise* a black woman. During her interview, a studio executive commented on the book she was holding entitled *Uhura* (Swahili for "freedom"), and Lieutenant Nyota Uhura became Nichelle's *Star Trek* name. Her character was not a glorified intergalactic telephone operator: she was the head of communications on the starship *Enterprise* and a top graduate of Starfleet Academy, a protégée of Spock. A black woman who had the responsibilities of a bridge crew officer—even in the fictional setting of space—was unheard of in the TV landscape of the 1960s, and the role came with collateral damage. Nichelle was thrilled with the prospect of a regular paycheck that would allow her to finally spend time with her son, buy her mother a house, and trade in her old Renault. However, when the bigwigs discovered Uhura's role was to be more than as eye-candy in a mini, form-fitting red dress, whose lines were to extend beyond, "Yes, Captain!" they ordered Gene to fire her. Their concern was that the network affiliates in the Deep South would cancel the show. Gene refused to comply, and the compromise was Nichelle worked on an as-needed basis. Further acts of racism occurred with slights, comments such as the studio was better off with a blue-eyed blonde, and the withholding of fan mail. Nichelle, having arm-wrestled Jim Crow for years, told Roddenberry she was disembarking from the *Enterprise*. His response was if she did so, then the racists had won; however, she took the view that if she stayed to be treated as less of a person than her co-workers, the racists, had won.

The following evening, Nichelle attended an NAACP fundraising event in Beverly Hills where a man informed her a big fan wanted to meet Uhura. She was speechless when the Trekkie turned out to be Dr. Martin Luther King, Jr., who told her that *Star Trek* was the only show he and Coretta allowed their children to stay up to watch. When she informed him she was quitting, he used his considerable power of oratory to point out that in the streets, the police were hosing African-Americans for wanting to sit down in a whites-only restaurant while she was portraying an astronaut of the legendary Starfleet. He argued Uhura was inspirational, and that hers was the only black portrayal on television in a worthwhile role. He continued, "Here we are marching, and there you are projecting where we're going. You cannot leave the show." His argument proved prescient. Caryn Elaine Johnson (later Whoopi Goldberg) remembered watching *Star Trek* as a nine-year-old who yelled, "Momma, there's a black lady on TV, and she ain't no maid!" Nichelle rescinded her resignation. Upon relating the event that had changed her mind, Roddenberry replied, "God bless Dr. Martin Luther King. Somebody does understand me." A month later Nichelle sang at the slain civil rights leader's funeral.

One of the most groundbreaking shows of the series was 1968 "Plato's Stepchildren;" it featured a kiss where no kiss had gone before. The interracial smooch was between Captain Kirk (who had a girl in every port of every planet) and Uhura. To offset any repercussions in the South, the plot made the couple unwilling lovers, made to embrace because of sadistic, humanlike aliens who forced the dashing white captain to lock lips with the beautiful black communications officer. To help lessen any backlash, producers filmed the kiss with their lips obscured by the back of Nichelle's head. Asked if she enjoyed the dozens of takes the scene entailed, Uhura, ever the lady, refused to kiss and tell. The episode received more fan mail than ever, mostly positive. In her autobiography, *Beyond Uhura,* she quoted one of the letters that William Shatner shared with her, "I'm a white Southern gentleman, and I like *Star Trek.* I am totally opposed to the mixing of the races. However, any time a red-blooded American boy like Captain Kirk gets a beautiful dame in his arms that looks like Uhura, he ain't gonna fight it."

The *USS Enterprise*'s warp speed drew to a halt in 1969, the end of a TV era. At the same time, Nichelle married Duke Mondy; however, their mutual love of music was not enough to salve their differences, and they divorced several years later.

Nichols went onto star as Uhura in the first six *Star Trek* films until 1991, by which time she was in her mid-fifties. Although she retired the miniscule red dress, retirement was not in the stars for its owner. In 1975, she attended a Chicago convention that had attracted 30,000 Trekkies; also in attendance was Dr. von Puttkamer, NASA's distinguished representative. In response to why he had come to an event celebrating a TV show, he answered that what made the sci-fi series so critical was the sense that, "the universe is worth living in, the equality of men and women in peaceful exploration, knowing we are

better than what we think we are. It is not even that."
Then he added, "What I have come here for today is to
find out for myself if Miss Uhura's legs are as beautiful in
person as they appear on the TV screen." In *Beyond Uhura,*
Nichelle did not say how she reacted to the good doctor's
words, but the presence of NASA led to another frontier.
In the 1980s, Nichelle worked for the space program as
an ambassador with the duty of recruiting minority and
women astronauts. Her efforts proved pivotal, and like
the USS Enterprise, subsequent flights into space carried
females and African-Americans. Dr. Mae Jemison, an
African American member of the Discovery Space Mission,
told Nichelle that seeing Uhura when she was young had
inspired her to seek a career in space, and she became
the first African American astronaut.

The trajectory of Ms. Nichols' life had taken her far afield
from Robbins: she had been a guest of Prince Andrew
and his then wife, Fergie; Nichols graced one of *Ebony
Magazine's* 1967 covers; and she was a guest of Trekkie
Barack Obama, who posed with her as they both gave
the Vulcan salute. (The Chief Executive also confessed
to having had a crush on her in his younger years.) In
1992, the fifty-nine-year-old Nichols became the first
black entertainer to place her hands in the cement at
Grauman's (now Mann's) Chinese Theater in Hollywood.
Never one to rest on her laurels, Nichelle turned her eyes
to another quest. Even in her eighties, Nichelle is not
one to repeat her TV closing line, "This communication
channel is now closed. Uhura out."

In her eighth decade, Ms. Nichols has gone up in space onboard NASA's C-141 Astronomy Observatory, which analyzed the atmospheres of Mars and Saturn. She also garnered praise for her role as the aging mother on the soap opera *The Young and the Restless.* On her eighty-fifth birthday, at a fan meet-and-greet in Los Angeles, she was asked what she wanted for her birthday, and she replied, "All I want is my two front teeth. Well, I have all my teeth...I just want to keep on keeping on. I love what I do." And to a reporter who asked if she ever planned to stop working, she responded, "Getting tired of work is like getting tired of breathing. The only time I will retire is to a casket."

The shot heard around the world started the American Revolution and the first interracial embrace helped change attitudes about what was permissible both on and off the small screen. The theme song of *Casablanca* does not apply, "A kiss is just a kiss..."

For integrating the USS Enterprise and NASA, for standing up to racism, let's raise our hands in the Vulcan salute in honor of Nichelle, "Live long and prosper."

Chapter 15

The Female of the Species (1969)

After a gestation period of a millennium, Israel became a phoenix, reborn from the ashes of the Holocaust. Immediately, the Middle Eastern nation became a powder keg as Palestinians and Jews waged war for the bitterly contested land. In a move that resulted in the world's collective gasp, Golda Meir became Israel's first (and only) female Prime Minister.

A stranger-than-fiction life began with Golda Mabovitch, who hailed from Kiev in the Russian Empire. Her first memory was of her father, Moshe, nailing boards over the front door during a rumor of an imminent pogrom. In addition to the anti-Semitism, there was poverty: her parents sometimes gave her food to her younger sister

Zipke, and her older sister Sheyna often fainted from hunger. Golda remembered, "I was always a little too cold outside and a little too empty inside."

After working for three years for steamship *shif skarte* (steamship fare), in 1906 Mr. Mabovitch had enough money for his family to immigrate to the United States. When he could find employment, he worked as a carpenter; his wife started a dairy store. At age eight, Golda had to work while her mother bought supplies at the market. Humiliated, she arrived late to school every morning.

At age eleven, to raise money for classroom textbooks, Golda organized her first public meeting and delivered her first public speech. A few years later, mother Bluma and daughter Golda got into a terrible fight when Golda announced she wanted to become a teacher. The decision did not sit well with her parents as a Wisconsin law did not allow teachers to be married, and they feared their child's 's destiny would be that of an old maid. Desperate not to become the wife of twice her age Mr. Goodman, the fourteen-year-old fled to Denver, where her sister Sheyna—a fiery revolutionary—lived. Listening to the young socialists who congregated at her sister's home solidified her belief in Zionism. After a sibling argument, the sixteen-year-old Golda moved out with friends and started a job measuring skirt linings. In later years, she found herself habitually glancing at hems. Her father poured on the guilt when he wrote that if she valued her mother's life, she would return to Milwaukee. The prodigal daughter reluctantly complied and worked in a local school. After she heard of attacks on Jews in the Ukraine and Poland, Golda organized a protest march. She turned the Mabovitch home into a Mecca for visitors from Palestine. She recalled, "I knew that I was not going to be a parlor Zionist."

In 1917, Miss Mabovitch met Morris Myerson, a poetry-loving sign painter and a fellow émigré from Russia. They started dating although they had little in common other than a mutual love of classical music. At age 19, when Morris agreed to be part of the third Aliyah (wave of immigration to Palestine), Golda became Mrs. Myerson. In 1921, the couple sailed on the *Pocahontas* to their second adopted country.

The newlyweds settled in Tel Aviv and joined the Kibbutz Merhavia, whose name translates to "God's wide spaces," situated a few miles south of Nazareth. The members of the commune grudgingly accepted them, though Golda felt they only agreed because of her phonograph and records. Following disagreements with the other members, she realized Merhavia would gladly have "accepted the dowry without the bride." Golda raised chickens, worked the land, and studied Hebrew, a language in which she never felt comfortable in conversing. Regarding her new homeland, she echoed her compatriots' complaint against Moses with the statement, "He dragged us forty years through the desert to bring us to the one place in the Middle East where there was no oil." Although the kibbutz was in a malaria-ridden area and the work difficult, she embraced her new country. The frail Morris did not share her enthusiasm, and they moved to Jerusalem, where she gave birth to son Menachem and daughter Sarah. Golda admitted the four years they stayed in the capital were grueling as the family could barely subsist on Morris's income as a bookkeeper. Mrs. Myerson did laundry in exchange for Menachem's tuition. In 1928, Golda, driven to work outside the confines of home, became the secretary of the women's labor council of Histadrut, supervising the vocational training of immigrant girls. She put in such long hours that Menachem and Sarah were happy when their mother had one of her regular migraine headaches as it meant she would be home. Golda's less than maternal nature manifested itself when she later insisted that one of her grandchildren, born with mild Down syndrome, be sent to an institution.

Golda had accepted her position knowing it meant frequent travel and that her absences would put a strain on her marriage, which was already on the rocks. Not willing to live a lie, with son and daughter in tow, she moved to a tiny apartment and slept on the living room couch. When not making speeches, working as a laundress, or looking after her family, Golda embarked on affairs, sometimes juggling two lovers at once. The Myersons were still officially married when Morris died six years later. Until the day she passed away, Golda kept a photograph of herself and her husband on her night table.

Despite Golda's lasting affection for her husband and her passion for her romantic liaisons, her greatest love affair was for her spiritual homeland. After the United Nations Special Committee on Palestine approved the establishment of a Jewish state, the Arab states refused to accept the decision. The Jews realized war was imminent and that they would need arms and money. Golda—few now bothered to use Meir—left for America and returned with $50 million. David Ben-Gurion, the Prime Minister of Israel, remarked, "She was the Jewish woman who got the money which made the state possible." Part of her success stemmed from her powerful oratory. As Golda spoke, her diminutive stature receded, and her audience was left with the image of an imposing woman who radiated strength. When she became Prime Minister of the country she had helped birth and spoke in front of thousands, it seemed she was talking in her living room to a gathering of intimates.

On her return, she undertook the diplomatic, political negotiations with King Abdullah of Transjordan. Disguising herself as an Arab woman, she traveled to Amman to urge him to keep his promise not to join other Arab leaders in an attack. He asked her not to hurry the proclamation of a state. "We have been waiting for two thousand years," she replied. "Is that hurrying?" On May 14, 1948, she was one of twenty-five signers of Israel's declaration of independence, a woman among Israel's founding fathers. Golda remembered that after affixing her signature to the document, she wept. By May 15, Israel was under attack by Egypt, Syria, Lebanon,

Transjordan, and Iraq. The fifty-year-old Golda showed her mettle when she dug in her orthopedic heels. Bearing what was in effect Israel's first passport, Mrs. Meir returned to the United States to raise more money. Implacable in her condemnation of those who threatened the existence of Israel, she stingingly declared her contempt, "The Arabs have become so rich they can buy anything—even anti-Semitism."

Bitten by the political bug, Golda became the Minister of Labor; when asked if she felt handicapped being a woman minister, she replied, "I don't know. I've never tried to be a man." She continued in this position until 1956, when she became the Foreign Minister and served under Prime Minister Ben-Gurion. A man of strong ideas— he was the one who had prevailed on Golda Myerson to change her name to the Hebrew equivalent Meir, he called her the only man in his cabinet. In this capacity she put in eighteen-hour days; she was what the Israelis call a *bitzuist*—a doer. In 1969, the Labor Party selected her as its candidate for Prime Minister. That was not exactly the retirement she had in mind. She said, "Being seventy is not a sin. It's not a joy either." The party's decision sent seismic shock throughout the country— and the world. She looked like a chain-smoking grandmother with a gray bun, stout frame, and Midwestern accent. Golda accepted the nomination, thereby traversing the improbable road from pogrom to Prime Minister. Golda had need of perseverance as her tenure coincided with the Palestinian movement, embracing terrorism, hijacking planes, and murdering Olympic athletes.

In 1973, Meir was upset when she did not hear from the
Vatican about her plea to help broker peace; this silence
was not surprising as His Holiness had never recognized
the legitimacy of Israel. Undaunted, Golda flew to meet
Pope Paul VI. "Before we went to the audience," she
recalled, "I said to our people: 'Listen, what's going
on here?' Me, the daughter of Moshe Mabovitch, the
carpenter, going to meet the Pope of the Catholics?' So,
one of our people said to me, 'Just a moment, Golda,
carpentry is a very respectable profession around here.' "
After the head of the Church told her the Jews should
be more merciful to the Palestinians, Golda responded,
"Your Holiness, do you know what my earliest memory
is? A pogrom in Kiev. When we were merciful and when
we had no homeland and when we were weak, we were
led to the gas chambers." Of the historic meeting, Golda
recalled there were moments of tension—something of
which there can be no doubt. She stated of her interior
turmoil, "I felt that I was saying what I was saying to
the man of the cross, who heads the church whose
symbol is the cross, under which Jews were killed for
generations..." Meir's position knew no gray area; the
situation boiled down to them or us. Her hardline stance
was that after the Diaspora, the Inquisition, the pogroms,
and the Holocaust, the world owed the Jews their
ancestral homeland.

In 1974, at age seventy-six, Mrs. Meir relinquished the
reins of government to Yitzhak Rabin, telling her party
she no longer had the stamina to carry the heavy mantle
of leadership. Surprisingly, toward the end of her life, the

powerhouse revealed she was still nursing guilt about the years during which she had neglected her children in her drive to be a mother to her nation. Her mea culpa was, "There is a type of woman who does not let her husband narrow her horizons. Despite the place her children and family fill in her life, her nature demands something more; she cannot divorce herself from the larger social life. For such a woman there is no rest."

Rest finally came for the restless woman in 1978 when she passed away in Jerusalem's Hadassah Hospital at age eighty. In announcing her death, hospital officials disclosed one of Israel's best-kept secrets; she had been suffering from cancer since the late 1960s even as she was leading Israel through its 1973 war. Ms. Meir did not permit disclosure of her illness even at the end. Ironically, death came for Golda with Israel on the brink of peace with Egypt, a goal she had sought for almost six decades of a Sisyphean struggle. In 1974, she stated, "Someday peace will come, but I doubt that I will still be here to see it." In honor of her selfless devotion, the government laid their own iron lady to rest near the visionary of Zionism, Theodor Herzl.

Golda had always downplayed her femininity, perhaps a necessary tactic to scale the ranks in a patriarchy. And yet she was at her core a mother lion who proved the truth of Kipling's words, "The female of the species is more deadly than the male."

Chapter 16

Stirring Salute
(1970)

If asked to list three iconoclastic generals, those who might spring to mind: Napoleon, Patton, MacArthur. The common denominator among those named is they all carved out a niche in military history, and all were men. The established paradigm shifted when Anna Hays became the country's first female general in a ceremony sealed with a kiss.

Dorothy Parker remarked, "It's a man's world," an observation that rang true regarding America's armed forces. For many years, women could not enlist, and when admitted, they knocked against a camouflage ceiling. A mild-mannered warrior was the catalyst for change. During the ceremony that made her a general, Anna stood at the lectern and quoted Albert Einstein with his words, "What I am I owe to the lives of other men."

The lives of other men—and women—likewise owed much to her.

The unfailingly polite and kind Anna Mae Violet was born in Buffalo, New York, in 1920, to Daniel Joseph and Mattie McCabe, who both worked for the Salvation Army during the Depression. When Anna was twelve, the family relocated to Allentown, Pennsylvania, a move necessitated by her parents' careers. In her early years, she dreamed of becoming a nurse and practiced wrapping bandages around the legs of a kitchen table on which her parents invited the infirm and destitute to eat.

Anna graduated from Allentown High School with two passions: nursing and music. Although she played the piano in church and the French horn in her school band, she abandoned her dream of Juilliard because of limited finances. Putting practicality over passion, Anna enrolled in the Allentown Hospital School of Nursing, graduating first in her class in 1941. A day that would live in infamy altered the trajectory of her life and the status of females in the military.

After learning of the devastation in Hawaii caused by Pearl Harbor, with her brother in the Marines and a younger sister living with her widowed mother, Anna enlisted as "it was the patriotic thing to do." She took the Liberty Bell Trolley to Philadelphia, where she joined a reserve unit affiliated with the Hospital of the University of Pennsylvania. From there, she was off to Louisiana for training. Never having been away from her parents and siblings, she said, "I was truly scared to death."

The novice nurse spent her deployment caring for US troops in the world's most desolate areas. In 1943, Anna shipped out for the state of Assam, India, on a troop transport with seven thousand men, facing the danger of attack from Axis submarines and planes. She recalled of those heady days, "It was a strange mix of fear and excitement. For someone who had never really been away from home, it was like an adventure." At the 20th Field Hospital, she worked in a malaria-infested stretch of the China-Burma-India corridor, treating construction workers who were building a new roadway that supplied the Chinese military, as well as the lice-infested special operations Army unit, Merrill's Marauders, who staged raids against the Japanese. "All in a day's work" for Anna entailed burning leeches off her skin and fending off snakes—one wrapped itself around the mosquito netting in her hut, and a cobra made itself at home under her bed. In lieu of a scream, she calmly asked a guard to shoot the snake and remarked, "When one lives in the jungle, one can expect that sort of thing." Malarial monsoons drenched mud floors in eight inches of water. Combat casualties from Burma arrived caked in mud and riddled with lice; ward after ward filled with men stricken with typhus; and gangrene amputations haunted the twenty-three-year-old New York state native. She also endured bouts of severe illness. "We were living under quite primitive conditions," Hays recalled. "Disease was rampant...everybody was sick. I had dysentery." In lighter moments, a sacred cow or jackal would run through the hospital or the nurses' quarters, of which she stated it was, "quite an experience." She ate coconuts fresh from the tree, admired orchids, and attended the occasional dance. She reminisced, "The pilots would come from all over the jungle, as far as fifty miles, just to visit with us for a couple of hours." Two years and 49,000 patients later, the Army promoted her to First Lieutenant.

When World War II ended, Anna contemplated what to do with the rest of her life. Most women returned home to the traditional role of mother and wife, but that was not a path Anna cared to tread. She considered becoming an airline stewardess (a job that often required a nursing degree) but decided to re-enlist. One of her positions was at Tilton General Hospital at Fort Dix, New Jersey, and Valley Forge General Hospital in Phoenixville, Pennsylvania, the latter a facility where the severely disfigured underwent plastic surgery.

After war broke out in Korea, she served as a nurse in the 4th Field Hospital, one of the first medical units to arrive in Inchon after the United Nations invasion of the Korean peninsula's west coast. She described the conditions in the Korean hospital as even worse than those in India thanks to the frigid temperatures and lack of supplies in the operating room; she even had to wear an overcoat under her scrubs because of the cold.

When "Johnny came marching home again," Anna was in charge of the emergency room at Walter Reed Army Medical Center in the Washington area. As the personal nurse for President Eisenhower, who had undergone intestinal surgery, she stayed by his bedside at night and held his hand. Vice President Richard Nixon came to visit,

and Eisenhower, on Anna's recommendation, declined
to see him. She went outside, shook Nixon's hand, and
explained the President was resting. A lifelong friendship
developed between Anna and Ike and Mamie Eisenhower,
and they invited her several times to their Gettysburg
farm. As a further mark of his regard, Eisenhower sent
her a letter or flowers in honor of her promotions as she
ascended the Army's hierarchy.

During her career, the daughter of Salvation Army
workers met Vietnam War Commander William C.
Westmoreland, China's General Chiang Kai-shek, and
Britain's Admiral Louis Mountbatten, the supreme Allied
commander in Southeast Asia. She danced with comedian
Jack Benny in Tokyo. On the romantic front, she fell in
love with William A. Hays, who directed the Sheltered
Workshops in Washington, DC, a nonprofit that provided
jobs for the disabled. They married in 1956; he died six
years later.

Due to Anna's accomplishments, she rose to the rank
of Chief of the Army Nurse Corps in 1967, and she was
deployed to Southeast Asia on several occasions. Through
dogged diplomacy, she successfully argued pregnant
married women should not be compulsorily discharged,
upped recruitment efforts to send more nurses to aid in
the war effort, and helped bring about maternity leave for
military personnel, all hard sells at the time.

Yet Hays resisted an association with feminism. "Let's not
talk about this" she told the *New York Times* when asked
about the burgeoning women's liberation movement;

she remained committed to her belief only men should participate in combat. Ironically, she became a symbol of unprecedented female achievement when the Army—under President Nixon's auspices—promoted her to the one-star rank of brigadier general, the first time a woman ever achieved the distinction in the United States Armed Forces. Only three years earlier, the position had been unattainable by law until President Lyndon B. Johnson opened up the possibility of a female attaining the privilege—who would be the first "in the Western world since Joan of Arc" General Westmoreland quipped. Hays described the breakthrough as "a giant step forward."

In a Pentagon ceremony, Westmoreland introduced Anna as an "able and attractive lady," then gave her the Silver Star insignia and what *Time* magazine described as "a brassy kiss on the lips." Of the smooch, the Army chief of staff joked, it was all part of "a new protocol for congratulating lady generals." *Time* magazine added, "They do it in France, but US generals caught kissing each other would be likely to lose their stars." General Hays laughed, though after a second—and a third—kiss from two other senior officers, she shook her head and stood at the lectern to accept her high honor. Mamie Eisenhower presented the new General with the stars her husband had received when he had been promoted to brigadier general in 1941.

The news elicited elation from some quarters and derision from others. A political cartoon showed two men at a bar with the caption, "Well, we've got everything,

Sarge, the atomic bomb, guided missiles, the M16 rifle, and now a lady general." A *New York Times* article that covered the historical event devoted more column inches to General Hay's hemlines (she liked them above the knee, and two inches higher still for civilian outfits) and dress size (a twelve), than her career saving lives during three American wars. But she appreciated her new status: a military policeman who saluted the flag at the front of her car gaped when he saw there was a woman in the back.

Westmoreland, who became a lightning rod for controversy not for kissing lady generals but for his running the Vietnam War, shared an anecdote. He said his wife Katherine (a.k.a. Kitsy) had run into Anna at the hairdresser and told her that she wished Anna would marry again. When Hays asked why, Mrs. Westmoreland replied, "I want some man to know what it's like to be married to a general." As it transpired, Hay's gender was not the only distinguished aspect of her high command. The army bestowed on her the Distinguished Service Medal—the Pentagon's highest noncombat award—and the Legion of Merit. However, when recalling her storied career, one that had entailed wearing gas masks, she did not mention her three tours of duty, the A-listers she had met, or her groundbreaking role in history. The brigadier general recalled, "I was always disgusted with most of the other girls in my unit because they couldn't keep in step."

After three decades in the army, General Hays lived in Spain and then Virginia. Her only regret was retiring in 1971, and she said of her career, "If I had to do it over again, I would do it longer." When asked how she wanted to be remembered, Hays replied, "First of all, as the first woman general, but as a very honest person, as a kind individual who did her best—and succeeded."

Anna passed away from complications following a heart attack in a Washington, DC, nursing home at age ninety-seven. Because of her military rank and high profile, Anna could have been buried at Arlington National Cemetery, but she had decided to lie next to her father in Grandview Cemetery in Pennsylvania's South Whitehall Township. For a lifetime of dedication, for breaking the army's 195-year history on banning women from the top brass, General Hays deserves a stirring salute.

Chapter 17

A Little Footprint
(1970)

Since the dawn of civilization, there has always existed a bond between man and horse: the ancient Greeks and the centaur, Emperor Caligula and Incitatus, the Confederate Generals and their steeds. A magical connection also exists between a woman and a horse, as illustrated by the life of Diane Crump, the first female jockey to compete in the Kentucky Derby.

An iconoclastic photograph from 1968 captured the image of American sprinters Tommie Smith and John Carlos raising their fists in the Black Power salute at the Mexican Olympics. The following year, another sports photograph portrayed an act of feminine protest: an armed escort protecting a teenaged jockey from hundreds of hostile hecklers.

At any of today's racetracks, a female astride a horse would not raise an eyebrow. Women have been triumphant in Triple Crown events, Breeders Cup races, and the Pacific Classic. However, if we were to turn back the hands of the clock to the 1960s, the track was a testosterone only zone. In the waning year of the decade, a young woman held her ground in the face of gender prejudice and paved a path for future female jockeys.

Diane Crump was born in 1948 in Connecticut on the Long Island Sound; her passion for ponies ignited at age four when her parents took her to a carnival and she first sat in a saddle. She devoured books such as *The Black Stallion*, *My Friend Flicka*, and *Black Beauty*. While for other girls, horses serve as the period between toys and boys, the four-footed remained her passion. At age twelve, Diane moved to Oldsmar, Florida, where her father opened a marina. Yet it was not the sound of the sea that provided Diane's siren call; rather, it was the stables of nearby horse haven Tampa Bay Downs. A year later, she began riding lessons, and her parents arranged for the arrival of horses Buckshot, Patches, and Lulu. She rode through orange groves and watermelon patches and into the bay. In her early teens, she helped out at Lake Magdalene Farm, caring for foals and conditioning yearlings to be comfortable with a person onboard. In 1964, she developed her galloping skills and worked at a stable at Gulfstream Park. She remarked of her job, "There's nothing I didn't do." Crump worked hard and paid her dues; but the non-silver lining that hovered overhead was the realization a woman had as much chance of competing in thoroughbred racing as she did of fighting alongside men in the jungles of Vietnam.

The paradigm shifted in 1967 when a trio of women felt they had the right to infiltrate the band of brothers. The first of these was the United States Equestrian Team rider Kathy Kusner, who applied for a Maryland jockey's license only to have officials deny her request. A year later, a judge, citing the Civil Rights Act of 1964, ruled that the Maryland Racing Commission was required to certify Kusner; but a tumble from her horse that resulted in a broken tibia ended her aspiration. In the last months of 1968, Penny Ann Early was set to ride at Churchill Downs; however, male jockeys were so incensed they threatened to boycott if a woman were of their number. The "jockettes," as they were patronizingly termed, endured stones thrown at their trailers; one returned home to a hatchet embedded in her door. Crump recalled of those not so glorious days, "People were saying we weren't strong enough or smart enough to ride. They thought it would be dangerous for other people to ride against us because we wouldn't know what to do under pressure." Next was Barbara Jo Rubin's turn, but the jockeys at Tropical Park in Florida also threated a walkout, and a male replaced her. Nick Jemas, director of the Jockey's Guild, proved a vocal detractor. He conceded that Crump was "the best of the lot" but insisted she would be a distraction to the male jockeys. Vitriol streamed from the jockeys: "What's next? Topless go-go riders?" "Boycott the broads." Breaking into the Race of Kings was no easy ride.

There was a momentary hope of leveling the racetrack playing field at Florida's Hialeah Park when female trainer Mary Kleim named Crump as the candidate to ride a filly named Merr E. Indian. She told reporters, "Diane is cool and she's smart, and I think she'll make as good a rider as any boy." However, Merr E. Indian was not chosen to compete; Diane was forced to wait.

At the same period, officials had grown weary over the furor over women's participation. The Florida Racing Commission convened and stated it would stiffen penalties against jockeys who refused to ride. One supervisor issued the warning, "If the jockeys back out now, God help them."

Early in February, Crump learned that her first race would be on a 54 to 1 long shot named Bridle 'N Bit, and in preparation, Ms. Crump borrowed a saddle from friend Tom Calumet. The horse's trainer stated his wife Catherine, Bridle 'N Bit's owner, had made her demand clear, saying, "Put the girl on or I'll get another trainer." A newspaper article snidely asked if "the willowy blonde jockette would be able to keep her powder dry." Diane responded that the only powder she wore was mud that clung to her face from the track.

In 1969, a man landed on the moon, and in the same year, a woman debuted as a professional jockey. When the big day arrived, some riders chose to drop out and were immediately replaced. Diane put on her red-and-white-silks in the Horseman's Benevolent and Protective Association office rather than in the jockey's room, for obvious reasons. In the paddock, those in Camp Crump applauded while her detractors booed, catcalled, and shouted sexist slogans.

Despite boycotts, hecklers, and a cynical public, Crump joined the pantheon of women trailblazers to become the first jockey to ride in an American pari-mutuel race at Hialeah. The petite teenager with curly brown hair was in the midst of a crowd of five thousand vying for a look at the woman attempting to challenge the tradition of thoroughbred racing. She encountered a barrage of flashbulbs and mayhem and recalled of the event, "The hecklers were yelling, 'Go back to the kitchen and cook dinner.' That was the mentality at the time. They thought I was going to be the downfall of the whole sport, which is such a medieval thought. I was like, 'Come on people, this is the 1960s!'"

News of Diane's inclusion caused a flurry of protest. "A gal in the Derby? Next thing you know they'll be playing second base for the Dodgers," wrote one reporter. Jeff Lehman of Grand Rapids, Michigan, said her presence "took a lot of tradition out of the Derby." A further affront was hardly anybody placed a bet on Fathom, the horse Diane had ridden since he was a yearling, because a girl would be on the saddle. Willow Abraham of Louisville, walking away from an advance Derby window, groused, "I just won't bet on her. It's just not right." In contrast, Crump had earned the grudging respect of her fellow jockeys. Diane also had support from her father and sister, who had accompanied her, as well as the long-distance well-wishes of her soldier brother, Bert. In Vietnam, he and his buddies were glued to the radio, cheering her on from Southeast Asia.

Instead of the traditional "Boots and Saddles" call to post, the bugler played "Smile for Me, My Diane." A bystander yelled to jockeys as the horses filed through the tunnel on the way to the track, "Remember, ladies first!" And then they were off.

The contemporary centaurs flew by in a flash of silk and horseflesh with Diane in the rear. When they approached the final stretch, Bridle 'N Bit and Crump thundered by the last two horses to finish tenth of twelve. She said of her groundbreaking ride, "I think I did okay for the first time. Beat two horses." A photograph from the day she had her date with her destiny showed Crump's elated, dirt-encrusted face. When Crump returned to the post and the audience saw that the Florida sky had not fallen—in Chicken Little fashion, the cheers outweighed the jeers. The walls of male exclusiveness—like those of Jericho—came tumbling down.

The anthem of the decade was Bob Dylan's "The Times They Are a-Changin'," lyrics that proved prescient in 1970 in the Bluegrass State. Meriwether Lewis, Jr. (grandson of the famous explorer) established the classic in 1875 as an American counterpart to the British Epsom Downs. The Kentucky Derby evolved into the crown jewel of thoroughbred racing, celebrated with its signature drink of mint julep, outlandish hats, and a blanket of four hundred roses. The Derby also achieved notoriety when twenty-one-year-old Diane Crump became the first woman to ride in what is known as "The Most Exciting Two Minutes in Sports."

In the first Kentucky Derby, all the jockeys were African American males with one lone white man; in 1970, all the jockeys were male with one lone female. Her fellow rider was Hall of Fame bigwig Bill Shoemaker; in the crowd was journalist Hunter S. Thompson. In a nod to tradition, the bugler played the plaintive notes of Stephen Foster's "My Old Kentucky Home."

Millions watched on television and thousands from the stands as Diane Crump proved thoroughbred racing was also the Sport of Queens. Once again Diane beat two horses when Fathom finished fifteenth out of seventeen.

Diane's burgeoning career took her to competitions around the world, and Puerto Rico proved a singular experience. She was in the lead when the jockey behind her grabbed on to her saddle, granting him a free ride, something he could get away with before the scrutiny of sporting event cameras. Crump proved she could handle the competition quite handily when she whacked him with her stick. He ended up the winner; however, when he exited the track, the female spectators pelted him with tomatoes, eggs, and various other projectiles.

Diane married her trainer, Don Divine; despite the perk of the alliterative name and its celestial connotation, the marriage did not make it to the finish line. However, it did produce a daughter and three grandchildren. She continued with her first love; tragically, a riding accident left her bedbound for months. Her horse had fallen backwards, and the incident left Diane with a severely broken leg. Crump currently resides in Linden, Virginia, where she owns a horse sales company. Reflecting on her life, she stated, "I've never won the Derby. I never made much money. But I always lived my dream."

In the 144 years of the Kentucky Derby, a female jockey has yet to win the Tournament of the Roses, although three fillies proved victorious: Regret, Genuine Risk, and Winning Colors. What remains a source of pride for Diane is other female riders have followed in her tracks. Diane said of her contribution, "I like to think I was a little footprint on the path to equality."

Chapter 18

Goodbye, Dolly
(1972)

Super Bowl half-time shows are the Academy Awards of sports—with an audience of over 100 million. Even those who could care less about the fate of the pigskin ball tune in for the highly touted extravaganza. The spectaculars are built around one-name wonder celebrities such as Madonna, Beyoncé, and Lady Gaga; in contrast, the first three half-time performances consisted of marching bands. The paradigm shifted with the advent of the woman who waxed eloquent on diamonds: Carol Channing.

Put the words "hello" and "dolly" together, and one will invariably start singing the catchy Broadway tune, one forever associated with Carol Elaine, born in 1921 in Seattle and raised in San Francisco. The only child of George Channing and his homemaker wife, Adelaide,

Carol later shared she was both frightened and embarrassed by her mother, the possessor of wild mood swings, though she adored her father, a newspaper editor and Christian Science lecturer. Adelaide revealed to her that George had one black parent as well as one white parent and warned Carol to keep the secret under wraps.

Carol discovered her passion at the age of seven when she ran for school secretary; unable to think of a reason why her classmates should vote for her, she began doing imitations of her teachers. After the first peal of laughter, she was hooked, especially as she won the election.

Channing's introduction to the theater occurred when she was a teenager and accompanied her mother to distribute Christian Science brochures to actors at the Curran Theater; in an epiphany, Carol likened the stage with the church. In 2005, she told *The Austin Chronicle*, "I stood there and realized that this is a temple. This is a cathedral. This is a mosque. I stood there and wanted to kiss the floorboards."

At eighteen, Carol studied dance and drama at Bennington College in Vermont but dropped out to pursue her dream of Broadway. Determined to carve a niche, she stated, "I auditioned for anyone who would look." In 1941, she appeared along with Danny Kaye in *No For an Answer*, which folded after three days. The silver lining was a succinct but laudatory review in *The New Yorker*. She became the understudy for Eve Arden in Cole Porter's musical *Let's Face It*.

The turning point in Carol's career was her appearance in *Lend an Ear*, for which she won the New York Drama Critic's Award. Anita Loos, the author of the 1925 comic novel *Gentlemen Prefer Blondes*, was in the audience and proclaimed, "There's my Lorelei." She arranged for Channing to be cast in her first leading role as Lorelei Lee, whose aspiration was to marry a sugar daddy and who philosophized in her signature song, "When those louses go back to their spouses / Diamonds are a girl's best friend...." Critics heaped praised on the six-foot-tall, bleach-assisted platinum-haired Ms. Channing; *Time* magazine placed her on its cover. What dampened her joy was Marilyn Monroe received the role in the film version. For inspiration, Marilyn often came to the theater to watch Carol perform. Channing said that it was so distracting for the orchestra to have the sex symbol in close proximity that players missed notes—except for the pianist, who "was more interested if Marilyn had a brother." Ms. Channing had so seamlessly disappeared into the character of Lorelei that theater folk questioned whether she could ever play another part.

The actress with the mascara-laden lashes and mega-watt smile became a national star as the pushy matchmaker Dolly Gallagher Levi, who decides to get hitched "Before the Parade Passes By" in the hit *Hello, Dolly!* Its original soundtrack album was Billboard's second-biggest of 1964 (after the Beatles' *A Hard Day's Night*), and the Grammy Hall of Fame inducted it in 2002. Carol appeared in five thousand performances, and the production—then the longest-running in Broadway history—grossed more than $17 million. She took pride in the fact she had only missed one show after a bout of food poisoning in Kalamazoo, Michigan. She was also still seen on stage despite her battle against ovarian cancer. Her work ethic was apparent in her comment to understudies, "Don't worry about learning the part. You'll never have to go on." Ms. Channing earned a Tony, triumphing over Barbra Streisand in *Funny Girl*. What offset her victory was Streisand played Dolly in the 1969 movie; Carol said it was "like somebody had kidnapped my baby." A dose of schadenfreude arrived when the show tanked, and her comment to an interviewer was revealing: "Barbra is one of our great creative forces, but a barrel of laughs she ain't." Perhaps it was fitting that the Broadway mainstay never really broke through in the movies; the silver screen was too small to contain her oversized personality. Despite her disappointment in never succeeding in that medium, she commanded such a niche in theater, she had the opportunity to sing "Hello, Lyndon!" at the Inauguration of President Johnson. Ms. Channing and the Johnson family became close friends, and that relationship contributed to the appearance of her name on President Nixon's infamous enemies list, a source of great pride for the star.

The lady who dominated the stage also enjoyed a parallel career on television, making guest appearances on variety shows such as Perry Como, George Burns, Carol Burnett, Dean Martin, Dinah Shore, and Red Skelton. And it was on the small screen that she ushered in the era of the celebrity infused Super Bowl.

In 1970, Broadway and the NFL seemed like strange bedfellows; the reason for their union was the NFL bigwigs realized the need to create a flamboyant, half-time spectacle starring big names to keep fans from channel surfing during the twenty-three-minute intermission. That was why Carol Channing came marching in. The venue for Super Bowl IV was New Orleans' Tulane Stadium when the National Football League added the three-time Tony winner, Oscar nominee, Golden Globe winner, and possessor of a star on the Hollywood Walk of Fame who had bumped the Beatles off the charts. If Carol had been less than thrilled at being supplanted by Monroe and Streisand, one can imagine how she felt when the main attraction of the show was the Southern University marching band performing a tribute to Mardi Gras. Her other competition was a reenactment of the 1815 Battle of New Orleans, waged by actors in period costume who melodramatically played dead on the turf after firing cannons. The diva admitted that she was not a sports fan and did not know what teams were playing (the Kansas City Chiefs and Minnesota Vikings). Her mea culpa went, "When you are working on a Broadway show, you have no idea what's happening beyond 41st and 54th Street." Nevertheless, Channing, clad in a floor-length white coat with white fur trim, dazzled enough in her rendition of "When the Saints Go Marching In" for the NFL to invite her back two years later.

In 1971, Louis Armstrong passed away, and as the big game was set to be played in New Orleans—the jazz great's hometown—the theme was dedicated to his memory. The two celebrity guests were Ella Fitzgerald (the first African American half-time performer) and Carol Channing, who crooned, "Hello, Louis."

The star once remarked that she did not have time for hobbies; nevertheless, she did not want the matrimonial parade to pass her by. Her first two marriages, to Theodore Naidish, a writer, and Alex Carson, a professional football player in Canada, ended in divorce. Her only child from Alex was son Channing, who took the last name of his mother's third husband, television producer Charles Lowe. She lamented that though she had given him unique opportunities such as a White House invitation, she had been too busy performing to be a mother. In 1998, aged seventy-seven, she filed for divorce after forty years, charging that Charles was physically abusive and had mismanaged her financial affairs. Another bone of contention was her claim that she had not had sex with her husband since Eisenhower had been president. Reading her kind words about him in her memoir that she published in her eighties, her junior high school sweetheart, Harry Kulijian, contacted her, and seventy years after their youthful romance, he became her fourth and last husband.

The diva was one of the most recognizable women in the theater world. Her tousled platinum hair, headlight-sized eyes, and outlandish clothes were the subject of countless caricatures and impersonations. She was immensely proud that one year at a San Francisco Pride event where they crowned a ceremonial "empress," she had been the one who wore the tiara. In a similar vein, she attended a Carol Channing lookalike contest with drag queens—and came in third. In her later years, she always wore a wig as her hair was frazzled from countless rounds of bleaching. Her spiky false eyelashes that she had used since a teenager led to the loss of her natural lashes, and to avoid further complications, she painted on long spiky ones.

Carol Channing was the embodiment of the actor's creed, "the show must go on," and she scoffed at retirement. In the early 2000s, she toured her one-woman show, "The First Eighty Years are The Hardest." Carol said she did not observe her birthday until 1993, her seventy-second, when she was a guest at a White House dinner; to her surprise, President Clinton noted the occasion in his speech. When she responded that she had never celebrated it, he responded, "Well, then this is your first birthday." In her seventh decade, she insisted she had not yet reached her potential, "Shirley Temple peaked at seven. I haven't got myself together yet." Defying age, the star was still bringing audiences to their feet night after night in a revival of "Hello, Dolly!" singing, "Wow, wow, wow, fellas / Look at the old girl now, fellas." *Variety* Magazine wrote, "Certain products of Western civilization exist beyond criticism and the ravages of time: Grant's Tomb, the Hollywood sign, Carol Channing in "Hello, Dolly!" Broadway agreed, and Channing received a lifetime achievement Tony Award. In 2001, the night before she was to co-star with Angela Lansbury,

Channing fell down a flight of stairs. Rather than be a no-show, the eighty-year-old Carol appeared with stitches on her temple; Harry Winston covered her cast in diamonds. For the first time, a sling needed its own security guards. A few days before her ninety-third birthday, she appeared at Town Hall in Manhattan as part of a celebration of the fiftieth anniversary of the night "Dolly" opened. The show became so iconic that Channing's red satin, sequin-covered gown she wore for her signature role is now in the Smithsonian. The star stated, "Performing is the only excuse for my existence. What can be better than this?"

Ms. Channing once said she hoped to die like David Burns, her original co-star in "Hello, Dolly!" who received a big laugh in 1971 in a tryout of the musical "70 Girls 70" and then keeled over onstage. The woman who had first garnered her own guffaws as a schoolgirl recalled, "He died hearing the laugh build. I can't think of a better way to go." Carol passed away at age ninety-seven at her home in Rancho Mirage, California. In tribute, Broadway theaters dimmed their lights. Goodbye, Dolly.

Chapter 19

The Nail That Sticks Up
(1975)

Because it was there. George Leigh Mallory made the statement when asked why he wanted to climb Mount Everest. He was referring to the alchemy between man and mountain, the challenge that beckoned to ascend to the world's highest elevation. Junko Tabei was the first of her gender to reach the sacred spot where heaven meets earth and showed her tradition-bound country that women could be more than housewives, more than geishas.

In the annals of great heroic exploits, the 1953 conquest of Mount Everest by Sir Edmund Hillary and Tenzing Norgay ranks with the first trek to the South Pole by Roald Amundsen in 1911 and the first solo nonstop transatlantic flight by Charles Lindbergh in 1927. They had conquered the unconquerable, a concept that endlessly appealed to the diminutive Junko.

Junko Istibashi was born in 1939, the fifth daughter of seven children, in Miharu, Japan, an agricultural town famous for its thousand-year-old cherry tree. Like many children of her generation, radiation from the atom bomb stunted her growth, and she never grew beyond four feet ten inches and a weight of ninety-two pounds. During World War II, her father struggled as a printer to support his family, and her neighborhood branded her as "a weak child" due to her physical frailty, exacerbated by several bouts of pneumonia. She fought against this demoralizing label when she was ten and a teacher took her and some classmates to hike the peaks of Mount Nasu, a volcano in the nearby Nikku national park that left her with a mountain high. She was drawn to both the volcanic landscape and the fact that the endeavor was a competition against herself. She said of mountaineering, "Even if you go slow, you can make it to the top. Or if you must, you can quit at the middle." The pattern of her life was made manifest.

Junko had to put the reins on her passion as conditions in Japan in the aftermath of World War II made it necessary to earn money for food, a commodity in short supply in the ravaged country. There were professional alpinists; however, cultural norms precluded the idea that a Japanese woman might take that road. Stymied, she decided to go into teaching, a career her society considered acceptable for her sex. Accordingly, in 1958 she enrolled in Tokyo's Showa Women's University, where she majored in English and American literature. After graduation, she abandoned the profession and found employment as an editor for a science magazine, the Physical Society of Japan. In her free time, she joined several climbing clubs that consisted mainly of men who teased her that she was only there to meet a husband. Ironically, Junko ended up falling in love with one of the clubs' members. She met twenty-five-year-old Masanobu Tabei during an ascent of Mount Tanigawa, the site of hundreds of fatalities. Her mother disapproved of the match as the prospective son-in-law was not a college graduate. Junko did not kowtow as Masanobu understood the mountains were her muse. But the demands of family did not stop Junko from climbing, and before long, she had scaled all of Japan's major peaks, the highest of which was Mount Fuji, 12,388 feet above sea level.

Four years later, Junko defied the expectation of her tradition-bound country when she founded the Ladies Climbing Club of Japan, whose motto was "Let's go on an overseas expedition by ourselves." The dual impediments were money and time—the average person only had two weeks of vacation per year. Nevertheless, by 1970, the fourteen members felt ready to tackle Annapurna III in Nepal. Junko was shocked at the extremes of wealth and poverty, first in Calcutta, then in Nepal. Despite heavy snow, the band of sisters persevered; Tabei was one of the four participants to reach the summit. The temperature was so cold the film in their camera broke. The experience profoundly changed Junko: no longer would she agree to slave long hours to prove she was her company's most loyal worker. And, if people wanted to refer to her as "that crazy mountain woman," then so be it.

Upon her return, the club members applied to the Nepali government for a permit to scale the mountain where the summit met the sky: Everest. The Himalayan peak on the Nepal-Tibet border, the highest point on Earth, was an otherworldly realm of hundred-mile-an-hour winds, perpetual cold, and air so thin that the human brain and lungs cannot properly function. The unyielding slope doubled as a graveyard for those with the requisite hubris: one of its myriad frozen corpses was that of Mallory, discovered two thousand feet below the summit, seventy-years after his demise. The club was stymied when officials replied they would only allow one expedition per season, and the ladies had to cool their heels until the spring of 1975. Another obstacle was many members had gotten married, had children, or lost interest, and their numbers shrank to five. Tabei knew she needed at least fifteen participants, given the expenses and the certainty that half would drop out during the climb. Junko went recruiting, heading for the Shinjuku train station in Tokyo where alpinists gathered before their weekend expeditions. After she had gathered the required number of members, raising the necessary funds proved another metaphorical mountain. Men repeatedly admonished her Everest was no place for a woman and preached that rather than raising funds, she should be raising her daughter, Noriko. (The family later included a son, Shinya.) She reasoned males wanted to keep women at their beck and call, serving tea or sake, not standing on some distant peak with an icepick raised triumphantly in the air. To subsidize the trip, in addition to working a full-time job and caring for her husband and daughter, Junko gave piano and English lessons. She also saved money by recycling car seats into over gloves and sewed her own sleeping bags. An infusion of funds arrived from Nippon television, one of the country's major networks, which surprisingly sponsored the women. After obtaining $300,000, Tabei left for Katmandu, leaving her saint of a husband with dad duty in their home in suburban Tokyo while her sister picked up the slack when Masanobu was at work as a supervisor for Honda Motor Company. The only complaint Junko ever made of her hubby was he left his dishes in the sink. She spent the next two months overseeing the transport of fifteen tons of food and equipment to the trekking center of Lukla. The indefatigable Junko hired six hundred porters to carry the goods through forests to the Everest Base Camp.

Along with six Sherpas and the sponsors' journalists, the members of the Ladies Climbing Club of Japan began their rendezvous with history. A harrowing episode that almost signified 'game over' occurred at Camp II, 21,326 feet above sea level on a freezing, windswept peak between Mount Nuptse and Mount Lhotse. Junko was jolted awake at 12:30 a.m. when a thunderous sound filled her with unspeakable dread. She had never heard that noise before, but she knew what it signified: an avalanche, a wake-up call from the mother of mountains.

Tabei and her team tumbled chaotically, trapped under a white wave of snow and ice. Their tent collapsed; equipment slammed into bodies, and a teammate's hair covered Junko's face. Their terror slowed time to the torturous pace of a waking nightmare. Junko recalled, "I couldn't move at all in the snow. Suddenly, the image of my three-year-old daughter appeared before my eyes. For a short time, I thought, 'If I die, what will happen to her?' But then I thought, 'I have to stay alive—for my daughter, for myself, for everybody.'" The Sherpas dug the four women out from their tent and dragged them to safety by their ankles. When she became conscious and discovered everyone was alive, she determined to continue. Persistence alone, however, could not enable her to walk; her body was a checkerboard of welts and bruises, and she had wrenched her lower back and legs. The male journalists wanted to turn back, and Mrs. Tabei had to pull rank. In 1991, she told *The Washington Post*, "If you climb with men, there are so many troubles."

Tabei's final ascent, accompanied only by Ang Tsering, her Sherpa, took six hours as she trekked through heavy snow, carrying twenty kilos on her back. On the morning of May 16, she arrived at Everest's south summit, the border between China and Nepal that led to the highest summit. A misplaced footing could send a climber plummeting thousands of feet in either direction. To cross, Tabei had to crawl sideways while straddling the ridge; her upper body was on the Chinese side, and her lower body was on the Nepalese side. She later recalled she had never felt that tense in her entire life and that her hair was standing on end. Undaunted, she arrived at a relatively flat rectangular area that she described as "smaller than a tatami mat" and peered down at a tranquil valley in Tibet, the first woman to reach the summit of Mount Everest. She unfurled a Japanese flag and remained at the pinnacle of the world for fifty minutes. Her elation was mingled with trepidation; she still faced the treacherous descent.

When Tabei returned to base camp, a telegram from the Prime Minister of Japan awaited. Then the King of Nepal awarded her a medal and a parade in Kathmandu. In New Delhi, Indian Prime Minister Indira Gandhi, also a mother of two, asked Junko how she managed to climb mountains with two little ones at home. Back in Tokyo, a crowd of thousands welcomed her at the airport. A sought-after guest speaker, she gave a presentation at a Japanese university where a student asked whether it was true that female mountaineers weren't good-looking. Junko replied, "If you look at me, you know that isn't the case." Reunited with her family, she refused to feel guilty. She never wanted Noriko to feel that because of her, her mother had not pursued her dream.

Tabei went on to tackle summits in more than seventy countries and became the first woman to scale the highest peak on each of the seven continents—collectively known as the Seven Summits. Her final journey was to Mount Fuji, accompanied by high school students, survivors of the nuclear disaster at Fukushima. The only opponent that eventually stopped Junko was abdominal cancer; she passed away in 2016, at the age of seventy-seven. On her deathbed, she drew a sketch and handed it to Masanobu: a drawing of Mount Everest.

In a 1991 interview for *The Washington Post,* Junko said, "I don't think people should leave behind a fortune, or things. When I die, I want to look back and know that my life was interesting." However, she did possess a cherished memento: the old wooden ice ax from her famous exploit.

The diminutive Junko proved what is good for the goose is good for the gander, and eleven days after she departed Everest, a Tibetan woman, Phantog, attained the same summit. Stacy Allison was the seventh woman—and the first American female—to stand at the same rarified height, a feat she accomplished three years later. To date, more than four hundred females have followed in Junko's footsteps, including thirteen-year-old Malavath Poorna, and Lakpa Sherpa, who has done so more times than any other woman. In 2018, a female dog named Mera became the first canine to reach the summit of Baruntse, just south of the Himalayan peak. The essence of Junko's indomitable spirit was her refusal to follow the admonishment of the Japanese adage, "The nail that sticks up will be hammered down."

Chapter 20

A Larger Circle
(1977)

In a Langston Hughes poem, a mother tells her son, "Life for me ain't been no crystal stair." One who could well have related to the metaphor was a woman who had to combat the trifecta of racism, sexism, and homophobia. Despite these societal handicaps, Pauli Murray became the first African American woman ordained as an Episcopal minister.

The woman who interacted with as many pivotal moments in American history as Forrest Gump was born in 1910 as Anna Pauline Murray; she preferred the name Pauli. She recalled of her formative years, "The most significant fact of my childhood was that I was an orphan." At the age of three, Agnes, Pauli's mother, suffered a cerebral hemorrhage on the family's staircase and died on the spot. Three years later, her father,

William, unable to cope with raising and supporting six children under the age of ten, entered the Crownsville State Hospital for the Negro Insane. In 1922, a white guard taunted him with racial epithets, dragged him to the basement, and beat him to death with a baseball bat. Twelve-year-old Pauli's final glimpse of her father was as he lay in a casket, skull split open, sewed together with jagged stitches.

Bereft of parents, Pauli lived with her Aunt Pauline, after whom she had been named, in Durham, North Carolina, in the home of her maternal grandparents, Cornelia and Robert Fitzgerald. Cornelia had been born into bondage; her mother had been a part-Cherokee slave, her father the owner's son and her grandmother's rapist.

During high school, Murray impressed her teachers with her hunger for knowledge, and when she graduated at age fifteen, she was editor of the school newspaper, president of the literary society, class secretary, a member of the debate club, the top student, and a forward on the basketball team. With her impressive credentials, Pauli could have attended the North Carolina College for Negroes, but as her whole life had been colored by segregation, she did not want to attend college in a system dominated by Jim Crow. Pauli set her sights on Columbia University and prevailed upon her aunt to take her north. In New York, she realized her ethnicity was not the only barrier: Columbia did not admit women. As she could not afford Barnard, her third alternative was Hunter College, but it would not accept her transcript because black high schools in North Carolina did not offer the requisite courses. Murray persuaded her family to allow her to live with a cousin in Queens and attended Richmond High School, where she was the only African American in a student body of four thousand. Two years later, Pauli enrolled in the college—one open only open to women—a fact she viewed as another form of segregation. She rented a room in the Harlem YWCA, where she befriended Langston Hughes, met W.E.B. Du Bois, attended lectures by the civil rights activist Mary McLeod Bethune, and visited the Apollo Theater to hear Duke Wellington and Cab Calloway. Pauli was living the life she had always envisioned; but it came to an abrupt end with the onset of the Great Depression. She lost her job as a waitress and was unable to find another. By the end of her sophomore year, she had lost fifteen pounds and suffered from malnutrition. In solidarity with the hoboes, she rode with them across the country on freight trains.

In 1930, when Pauli was twenty years old, she met William Wynn, with whom she shared the commonalities of age, poverty, and separation from family in the South. After a brief courtship, the two married in secret and spent a less than fulfilling two-day honeymoon at a cheap hotel. Their "dreadful mistake" did not last the weekend. After the breakup, Pauli wrote in her diary, "Why is it when men try to make love to me, something in me fights?" The question was not merely rhetorical; she went to the New York Public Library and read every book on sexual deviance. Murray became convinced she was only attracted to women because "she had secreted male genitals." Her awareness of her unconventional sexuality did not come as a shock. Her Aunt Pauline had referred to her as a "little boy-girl" as she had rejected her birth name Anna and dressed in boy's clothes. Partially due to her same-sex leanings, from the time she was nineteen, she had a psychological breakdown resulting in hospitalizations. She wrote to a doctor, "Anything you can do to help me will be gratefully appreciated, because my life is somewhat unbearable in its present phase." The climate of her era was not kind: Until 1973, the American Psychiatric Association classified homosexuality as a mental illness.

Pauli's only significant romance was with Irene Barlow, one that lasted a quarter of a century. Nevertheless, the couple never shared a residence and left behind no correspondence, as Murray, otherwise a pack rat, destroyed their letters. She revealed little of their relationship in her 1987 memoir, *Song in a Weary Throat: an American Pilgrimage,* and only when Barlow lay dying of a brain tumor in 1973, did she describe her as "my closest friend." In 1985, when Pauli passed away from cancer, her final resting place was a Brooklyn cemetery, where she shared a headstone with Irene.

Lacking employment, Murray applied to the graduate program in sociology at the University of North Carolina despite its whites-only policy. However, Murray saw a loophole: her slave- owning ancestor had served on its board of trustees. The school sent their decision, "Dear

Miss Murray. I write to state that...members of your race are not admitted to the University." Infuriated, the twenty-eight-year-old Pauli sent a letter of protest to President Roosevelt, but it was the First Lady who responded, "The South is changing, but don't push too fast. There is a great change in youth, for instance, and this is a hopeful sign." Thus began a decades-long correspondence between the radical Murray and the genteel First Lady, who met at the White House and at Eleanor's homes in New York City and Hyde Park. Murray influenced the FLOTUS to resign from the Daughters of the American Revolution after the organization refused to allow Marian Anderson to sing at Constitution Hall. Pauli also pleaded with Eleanor to have the president intervene when the court sentenced Odell Waller, a black Virginia sharecropper, to death. Murray delivered such a powerful speech on his behalf the audience—one of whom was Thurgood Marshall—was reduced to tears. Though Eleanor was swayed, FDR was not: Waller died in the electric chair.

The University of North Carolina never admitted Pauli, although she did get into two other notable American institutions: jail and law school. In 1940, Murray boarded a southbound bus in New York in order to spend Easter with her family in Durham. She and her friend Adelene McBean changed buses in Richmond, Virginia, and as the seats in the back were in disrepair, they sat closer to the front. When the driver asked them to move, they politely refused, and their road trip ended with their arrest. The NAACP wanted to use the incident to challenge the constitutionality of segregated travel; Virginia steered clear of the powder keg when Murray and Adelene only faced charges of disorderly conduct. The court found them guilty and fined them forty-three dollars; without funds, they again ended up behind bars.

Pauli enrolled in law school at Howard University, a historically black institution of higher learning, and although race was no longer an issue, her gender proved problematic as her professors and classmates were all male. When a professor remarked he didn't know why a woman would enroll in law school, Pauli was determined to become its top student. She termed the school's form of degradation "Jane Crow" and vowed to spend her life fighting sexism. In keeping with her promise, during the Nixon administration, she sent a letter to the president wherein she requested her appointment to the Supreme Court, knowing full well the futility of her application based on her race, gender, and sexuality.

After graduating, Murray applied to Harvard for graduate work and received a letter, "You are not of the sex entitled to be admitted to Harvard Law School." Even President Roosevelt's intercession bore no fruit, and she enrolled at Berkeley for her masters. With the prestigious degree under her belt, she headed for New York City; due to the negative light in which female attorneys were held, she had to subsist on low paying jobs. At last, in 1953, the law firm Paul, Weiss, Rifkind, Wharton & Garrison hired her. Of its sixty-some attorneys, she was the only African American and one of three women.

(Two soon left, although a fourth briefly appeared by the name of Ruth Bader Ginsberg, a summer associate with whom Murray crossed paths.) Years later, as a member of the Supreme Court, Justice Ginsburg named Pauli as an honorary co-author in a brief based on her work on gender discrimination. In her final year in the corporation, Murray received the distinction of being able to practice before the United States Supreme Court. In 1960, frustrated with her work environment, she took a job at the recently opened Ghana School of Law. When Ghana veered toward dictatorship, Pauli returned to the States, a country caught up in the civil rights movement. However, she spent most of her efforts in the women's movement, from arguing sex discrimination cases to serving on President Kennedy's Presidential Commission on the Status of Women. Along with Betty Friedan, she was a founder of the National Organization for Women. A female Faustus, Murray attended Yale Law School, which in 1965 awarded her as a Doctor of Juridical Science, the first African American to be so recognized.

Dr. Murray was a tenured professor at Brandeis when she resigned her post at age sixty-two; she had decided her life's calling was in the Episcopal ministry. In classic Pauli fashion, the position she sought was unavailable: The Episcopal Church did not ordain women. Fortunately, while she was in divinity school, its ecclesiastic branch voted to change their policy. In a ceremony in the National Cathedral, Murray became the first African American woman to be vested as an Episcopal priest; the clergy ordained Pauli at the National Cathedral in Washington. A month later, Reverend Murray administered her first Eucharist at the Chapel of the Cross—the little church in North Carolina where, a century earlier, a priest had baptized her grandmother Cornelia, a slave, one of the servant children belonging to Miss Mary Ruffin Smith.

Three years later, Pauli encountered her fourth form of discrimination—ageism, when the church enforced their rule mandating retirement at the age of sixty-five. Not one to be idle, she worked in a smattering of fill-in preaching positions for twenty-five dollars a sermon. Although Pauli held four advanced degrees and had friends on the Supreme Court and in the White House, she died as she had lived, on the periphery of penury. Nevertheless, her trailblazing accomplishment in the Episcopal Church—followed by her 2012 sainthood— paved the way for fellow black women.

Rather than give in to the hydra heads of hate she battled all her life, Murray's message was one of love: "When my brothers try to draw a circle to exclude me, I shall draw a larger circle to include them."

Chapter 21

A Good Judge
(1981)

Before the first female presidential nominee of a major political party was a twinkle in the nation's eyes, before there was a female speaker of the House of Representatives, a female attorney general, or a female secretary of state, there was the F.W.O.T.S.C.—the first woman on the Supreme Court—an acronym Sandra Day O'Connor used when she ascended America's loftiest bench.

The fact a tomboy would one day join the United States' most exclusive male club serves as a harbinger of hope. Born in 1930, the oldest of three children, Sandra's childhood was spent at the Lazy B Ranch, situated on 160,000 rain-starved acres on the Arizona-New Mexico border. The little girl did not own a pet cat; she had a pet bobcat. While her contemporaries played with Shirley

Temple dolls, Sandra held a rifle. Her family kept one in their truck, and if they saw a coyote, Sandra would take aim from her window to kill her prey in order to save the ranch's small calves. Life on the homestead provided a litany of lessons: caring for sick animals without access to a veterinarian, heating water using only the sun's rays, finding entertainment without television. Sandra's early years left her with a sense of self-sufficiency and an aversion to whining. Years later, her orders to her law clerks left no doubt as to her expectations, "No excuses. Get the job done." Her early grit was to serve her well.

Sandra's parents wanted more for their bright daughter than pet bobcats and moving target practice, and at age six, they sent her to her maternal grandparents in El Paso, where they enrolled her in a finishing school. Unlike meals at the Lazy B, Sandra ate in a home with white tablecloths and studied Latin and Greek. Her father held hope his daughter would attend Stanford, his own youthful aspiration that had fallen by the wayside.

As an attractive sixteen-year-old, Sandra left for college, followed by law school at Stanford, an extremely unconventional route for a woman of her era. To her surprise, the male student body was not intimidated by her combination of beauty and brains. World War II had just ended, and the returning GIs crowded the campus, many looking for relationships. She received four marriage proposals, one from a lanky Midwesterner with a flattop haircut, William Rehnquist, slated to become the Chief Justice of the Supreme Court. They met in class and bonded over picnics, bridge, and charades. His intentions imploded when he failed to please her papa. Mr. Day offered his daughter's beau a bull's testicle he had grilled on a branding fire, and William flinched. After he struck out, a man with a stronger stomach wooed and won Sandra's heart: John O'Connor III, her colleague on the Stanford Law Review. Nevertheless, William persisted; during his tenure as a clerk on the Supreme Court, he wrote to her in a lawyerly style—the equivalent of flinching at bull testicles: "To be specific, Sandy, will you marry me this summer?"

Sandra's marriage to John proved to be of the ilk said to be made in heaven. The O'Connors and their three sons settled in Phoenix, as did Rehnquist and his wife. Despite the demands of motherhood, the future justice actively sought a job in a law firm. Although she had been third in her class at Stanford Law, she only received offers as a legal secretary. The country was not yet ready to embrace an ambitious, married mother who could argue legalities as well as shoot a jackrabbit at fifty yards. She recalled of those not-so-good-old-days, "No one gave me a job. It was very frustrating because I had done very well in both undergraduate and law school and my male classmates weren't having any problems. No one would even speak to me." Exhibiting the persistence and initiative for which she would later become renowned, Sandra sought out a county attorney in San Mateo, California, who had once had a woman on his staff, and agreed to work as a volunteer. Four months later, she was a full-time employee and only left to work as the Judge Advocate

General's Corps in Frankfurt during the Korean War when the government drafted her husband.

When the O'Connors returned to Arizona in 1957, Sandra again struggled to find work until she eventually convinced a man to co-own a law office. They primarily took on cases for clients with limited funds, and soon the firm garnered a sterling reputation. Consequently, the Republican Party elected Sandra a precinct committeeman and later promoted her to a vacancy in the Arizona State Senate, where she served two terms. After infiltrating the senatorial band of brothers, in 1973, to everyone's amazement—including her own— she became the majority leader. Obtaining the lofty position was a momentous event as it was the first time a woman in the United States had ever held a legislative leadership position.

Sandra's life was the embodiment of the cliché of "having it all." In addition to her unprecedented political successes, her marriage was a happily ever after one. John and Sandra skied and golfed; hobnobbed with bigwigs such as Chief Justice Warren Burger, and raised their Stanford-educated sons. One of their boys also ascended a lofty height when he went on to climb Mount Everest.

Mrs. O'Connor eventually returned to law in 1975 as an elected county judge, and four years later became a member of the Arizona Court of Appeals. If these laurels were not heady enough, in 1981, she had the shock of her life. During Ronald Reagan's presidential campaign, he had promised to appoint the first woman to the Supreme Court, a commitment he had undertaken to woo the female vote. When he chose Sandra Day O'Connor for the singular honor, the gobsmacked future justice stated, "I had never worked at court. Had never worked as a law clerk there. Had never tried a case at court. It was far removed from our life in Arizona and I was not trying to move to Washington, DC. I was not sure if I went to the Supreme Court that it would be a comfortable choice for me." John helped quell her self-doubt, telling her, "Come on, you'll be fine." In the first televised confirmation, the Senate Judiciary Committee confirmed her in 1981 by a sweeping majority of 99-0. The missing senator, Max Raucus of Montana, sent her a copy of Norman MacLean's *A River Runs Through It* as an apology for his absence. The bench broke its trend: it had been populated exclusively by men for the previous 192 years.

Although it was not easy to be a sister among the band of brothers, Mrs. O'Connor was clearly a popular choice, even if her approval was due in large part to the President's popularity. Had Sandra chosen William over John, she would have achieved another historical landmark—as part of the first married couple on the Supreme Court. With her entry, the term Mr. Justice went the way of the dodo. By age fifty-one, Sandra had shattered the seemingly impenetrable glass ceiling of the Supreme Court.

Over her twenty-four years wearing the black judicial robes, Sandra left her brand: her vote saved abortion rights, her decision preserved affirmative action, and her voice delivered the presidency to George W. Bush in 2000. Not a bad résumé for the girl from the Lazy B Ranch. Her presence on the bench proclaimed that women had a niche on it, and since they belonged there, there was no place they did not belong. Because of her singular accomplishments, she became one of the most consequential women in American history, something that makes her as notorious as the next woman to occupy the precipice of power, Ruth Bader Ginsburg.

In her spare time, Sandra—apparently a member of some more evolved species—cooked every recipe in Julia Child's *Mastering the Art of French Cooking.* A friend commented, "Oh, for God's sake, Sandra, do you always have to overachieve?"

Sandra, a pivotal pioneer in jurisprudence, enjoyed a magical life, but her golden years were tarnished. At age seventy-five (still a spring chicken for those who preside over the bench), she retired in order to nurse John through the onslaught of Alzheimer's. Hours after her announcement, the other members of the nation's highest court and three retired justices released statements praising Justice O'Connor. Ruth Bader Ginsburg stated, "She strived mightily to make what was momentous for women in 1981 no longer extraordinary, but entirely expectable. I am among legions of women endeavoring to follow her lead." The disease proved the only obstacle Sandra could not successfully arm-wrestle; John quickly slipped into a place his wife could not reach. With the grit she had learned from her early years, she turned down her doctor's prescription for antidepressants as it went against her philosophy of tackling troubles head-on. When John's condition worsened, Sandra had to make the heartrending decision to place him in an assisted living center. In the facility, her husband of fifty-five years carried on a romance with another patient; when Sandra came to visit, she observed him as he sat on a porch swing with the other woman as they held hands. Sandra was pleased to see him content and was devastated when John passed away in 2009.

Former Justice O'Connor determined there was life after loss, and the widow became far from the conventional octogenarian grandmother. In addition to raising awareness for Alzheimer's research, she heard cases in appeals courts, lectured, and demystified the judicial process for teens. After discovering that only a third of young people could name the three branches of government, Sandra established ourcourts.org as an educational tool that proved a resounding success.

In 2018, at age eighty-eight, Sandra announced her departure from public life. She wrote, "While the final chapter of my life with dementia may be trying, nothing has diminished my gratitude and deep appreciation for the countless blessings in my life. As a young cowgirl from the Arizona desert, I never could have imagined that one day I would become the first woman justice on the US

Supreme Court." The words echoed an earlier letter, one penned by President Reagan, who had encountered the same struggle, "I now begin the journey that will lead me into the sunset of my life." In an ironic twist, the man who had put Justice O'Connor on the Supreme Court and the man for whom she had left it ended up arm-wrestling the same disease with which she now struggles. Although she may no longer have a memory of the country she served, America should remember her as a trailblazer.

Sandra knew what she wanted her legacy to be. While she was a justice, she told her sons that she hoped she had helped pave the pathway for other women. And pave it she did: Ruth Bader Ginsburg, Sonia Sotomayor, and Elena Kagan have followed in her footsteps. However, the balance of justice is still lopsided, considering that of the one hundred thirteen justices, only four have been women. Mrs. O'Connor was clear on what she wanted on her tombstone: "It was what I told Congress when they were interviewing me. Here lies a good judge."

Chapter 22

Ride Sally Ride
(1983)

The monologue that introduced the television series *Star Trek*, "Space: the final frontier. To boldly go where no man has gone before," echoes the fascination man has always had with the heavens. The men who have heeded the siren call of the skies are legendary: Shepard, Glenn, Armstrong, Aldrin. Then came Sally Ride, who blazed a cosmic trail when she became the first woman astronaut and shattered the glass dome of the galaxy.

The trailblazer of the stars was Sally Kristen, born in 1951, in Los Angeles' San Fernando Valley. Her father, Dr. Dale Ride, was a political science professor at Santa Monica College; her mother, Joyce, worked as a volunteer counselor at a women's correctional facility and founded the Mary Magdalene Project to help prostitutes escape the streets. Both parents were elders in the Presbyterian

Church. Her only sibling was her younger sister, Karen, known by the nickname Bear, and later as the Reverend Karen Ride (with the 'Reverend' coming from her position as a Presbyterian minister). From an early age, Sally was enamored of science and played with a chemistry kit and telescope; when asked what she wanted to be when she grew up her invariable answer was a physicist. The possessor of brains as well as brawn, Sally became so obsessed with playing football in the street her parents gave her tennis lessons as a safer alternative. Soon she was competing in national junior tournaments.

Sally attended Westlake School for Girls in Beverly Hills on a tennis scholarship but felt out of place among the actors' daughters and "Bel Air belles." One shining light was her science teacher, Dr. Elizabeth Mommaerts, whom she described as "logic personified." The esteem was mutual, and Elizabeth invited Sally to her home to sample French food and wine.

After graduation, Sally left for Swarthmore College in Pennsylvania but quit after three semesters. She was homesick for California and had decided to pursue a career in tennis. Driven, she practiced several hours a day and took physics courses at the University of California at Los Angeles. In 1970, she enrolled at Stanford as a junior, where she was her tennis team's number one women's singles player and garnered a national ranking. During summer vacation, Ms. Ride taught tennis; there she met Tam O'Shaughnessy, who was to play a pivotal role in her life. Billie Jean King urged Sally to quit college and turn pro. Years later, when asked why she decided to be a scientist instead of an athlete, Sally quipped, "A bad forehand." The Renaissance woman received bachelor's degrees in physics and English (her specialty was Shakespeare, whose works she viewed as a jigsaw puzzle), a master's degree in physics, and a Ph.D. in astrophysics. Sally, who accrued degrees like other girls collected charms on their bracelets, was once asked if she got her brains from her professor father: "I must have, because my mother still has hers."

A NASA advertisement in the Stanford student newspaper altered her aspiration to become a professor. Out of eight thousand applicants, the space agency selected Sally along with five other women and twenty-nine men. They were referred to in NASA circles as "the thirty-five new guys," and the six who did not fit that description remained tight-lipped. The successful candidates brought scientific and engineering skills to a field that had been the preserve of male military test pilots. Ride said that upon first hearing she had made the cut, the one person she had wanted to call was Dr. Mommaerts; that was not possible as her former teacher had committed suicide.

As part of her training, Dr. Ride practiced parachute jumping, operating a jet plane, and coping with weightlessness. Sally was not old enough to have applied for the position when women in the space program were either wives, mothers, or spacesuit seamstresses—a nod to "those who serve also stand and wait." When the space agency lifted their iron curtain of gender, the gesture was simply an act of bureaucratic box-checking. The ladies still had to prove—to use the name of the 1983 movie about the space race—they had "The Right Stuff."

Ironically, NASA chose Sally to be the first woman for their 1983 shuttle launch just weeks before the Equal Rights Amendment dissolved in defeat. The name of the spacecraft that carried Sally and four male crew members beyond the confines of Earth captured her trailblazing spirit: the Challenger. NASA's historic flight was the first step of the crumbling of the space program's old boys' club, and the news sparked a media frenzy. Speaking to reporters before takeoff, she politely endured a barrage of questions: Would spaceflight affect her reproductive organs? Would she wear a bra or makeup in space? Did she cry on the job? How would she deal with menstruation in space? On *The Tonight Show*, Johnny Carson smirked that the shuttle flight would be delayed because Dr. Ride had to find a purse to match her shoes. Such were the times. Before the flight, *People Magazine* featured Sally on its cover with the headline: "O WHAT A RIDE!" and its accompanying caption, "Fed up with those dumb chauvinist questions, America's first woman in space is ready to prove herself." Sally said of the hoopla, "It may be too bad that our society isn't further along and that this is such a big deal."

Cape Canaveral turned carnival the day of the launch, and among the crowd of 250,000 were her proud parents rooting for Sally. Gloria Steinem said of the takeoff,

"It's an important first because it means that millions and millions of little girls are going to sit in front of the televisions and know they can become astronauts after this." When the shuttle returned to Earth, Sally told the reporters, "I'm sure it was the most fun that I'll ever have in my life." The woman in the eye of the storm refused to accept a bouquet of flowers since the same gift had not been presented to the rest of the crew. President Reagan congratulated the astronauts and told Dr. Ride, "You were the best person for the job."

The golden girl of the galaxy made headlines when she married astronaut Steve Hawley, the first time two active astronauts wed. She piloted a plane to the family-only wedding at his parents' home in Kansas; the bride wore Levis and a rugby shirt. The couple fiercely safeguarded their privacy and never appeared together in public. She explained her reticence, "I've spent my whole life not talking to people, and I don't see any reason why I should start now." Steve appeared an ideal husband; he did not care that his wife was an indifferent housekeeper, a trait she inherited from her mother. He backed her decision not to have children and was fine with standing in her considerable shadow. The Hawley house was "laced with mementoes of the space age," such as shuttle dishes, and bedroom décor was a large photograph of astronauts on the moon. Despite their commonalities, the marriage hit a roadblock as Sally realized the love of her life was not her husband. The truth was something even her ideal husband could not overlook; they divorced in 1987.

The second and last time Ride voyaged into space was in 1984, accompanied by Kathryn Sullivan, who became the first American woman to walk in space. NASA cancelled her third flight when the Challenger exploded after seventy-three seconds on its 1986 flight, resulting in the deaths of all its astronauts as well as the first civilian in space, schoolteacher Christa McAuliffe.

President Reagan ordered a panel to investigate the twin space disasters of the Challenger and the Columbia, and Ride became the only person to sit on both committees. After the grueling tasks of investigating the death of her colleagues, Sally retired in 1987. At that time, she donated her first flight suit to the Smithsonian National Air and Space Museum, where it hangs inside a mock-up of a space shuttle. The light-blue jacket bears a name tag: Sally. Dr. Ride told interviewers that her motivation had never been fame or to make history as the first woman in space. All she had wanted to do was "to fly, to soar into space, float around weightless inside the shuttle, look out at the heavens and gaze back at Earth."

After leaving NASA, Ride joined the Stanford University Security Research Institute, and later she became a physics professor at the University of California at San Diego. In 2001, she founded and served as president of Sally Ride Science, a company whose mission was to motivate middle-school girls to study math, science, and technology and to urge parents and teachers to discourage gender stereotypes. With Tam O'Shaughnessy, a professor emerita at San Diego State University, Ride co-authored five science books for children, one of which explained how to make a sandwich in space. (She advised eating it fast before it floated away.) When autographing her books, she always wrote, "Reach for the stars." Interestingly enough, she said educating the young was her greatest accomplishment.

At age sixty-one, Sally passed away from pancreatic cancer at her home in La Jolla, California. She achieved another first through her obituary, which she used as a vehicle to come out of the closet. The brief announcement she had co-written with Tam stated, "Dr. Ride is survived by her partner of twenty-seven years, Tam O'Shaughnessy; her mother, Joyce; and her sister, Ms. Scott, who is known as Bear." Sibling and lover confirmed to reporters that no one should mistake "partner" for business partner. The outing revealing that Sally had been the first gay astronaut generated an avalanche of controversy. Andrew Sullivan, a journalist for *The Daily Beast*, called Dr. Ride an "absent heroine" who could have used her iconic status to serve as role model for the LGBT community. Those in Camp Sally argued that public figures have a right to their privacy; moreover, she might have felt the disclosure would have engendered repercussions. Conservative NASA would have welcomed a bride marrying a bride as readily as they would have welcomed an invasion of Klingons; mothers would not have purchased books penned by two lesbian authors. The precious privacy she had always sought would have been forfeit had she served as a poster child for gay liberation. Perhaps the most poignant anecdote was shared by Lynn Sherr in *Slate* when she asked the ninety-two-year-old Joyce Ride if her late husband would have been more concerned that his daughters were gay or that that they were Democrats. "Probably," Joyce responded, "that they were Democrats."

President Obama called Sally "a national hero and a powerful role model." In a statement, he said she "inspired generations of young girls to reach for the stars." He also honored her memory with a Presidential Medal of Freedom, one Tam accepted on her late partner's behalf, making her the first woman to do so for a same-sex partner. The post office issued a Forever stamp with the image of a smiling Dr. Ride in her blue astronaut garb, the space shuttle blasting off in the background.

As the hatch closed on the Challenger, a different door opened, one that allowed American women access to the galaxy. In the crowds of onlookers who had watched the historic launch—among them Jane Fonda and Gloria Steinem—many wore T-shirts alluding to the 1966 pop song "Mustang Sally," whose lyric was a fitting send-off for the lady in blue, one who had reached for the stars: "Ride Sally Ride."

Chapter 23

I Did What I Could (1985)

C razy Horse, Sitting Bull, Geronimo: The names conjure the legendary Native Americans of yesteryear, the era when the buffalo and the teepee dotted the landscape. In 1985, Wilma Mankiller joined the trio as the first principal female chief of the Cherokee Nation.

Southern writer William Faulkner wrote in *Requiem for a Nun*, "The past is never dead. It's not even past." His words can apply to the 1838 federal government's removal of the Cherokee people from their homes in the southeast in a forced resettlement to the Indian Territory of latter-day Oklahoma. The victims called the experience *Nunna daul Tsuny*, which translates to "the trail where we cried," but it is mostly referred to as the Trail of Tears.

The descendant of the displaced was Wilma Pearl Mankiller (whose family name originated from a tribal military rank), born in 1945 in Tahlequah, Oklahoma. She was the sixth of eleven children of Charley Mankiller, a full-blooded Cherokee, and the former Clara Irene Sitton, of Dutch-Irish descent, who had become a bride at age fifteen. She christened Wilma as a shortened form of the Dutch name Wilhelmina and Pearl after her maternal grandmother. As a little girl, her family called her Pearl, and the thought of an irritant developing into a precious stone could serve as a metaphor for her life. Wilma spent her early childhood on Mankiller Flats, land deeded to her grandfather as a settlement for forcing him from his ancestral territory. The Mankiller home had no electricity or indoor plumbing; meals consisted of fried squirrel, and the girls' dresses were sewn from flour sacks. On the three-mile walk to school, white women offered the shoeless children rides accompanied by pitying looks. Their customary comment was, "Bless your little hearts," and the children nicknamed them the "Bless Your Heart Ladies."

In 1956, The Bureau of Indian Affairs (BIA)—the same bureaucrats who had "relocated" Japanese American during World War II—initiated a program to tempt the Cherokee to move from rural Oklahoma to urban California. Many felt the move was calculated to weaken reservation ties and diffuse the political clout of the tribe. The eleven-year-old Wilma described the move as her personal trail of tears. In her autobiography, *Mankiller A Chief and Her People* Wilma described the train ride for the journey to the West, "We must have looked like a darker version of the Joad family from John Steinbeck's novel, *The Grapes of Wrath*." The vouchers from the BIA for an apartment fell through, and they stayed for two weeks in an old hotel in a district of San Francisco called The Tenderloin. In the night, they saw flashing neon lights and garishly garbed prostitutes. Wilma recalled they had left behind the sounds of roosters, coyotes, and bobcats and instead heard sirens from police cars, ambulances, and fire engines. Wilma, who had never before heard the shrill sound, thought they were the screams of wild animals. Similarly, she was bewildered at the box that swallowed people and delivered new ones. Although she learned about elevators, she took the stairs. She felt alienated at school and especially dreaded roll-call, where her name never failed to elicit snickers. Miserable, her mother tried to help by giving her a home permanent that Wilma described as "the most awful" she had ever seen. She recalled, "We had no preparation, no way to conceptualize San Francisco or even a city. We'd never been past the Muskogee State Fair." Wilma said of the ordeal that the architects of the federal program felt the Native Americans would probably open liquor stores. The stereotype took a hit when Charley became a warehouse worker and a union organizer. In her new city, Wilma felt as if she were on the far side of the moon.

As a minority teenager without money, confidence, or self-esteem, Wilma found a sanctuary at the San Francisco Indian Center in the Mission District. However, she felt her escape route was marriage to her Ecuadorian boyfriend, whom she wedded at age seventeen in a Reno chapel. Wilma Mankiller became Mrs. Hugo Olaya and fell into the role of dutiful housewife and mother to Gina and Felicia.

Despite Wilma's domesticity, her latent activist spirit emerged, one aided by living in San Francisco, the epicenter of 1960s radicalism. The shy girl was caught up in the spirit of the Vietnam protests, feminism, and the Civil Rights Movement. Wilma swapped her ladylike pumps for sandals, her pantsuits for flowing skirts. Unwilling to be the housebound wife expected by her Hispanic husband, Wilma took college courses and became active in the causes that swirled around the city.

There is an old adage that states the times make the man, and an event that occurred in the dying days of a turbulent decade altered Wilma's journey. On November 9, 1969, Native Americans traveled to Alcatraz Island, the abandoned federal prison in the middle of San Francisco Bay, to stage a political protest. They claimed the island "in the name of Indians of all tribes," and during their nineteen-month occupation, Wilma was a frequent visitor and raised money for their cause. She said of the takeover, "I had felt there was something wrong with me because I wasn't happy being a traditional housewife. I started listening to what these people were saying. What Alcatraz did for me was, it enabled me to see people who felt like I did but could articulate it much better." No longer allowing herself to be marginalized, when people snickered at her name, she said that it was actually a well-earned nickname. In an act of rebellion, without asking her husband, she took money from their joint savings account and bought a car—a red Mazda—in a bid for independence. With sadness, she watched the cracks in her marriage widen; "I would look at Hugo and wish I could love him... Not wanting to live a lie led me to the final step." In 1997, she obtained a divorce and resumed using her Cherokee name. Though a single mother without money, she was able to accomplish what those who had endured the Trail of Tears could never do—she returned home to Mankiller Flats. She had twenty dollars in her purse. When she arrived in Oklahoma, she said, "I never felt home until I came home. When I came back here, then I began to understand, this is where I belong."

Anxious to improve herself, Wilma obtained a degree in social sciences from Flaming Rainbow University, worked a job as a community coordinator at the Cherokee tribal headquarters, and raised her daughters. Her not-a-minute-to-spare-days abruptly halted when, while driving on a rural road in the early morning, a car hit her head-on. The other driver, ironically her close friend, died at the scene of the accident. Wilma was barely alive when paramedics extricated her from the wreckage; the impact left her right leg almost severed and shattered her facial bones. When she regained consciousness, she felt death had bathed her in a feeling of love, yet she pulled back from its embrace for the sake of her daughters. Her seventeen operations were agonizing, but left her with a feeling of equanimity, "I knew I'd lost the fear of death and the fear of the challenges in my life." Post-surgery, she had to battle the new health problem of myasthenia gravis, and in the future lay a serious kidney disease that required an organ transplant from an older brother. She often had to rely on canes to walk without pain.

After her convalescence, Wilma returned to her job; her success as a community planner and grant proposal writer caught the attention of Chief Ross Swimmer, who nominated her as his deputy chief. When he resigned two years later for a position as Assistant Secretary of the Interior for Indian Affairs, she succeeded him as principal chief, thus becoming the first woman to head the country's second largest tribe. Upon the completion of her term, she campaigned for the position and found gender an impediment. An opponent, J. B. Dreadfulwater, argued tradition did not allow a woman to lead the tribe. At committee meetings, members said if her election passed, their tribe would become a laughingstock. Her enemies slashed her car tires, and she was the recipient of death threats. In a tight race, Mankiller prevailed. She received national attention for her work when she became the guiding spirit behind the rehabilitation of Bell, a rural Oklahoma slum she helped turn into a model town. Because of her accomplishments, nobody grumbled when the tribe chose Wilma at the poll. Feminist icon Gloria Steinem—who was married in Wilma's home—stated, "In a just country, she would have been elected president."

For inspiration, Mankiller turned to her hero, Chief Joseph, the brilliant Nez Perce leader of the 1800s who resisted overwhelming forces of white soldiers before finally making his peace. In 1990, she signed an unprecedented agreement in which the Bureau of Indian Affairs gave the Cherokee direct control over millions of dollars in federal funding, and the following year she served a second term after receiving 82 percent of the vote. As head chieftain, Mankiller headed a government with one full-time deputy chief, a part-time tribal council of 15,200 employees, and a budget of $78 million a year. She stated of her position, "It's a little like being the CEO of a tiny country and a social worker at the same time." Despite her prestigious appointment, jokes about her name persisted. She called it a cheap shot when an editorial page of *The Wall Street Journal*, in a nod to her attendance at Clinton's economic summit, wrote, "Our favorite name on the summit list is Chief Wilma Mankiller, representing the Cherokee Nation, though we hope not a feminist economic priority."

What helped Mankiller in her historic role was the support of her family and, since 1986, her second husband, Charlie Soap, a Cherokee community organizer and skilled native dancer. She also knew many traditional dances but claimed her favorite dancing song was Aretha Franklin's "Respect"—the title a nod to what she had fought for all her life. The marriage made Wilma a stepmother to Winterhawk, who shared her home. Wilma said in a tribute to her husband, who never resented standing in her significant shadow, "He is the most secure male I have ever met."

During her tenure, Wilma took her people's issues to the White House and met with three presidents. She successfully fought for a 1990 agreement with the federal government to give the tribe autonomy over millions of dollars, allowing them to aspire to self-government; she had well learned the lesson of the Bless Your Heart Ladies. Post-retirement, she was a guest professor at Dartmouth College, President Bill Clinton awarded Ms. Mankiller the Medal of Freedom, and the National Women's Hall of Fame inducted her as a member. Despite all her lofty accomplishments, one of which she was most proud was revealed in her comment, "Some high school girls have never known a male chief. They think this is the natural order of things."

Death finally embraced Wilma when she succumbed to pancreatic cancer in 2010. Ancient tribal traditions call for the setting of signal fires to light the way home for a great one whose spirit has passed; fires were lit in twenty-three countries. The indefatigable activist made good on her aspiration, "I hope that when I leave, it will just be said: I did what I could."

Chapter 24

Black Magic
(1987)

In 1973, Dobie Gray crooned, "I wanna get lost in your rock 'n' roll and drift away." Thirteen years later, the lyrics, rather than being a paean to romantic fulfillment, alluded to women who had to drift away from their dream of becoming the Founding Mothers of Cleveland's newly instituted Rock and Roll Hall of Fame. The gender gap reared its head when the music emporium listed its first ten inductees: Buddy Holly, Chuck Berry, Elvis Presley, Fats Domino, James Brown, Jerry Lee Lewis, Little Richard, Ray Charles, Sam Cooke, and the Everly Brothers. Apparently, the museum did not abide by First Lady Abigail Adam's admonition, "Remember the ladies." The decision did not sit well with those consecrated to the Women's Liberation Movement. Had society not read Germaine Greer's *The Female Eunuch*, perused Gloria Steinem's *Ms. Magazine*, listened to Helen Reddy's "I am

Woman"? Perhaps their struggle finally bore fruit: in 1988, Aretha Louise Franklin received her R-E-S-P-E-C-T when she became the first female inductee in the Rock & Roll Hall of Fame.

The Queen of Soul was born in Memphis, Tennessee, in 1942. Her mother, Barbara Siggers Franklin, was a gospel singer and pianist. Her father, Clarence LaVaughn Franklin, called C. L., preached black liberation theology, and his career as a pastor led the family from Memphis to Buffalo and then to Detroit. Her parents separated over C. L.'s wandering eye when Aretha was six, leaving her in her father's care. Barbara remained in contact with her children, who were devastated when she passed away four years later after a heart attack. A rock star among preachers, C. L. was known as "the man with the golden voice." His sermons, often delivered beneath a neon-blue crucifix, were broadcast on radio and released on vinyl. With his celebrity status, he charged $4,000 for appearances. Dr. Martin Luther King, Jr. stayed with the family when he visited Detroit, and C. L. helped him organize the historic Walk to Freedom.

The Franklin household door was always open to musicians such as Mahalia Jackson, who served as Aretha's music mentor. Future Motown artists such as Smokey Robinson and Diana Ross lived nearby. After hearing Clara Ward perform at her aunt's funeral, Aretha taught herself to play the piano before she was ten and emulated songs from the radio and her record collection. Proud of his daughter's magnificent voice, C. L. placed her on a chair in his church, and she became a star soloist. C. L. told her that with her God-given talent, she would one day sing for kings and queens. At age twelve, Aretha became pregnant and had son Clarence two months before her thirteenth birthday. His father was Donald Burk, a boy she knew from school. At age fourteen, she had a second son, Edward, whose father was Edward Jordan. She dropped out of school after having her children and ditching diaper duty went on tour with C. L., leaving Big Mama, her grandmother, with the baby rearing responsibilities.

Aretha left for New York City at eighteen, hoping to become a star in the music industry. John Hammond, the Columbia Records executive who had championed Billie Holiday and would one day bring Bob Dylan and Bruce Springsteen to his label, signed Aretha in 1960. The following year she met and married Ted White, who became her manager and the father of their son, Ted Jr.

In 1967, after her contract ended, Aretha moved to Atlantic Records. For her first session, Ms. Franklin traveled to FAME Studios in Muscle Shoals, Alabama, to record a smoldering blues ballad with an all-white group of studio musicians. Their song, "I Never Loved a Man the Way I Love You," detailed a woman's devotion to a no-good man. Ted got into a drunken fistfight with the trumpet player, and husband and wife returned to New York. The song recorded that evening went on to sell a million records and launched Aretha's reign as the Queen of Soul. On Valentine's Day, Aretha recorded

"Respect," a demand to be treated with dignity and the instruction to "give it to me when you get home." The song by the daughter of the preacher man caught on with the Black Power movement, feminists, and human rights activists across the world. In 2018, it became a symbol of the #MeToo Movement. Ms. Franklin stated, "I think women have to be strong. Some people will run all over you." The signature song surged to number one and garnered Aretha her first two Grammy Awards for best R & B recording and for the best R & B female vocal performance (an award she won each succeeding year through 1975). By the end of 1968, she had made three more recordings for her label, including the wildly popular "I Say a Little Prayer" and "You Make Me Feel Like a Natural Woman."

Janis Joplin said of Ms. Franklin that she was, "the best chick singer since Billie Holiday." Ray Charles's take was, "I don't know anybody that can sing a song like Aretha Franklin. Nobody. Period." *Time* magazine billed the eighteen-time Grammy winner as "The Sound of Soul," and she graced its 1968 cover. The feature article stated that Franklin's music channeled her own pain, sorrow, and resilience in a way that aligned with soul music's past. Her soaring notes also encompassed a nation's sorrow when she sang at the memorial service for the Reverend Dr. Martin Luther King, Jr.

Despite her runaway success, Aretha's personal life was in upheaval. The extremely private woman lifted the curtain of the confessional when she admitted, "I've been hurt—hurt bad." White, rather than making his wife feel like a natural woman, roughed her up in public, and the lyrics of her song "I Never Loved a Man the Way I Love You" took on a personal significance, especially with the line, "You're a no-good heart breaker." Before their 1969 divorce, she dropped White as her manager and filed a restraining order against him. She took to self-medicating with alcohol and went through a period of heavy drinking before she attained sobriety. In 1972, she had an affair with her road manager, Ken Cunningham, and had a son, Kecalf. His name was an acronym of Ken E. Cunningham and Aretha Louise Franklin. Having reclaimed her life, she released her blockbuster "Amazing Grace," which sold two million records, making it one of the best-selling gospel albums of all time. Aretha branched out to film with her appearance as a waitress in the movie *The Blues Brothers*, where she revived her former hit "Think." The song was Ms. Franklin's feminist anthem, giving an unprecedented voice to women. She took a fourth trip down the aisle with her marriage to actor Glynn Turman spanning the years 1978 to 1984. The split was amicable enough for her to sing the title song for his television series *A Different World*. The soul singer lamented, "Falling out of love is like losing weight. It's a lot easier putting it on than taking it off."

Despite Aretha's demanding schedule, she became an activist, well aware that she would be stepping on conservative toes. In 1970, Franklin offered to post bail for Angela Davis, a member of the Communist Party. Davis had been charged with conspiracy, kidnapping, and murder. C. L., concerned about the repercussions for his daughter's career, advised her to avoid any association with the radical. Despite his advice, Aretha continued to support Davis and offered to post her bail of $250,000.

Through Aretha's childhood loss of her mother, absences from her sons, and her two failed marriages, her one constant was her father. In 1979, robbers shot C. L. during a home invasion, and he remained in a coma until his death in 1984. During those pain-laden years, Aretha shuttled between her residence in California and her childhood home in Detroit—where she eventually relocated—to be at his side.

With the disco era, her popularity waned, but Aretha recorded duets with Elton John, Whitney Houston, and James Brown. She also rallied with televised triumphs such as a noteworthy appearance at the 1998 Grammy Awards, where she substituted at the last minute for the ailing Luciano Pavarotti by performing a Puccini aria. On *Divas Live* for VH1, she steamrolled fellow stars Mariah Carey and Celine Dion. Part of her appeal was that unlike these divas or Diana Ross, Ms. Franklin, with her considerable girth, looked like every woman, a fact that made her more relatable. If she were concerned about body image, she never let it show. Onstage she often wore tube tops and leotards, unapologetic for her weight. In her later years, she favored strapless gowns and upon occasion slapped her ample backside.

Aretha donned a more proper and prim demeanor when she sang "My Country 'Tis of Thee" at President Barack

Obama's inauguration. The auspicious occasion was one of the first times Ms. Franklin was *ever* upstaged—by her *hat*: adorned with a giant, angled bow and ringed with Swarovski crystals that ended up on display in the Smithsonian. (Ms. Franklin, a clotheshorse, had a favorite milliner and a preferred furrier. She also traveled with a valet who carried the singer's designer purse on and off the stage at concerts.) The diva had traversed this presidential path before: she had performed at preinaugural concerts for Jimmy Carter and Bill Clinton. Ever since Franklin's star had appeared in the music firmament, every powerhouse songstress—at least every one worth her weight in sequins—has been measured against the Queen of Soul. In addition to all her awards, the girl who had been a college dropout garnered several honorary degrees from Yale, Princeton, and Harvard. In 2005, Aretha received the Presidential Medal of Freedom.

Though Franklin's career cooled in the 1970s as Roberta Flack's star ascended, she rebounded in the mid-1980s. Even in her later years, Ms. Franklin never became a museum fixture. In 2014, Aretha recorded "Aretha Franklin Sings the Great Diva Classics," including her take on Adele's "Rolling in the Deep." In 2015, she entertained Pope Francis and brought down the house at the Kennedy Center when she sang "You Make Me Feel Like a Natural Woman." Carole King almost fell from her balcony in exuberance; President Obama wiped away a tear. Two years later, she appeared at the Cathedral of Saint John the Divine in New York City during Elton John's twenty-fifth anniversary gala for his AIDS Foundation.

The New York Times reporter, Rob Hoeerburger, met Ms. Franklin for lunch and asked if Dennis Edwards, the lead singer of the Temptations, who had been the final performer at her sixty-ninth birthday bash, had been the love of her life. She coyly responded, "The love of my life? I'm much too young to answer that question."

Aretha Louise Franklin opened the door of the Rock and Roll Hall of Fame, thereby allowing other women to enter: the Supremes, Janis Joplin, and Joni Mitchell. Currently, in the seesaw of gender, only 43 of the 317 inductees have been female. However, in the words of Dylan, "The times they are a changing," and the museum is becoming ever more open to the fact that women have a voice. For being the first possessor of estrogen to enter the emporium, Aretha deserves undying R-E-S-P-E-C-T. Because of her courage and indomitable spirit, she put a new spin on the term *Black Magic.*

Chapter 25

Checkmate
(1991)

The only piece on a chessboard that symbolizes a woman is the queen—its most powerful player, able to move in any direction. Ironically, females are treated as second-class citizens in the male-dominated game. A blow to sexism arrived when Susan Polgár became the first female grandmaster of chess.

Chess was not always a male domain. In medieval Spain, women indulged in the ancient art in bed while recovering from childbirth. A French tale from 1230 relates how a knight must triumph against an emir's chess-master daughter in order to win her hand. Around the seventeenth century, women disappeared from the chess scene until the advent of three sisters.

Tiger Mother Amy Chua had nothing on tiger father László Polgár, a Hungarian psychologist. The stepson of a rabbi and the product of a broken home, László grew up in an orphanage and wanted a far more ordered life for his future children. After studying the biographies of four hundred intellectuals from Einstein to Socrates, László came up with the theory that geniuses are made, not born. To support his hypothesis, he published *Bring Up Genius!* He also conducted an epistolary courtship with Klara, a Ukrainian foreign language teacher. His letters did not wax eloquent on her beauty or profess declarations of eternal love. Instead, they centered on a pedagogical experiment. In one he told her, "Miss Klara, we both agree that the school system produces the gray average mass. But give me a healthy newborn and I can make a genius." Klara fell for him as well as his plans for their future offspring, and the two wed in 1973. László delivered on his promise, not just once, but three times with daughters Zsuzsa, Zsofia, and Judit.

Although László knew he was to "specialize" his firstborn, he was unsure of the best discipline: mathematics, finance, or languages. The question was answered when Zsuzsa (who currently uses the Anglicized Susan), the highly energetic firstborn, discovered a chess set while rummaging through a cabinet in search of a toy. Klara, not familiar with a single rule of the ancient game, was delighted her daughter was quietly absorbed in the figurines and promised that her father would teach her the game. Rather than drilling his daughter in the rules, he described the pieces as characters in a fairy tale, filled with adventures of the king, queen, horses, and knights.

Chess, Polgár decided, was the perfect outlet as it was an art and a science, and as with competitive athletics, it could yield measurable results. He decided he had found his child's calling card—despite the fact that less than 1 percent of the top players were women. Six months later, Zsuzsa arrived at Budapest's smoke-filled chess club. One of the regulars guffawed when László asked him to play against a diminutive opponent; sitting on phone books and a pillow to reach the table, the little girl earned her first competitive victory. Soon afterwards, she dominated the city's girls-under-eleven tournament by achieving a perfect score. Judit, not one to stand in her sibling's shadow, was beating her father by age five.

László had read that Yehudi Menuhin's father had sacrificed his career to devote himself to his son's concerts, and although it meant living in a cramped apartment and bread dipped in gravy for meals, he decided to do likewise for his daughters. Hungary's communist regime threatened to throw Polgár into a mental institution when he refused to send his children to school. His rebuttal was he was paving the way for his girls' destiny as the best chess players in the world and would provide homeschooling for five to eight hours a day with instruction in German, English, Esperanto, history, and chess. To show he was not an adherent of all work and no play, he claimed he would slot time for table tennis and swimming as well as a twenty-minute break for jokes. Apparently, this latter activity bore fruit. For entertainment, the sisters challenged each other to blindfold matches, envisioning the moves in their minds. On one occasion, a Budapest restaurant owner invited them to perform in a local match. Observing Judit's smug smile when she took first place, he told her, "So you play chess well and I cook well." She responded, "With a blindfold?" Another indulgence was junk food. László stated he was very strict about their diet, but their mother and grandmother were more permissive. Their world was consecrated to sixty-four black-and-white squares.

The government informed Polgár that he could not treat his offspring as guinea pigs; however, what helped his case was that communist leader Janos Kadar was a chess fan. The authorities were also mollified by East Germany's dabbling in human engineering by creating athletic champions. But most people felt that rather than creating another Bobby Fischer, he was a contemporary Dr. Frankenstein. While László orchestrated his daughters' lives, Klara took care of the pragmatic aspects of their home, and in later years, coordinated her girls' travels to tournaments in forty countries. She was happy to follow her husband's lead and stated, "The thread follows the needle. I am the thread."

The Hungarian Chess Federation wanted the girls to compete against other girls, something which László opposed. He argued that they could only become the best by playing against the best—which meant men, the seasoned players. The dispute with the communist-controlled Chess Federation became bitter, and in 1981, Polgár renounced his Party membership. In retaliation, the government refused to allow the family to travel to tournaments in the West in fear of defection from the Iron Curtain. In 1988, László relented and agreed that his daughters could compete in the women's Chess Olympiad in Salonika, Greece. For the first time, Hungary beat the Soviets, a feat that thrilled their homeland and shocked the chess world. The Polgár sisters became the royal chess sisters.

At age nineteen, Zsuzsa had made more money than most Hungarians could dream of earning in a lifetime. Similarly, while most of her countrymen lived their entire lives in the communist bloc, Zsuzsa had traveled the world and met dignitaries such as President Bush. She also spent time with Bobby Fischer when he fled to Budapest to outrun criminal charges in America. He had chosen Hungary partly to pursue nineteen-year-old Zita Rajcsanyi and because Zsuzsa had recommended her homeland for its culture and prodigious chess talent.

Zsuzsa's accolades grew to include being the first woman to qualify for the Men's World Championship; nevertheless, she was not allowed to compete as females were not permitted. Because of Polgár, the World Chess Federation eventually changed its policy—as well as its name. In 1991, the twenty-one-year-old broke barriers once again by becoming the first woman to earn the grandmaster title. The lady who was once not permitted to play in men's tournaments competed against all the big boys: Bobby Fischer, Boris Spassky, Gary Kasparov, and Anatoly Karpov. In the process, Zsuzsa sent the entrenched belief that competitive chess was a man's domain the way of the chastity belt.

There was only one woman who achieved more in her field—her sister Judit—who became the youngest chess master at age fifteen and the greatest female chess player of all time. She beat the previous record of American prodigy Bobby Fischer, at a month older than he was when he achieved the eminent distinction. Zsofia, at age seventeen, held a ranking of No. 10 among female chess players.

After Zsuzsa's historic win, Joop van Oosterom, a Dutch billionaire, suggested the Polgárs adopt three boys from a Third World country to prove that racial barriers, as well as gender barriers, could be eliminated from the world of chess. At this suggestion, the thread defied the needle, arguing they had already proved their point.

The Polgár sisters triumphed over a communist regime and anti-Semitism; all four grandparents were Holocaust survivors, and the Arrow Cross had sent both grandmothers to Auschwitz. The girls' victories stirred up the deeply chauvinistic chess world, littered as it was with men who balked at playing with women. László called the world champion Gary Kasparov "the Stalin of chess" when he belittled the notion of female chess players.

The sisters turned out to be not only accomplished but also well-adjusted, proof positive Polgár was not a daddy dearest. While his daughters had no trouble holding their own while playing their game, László served as their father, trainer, manager, and protector. Whenever he felt his girls were under siege, he attacked with even greater vigor than the sisters displayed when competing.

The overreaching question remains: was raising three grandmasters a result of László's unique method of parenting, or was it an act of serendipity? By contrast, the British Brontë sisters produced literary masterpieces in spite of growing up without a mother and a mercurial father who looked after his parishioners more than his three daughters. Regardless of the answer, the Polgár girls fared better than the Brontës.

The Polgár sisters, once as joined as a row of paper dolls, currently live in different countries. Each is married and the mother of two: Zsuzsa in the United States, Judit in Hungary, and Zsofia in Israel and Canada. László must lament that he cannot be Tiger grandfather to the next generation. In 1994, Zsuzsa married the American computer consultant Jacob Shutzman, and they opened a private chess club in New York City. Unfortunately, lasting marriage proved more elusive than the moves on an ancient board, and after having sons Tom and Leeam, the couple divorced. Abiding by her philosophy of, "There's no crying in chess," Susan rebounded and tied the knot again with Paul Troung, who had been the chess champion of his native South Vietnam.

In 2019, the US Chess Hall of Fame inducted Zsuzsa Polgár in a special event in St. Louis, where she currently lives, the youngest woman ever to be so honored. Thus she joined members such as Bobby Fischer, Edward Lasker, and founding father Benjamin Franklin. In her speech, she spoke of her Hungarian and Jewish roots, as well as her determination to shatter the black-and-white-squared ceiling of chess. She began on a humorous note, "After I retired from competitive chess, I was told by some people that it would be harder for me to be inducted to the Hall of Fame than to go to Mars. OK, so after tonight, Mars is a piece of cake, right?" She then switched to a serious note and revealed her iron motivation stemmed from her desire to honor her parents who had sacrificed on her behalf and to pay tribute to the members of her family who had perished in the Holocaust.

Zsuzsa Polgár, chess prodigy, carved a niche in the game of kings where she made herself queen. And thanks to her father, she can say—in Hungarian, English, German, Russian, Spanish, Hebrew, and Esperanto—checkmate.

Chapter 26

Let History Make the Judgment (1993)

Historically, females could not be attorneys; nor could they be generals. Hence, when Janet Reno became the first attorney general, the splintering of the glass ceiling sent seismic shock waves throughout the country.

Born in Coconut Grove, Florida, in 1938, Janet's childhood provided her with the moral compass that stood her in good stead when she assumed the mantle of leadership that placed her in the eye of many a storm. Her father was born in Denmark as Henry Olaf Rasmussen; his parents changed their name from Rasmussen to Reno (chosen at random from a map of Nevada to make it sound American). Her father, a Pulitzer-Prize-winning reporter for the *Miami Herald*, covered crime for a city infiltrated by mobs. Her mother, Jane, also a reporter, built the family residence with her own hands at the edge of the Everglades, situated where paved roads ended and air-conditioning was considered a luxury for sissies. The house had two bedrooms for a family of six, and there was no door on the bathroom until a family friend arrived with tools and lumber. The surrounding property of twenty-one acres was the domain of alligators, cows, beagles, macaws, raccoons, goats, geese, ponies, pigs, and skunks—*not* descented. Jane raised peacocks, all named Horace. On one occasion, the police raided their house, having been summoned about a possible rape because the opera-loving Henry had been listening to La Traviata at full blast, driving the peacocks into a frenzy that neighbors misconstrued as an attack. In her early years, Janet had strong women as role models. Her aunt Daisy served as a nurse during World War II in North Africa and marched on Italy with General George Patton. Another aunt, Winnie, was a member of the Women's Air Force Service Pilots. After junior high, Janet traveled to Europe to stay with her uncle, a military judge, as he presided over a spy trial.

Henry died when his children were young, and Jane ruled as a disciplinarian who resorted to a bridle strap. The fact that Jane had once wrestled an alligator who had wandered into her kitchen served as a warning to toe the line. On a maternal note, she taught them to appreciate Beethoven, Coleridge, and Kipling, as well as how to use a rifle, scuba dive, and catch alligators (some of which she gifted to the London Zoo). She advised daughters Maggie and Janet that they should not marry unless a man made their hearts go "potato, potato, potato."

A debating champion at Coral Gables High School, Janet studied chemistry at Cornell with the aspiration of becoming a doctor. Instead, she decided on a legal career "because I didn't want people to tell me what to do" and was one of sixteen women in a class of five hundred at Harvard. She hoped to practice in South Florida, but prominent Steel, Hector & Davis turned her down on the basis of her sex, and she ended up in a smaller firm. Her foray into politics arrived when Richard Gerstein, the state attorney for Dade County, offered her a position. Forever forthright, she informed Gerstein that her father thought he was a crook; he replied that her candor was why he had offered her the job. Eschewing an official car, Reno drove her battered Chevy Celebrity.

As prosecutor-in-chief, there were many people to prosecute as Miami was in its "Miami Vice" days. She orchestrated a number of high-profile cases, including one where five white policemen had been charged with beating Arthur McDuffie, an unarmed black motorcyclist, to death. When an all-white jury voted for acquittal, rioting erupted during which eighteen people died, and damages were later estimated at $100 million. Governor Bob Graham called in thousands of National Guard troops to keep the peace. Mobs shouted "Re-no!" as they set fires. Detractors accused Reno of being a racist and received death threats and calls for her resignation. She refused with the words that, "To resign was to give in to anarchy" and set out to rebuild her reputation in the black community. Janet travelled without a bodyguard to impoverished African American neighborhoods where crowds vented their rage. Her calmness and candor diffused the situation. During her tenure, Reno cracked down on deadbeat dads, inspiring a rap song with the lyrics, "She caught you down on 15th Street, trying to hide your tail / She fined your ass and locked you up. Now who can't post no bail?"

During her bid for reelection, a contender she faced was a born-again Christian, Jack Thomson, who called the six-foot two Janet a lesbian. In response, she put her arm around his shoulder and said, "Don't worry, Mr. Jackson. I love big, strong, handsome, rational, intelligent, kind, and sensitive men, and I understand why you might be concerned." Jackson attempted—unsuccessfully—to sue for assault. After Gerstein announced he was leaving office, he made Reno the interim state attorney, choosing her over fifty other candidates. She was the first woman to obtain the position and remained at her post until the White House called.

President Bill Clinton announced his commitment to appointing a woman District Attorney. His first choice was the corporate lawyer Zoë Baird, but he rescinded the nomination over her having employed an undocumented immigrant as a nanny. The episode, dubbed "Nannygate," deepened when it turned out Clinton's second choice, Judge Kimba Wood, had committed the same offense. Ms. Reno had no children and no nanny issues. She also had no husband; apparently, no man had made her heart go "potato, potato, potato." Rumors circulated as to Janet's sexual orientation and led to her rebuttal, "I'm just an awkward old maid with a very great attraction to men." At her Rose Garden induction ceremony, Janet said, "It's an extraordinary experience, and I hope I do the women of America proud." Her mother had died a few weeks before the historic moment, and in her acceptance speech, she paid tribute to the woman who had been her life's guiding light. While Janet had wrestled alligators with the Miccosukee Indians and punched a hog between the eyes when it turned aggressive with her niece Karin, in DC, Reno had to circumvent sharks. She proved her detractors wrong when they scoffed at the gal from the swamp.

Despite her prestigious post, Janet insisted she not be addressed by the traditional title "General," and said, "Call me 'Hey, you!' or call me Janet." Reno was never part of the Clintons' inner circle, and her preference for kayaking on the Potomac River over hobnobbing on the capital's cocktail circuit made her a fish out of the capital's water. In her role, she proved a fierce advocate of guaranteeing federal protection to women exercising their Roe v. Wade rights and safeguarding abortion clinics that were under threat. Janet provided fodder for *Saturday Night Live*, where Will Ferrell showcased skits of "Janet Reno's Dance Party."

Janet was no drama queen, but she was in the eye of the storm in a number of dramas. Within weeks of her appointment, Reno faced off against the self-proclaimed prophet David Koresh, who belonged to an off-shoot of the Seventh-Day Adventist Church, at the Branch Davidian compound near Waco, Texas. Koresh had already killed four federal officers and had withstood a standoff with the FBI that lasted several weeks when Reno authorized a raid on what she called the worst day of her life. She gave the go-ahead for agents to attack armed with tear gas, acting under reports that cult members were endangering children. The assault went horribly awry. The compound went up in flames, leaving more than eighty dead, including twenty-five children. The debacle aired live on national television. Later that day, a haggard Reno stated that she took full responsibility and offered to resign. In the glare of the media spotlight, she stated, "The tragedy is we will never know what was the right thing to do." The public deluged her with letters of support, and she became the shining light of the Clinton cabinet. *Time* declared, "Reno is pure oxygen in a city with thin air and she's gone to its head." Celebrities such as Barbra Streisand flocked to meet the reluctant hero.

The Attorney General's plate was never empty. Reno authorized prosecutors to seek the death penalty for Timothy McVeigh, responsible for the bombing in Oklahoma City, and secured a guilty plea from the "Unabomber," Theodore Kaczynski. She was behind the anti-monopoly prosecution of Microsoft and a racketeering lawsuit against the tobacco industry. Ms. Reno oversaw the arrest of Sheik Oman Abdel Rahman for his role in the World Trade Center bombing. The A.G. handled the espionage case against former Los Alamos National Laboratory scientist Wen Ho Lee, held in solitary confinement for nine months after being charged with mishandling nuclear secrets. Near the end of her tenure, Ms. Reno arranged for the armed seizure by federal agents of Elian Gonzalez, a six-year-old Cuban refugee caught in an international custody battle between his father and his Miami relatives. Photographs of the terrified child taken with a gun-wielding border agent became media fodder. For each case, she stood behind her actions and took as her mantra Harry S. Truman's quotation, "The buck stops here."

Despite Janet's appointment by the President, her decision to allow an independent inquiry into a failed Clinton land deal in Arkansas, the so-called Whitewater investigation, expanded to include the President's sexual relationship with the White House intern Monica Lewinsky that led to his impeachment. Ms. Reno said first lady Hillary Clinton never forgave her for airing her husband's dirty linen—and the blue dress—in public. Nor did she endear herself to journalists, who dreaded her customary terse rebuke, "You haven't done your homework, have you?" However, her legacy was sterling as she operated on Jane's precept of, "telling the truth and being kind." When Reno stepped down from her post, only one person's in the nation's history had occupied the position longer, and that was back in the days of wooden whaling ships. Washington would have been glad to see her go before she did, but she was as immoveable as the limestone house her mother had built a century ago. Reno showed a more relaxed side when she appeared on *Saturday Night Live* alongside Ferrell the night she departed the Justice Department.

After her tenure as District Attorney, during which she had withstood a series of political cannonballs, all while suffering the ravages of Parkinson's disease, the formidable Floridian returned to her Everglades home. Unwilling to retire, in 2002, she ran for governor to oust Jeb Bush, brother of President George W. Bush, and campaigned by driving throughout the state in her red pickup truck. However, her popularity was undermined by the Cuban community, which still had undying enmity over her handling of Elian Gonzalez.

After Reno's 2016 passing, Loretta Lynch, the second woman to serve as US attorney general, praised her predecessor, "She was guided by one simple test, to do what the law and the facts required...regardless of which way the political winds were blowing." Asked to describe her legacy, Reno quoted George Washington, "If I were to write all that down, I might be reduced to tears. I would prefer to drift on down the stream of life and let history make the judgment."

Chapter 27

The Worst Gorings (1996)

Spain, the culture that invented the word *machismo*, has for centuries considered bullfighting an altar of testosterone. Hence, when Cristina Sánchez became Europe's first *mujer torero* (matador), it was the equivalent of waving a red flag at a male citadel.

The Latin controversy surrounding the ethics of bullfighting is as heated as the American one surrounding abortion. At one end of the spectrum was Ernest Hemingway, who wrote, "There are only three sports: bullfighting, motor racing, and mountaineering; all the rest are merely games." Picasso and Orson Welles were equally smitten. At the other end are those who feel the sport is a contemporary gladiator game. In either contingency, it is hard to wrap one's mind around why a lone matador, armed only with a red cloth and sword, would pit himself (or herself) against half a ton of infuriated animal equipped with horns for the merriment of the masses.

Cristina Sánchez, who made waves both in and out of the arena, was born in 1972 in working-class Parla, Spain, the second of four sisters. Her mother, Maria Carmen, worked in a leather factory; her father, Antonio Sánchez, was an undistinguished matador who became a *banderillero*—the man who rushes on foot toward the bull to thrust barbs in its neck, an action that facilitates the kill. Before his demotion, Cristina watched her papa perform, and even after witnessing several gorings was not swayed from following in his footsteps. Antonio tried to dissuade his headstrong daughter, "I told her you have to know that bullfighting is very difficult—sometimes impossible—for a man, so for a woman it will be [even] more difficult." But Cristina had the poison—a Spanish expression for obsession.

Senor Sánchez did not embellish the difficulty of becoming a matador. For every ten thousand who aspire to the calling, only one is successful. Thus, the likelihood of meeting a matador is as improbable as encountering a Nobel Prize winner or an Academy Award recipient. An episode of *Seinfeld* alluded to this rarity when Elaine claimed to have dated Eduardo Carochio. Jerry, waving a red hand towel, asked, "I wonder where on the Upper West Side a single girl might meet a matador? Perhaps Zabars? Or Ray's Pizza!"

At age fourteen, Cristina took trips to the Plaza de Torres to join the student matadors who practiced with her father. Many thought her audacity was "bull," and cries broke out, "Look! Look! A *girl* is bullfighting!" The shouts alerted Antonio, who lectured her about her unfeminine pursuit. What he did not tell her was, "Dios mio, she is *not bad.*"

The sixteen-year-old Cristina bowed to family and societal pressure and found a job at a hairdressing salon; in the evenings, she cried. While Prufrock measured his life out in coffee spoons, Cristina felt her life was slipping away in a bouillabaisse of hairspray, conditioners, and mousse. Her escape was an allergy to the chemicals, and her family arranged for her to work as a clerk in her uncle's fire extinguisher factory. In her after-hours, alone in her kitchen, she moved the dish towel as if it were a cape. Soon she was ditching her job and joining aspiring matadors at practice; her embarrassed papa assured everyone her obsession would pass.

Cristina wore Antonio down, and he took her to the plaza at Torrelaguna, where she killed her first bull. She decorated her bedroom walls with pictures of bulls, matadors, and cutouts from matchboxes that demonstrated the traditional poses of a torero. Fired with enthusiasm, Cristina enrolled in Madrid's elite La Escuela de Tauromaquia de Madrid, which she attended seven days a week. She graduated in 1992 third in her class, one of five women among one hundred men. The star pupil collected accolades over the next few years as a *novillera*, an apprentice bullfighter. During her successful run, Sánchez slew approximately 240 bulls. She said of her passion, "Every problem in your life goes away in front of a bull—because the problem, the bull, is bigger than all other problems. Of course, I have fear, but it is the fear that I will fail the responsibility I have taken on in front of all these people—not the fear of the bull. Death becomes unimportant when I am in front of him. I feel so good; it doesn't matter if he kills me." Her gender contributed to her visibility, but recognition also arrived for her flourishes that seduced the animal into coming ever closer. Cristina earned a trophy case of more than two hundred bull ears and one tail.

The beauty who faced the beast in the arena declared bullfighting was her drug, and like a drug, her career was fraught with peril. In a bullring in the tiny town of Loeches, Cristina had her "baptism of blood" when a 700-pound bull knocked her down with the force of a runaway car. The animal tossed her in the air with its twenty-four-inch horns, stamped on her, tossed her again, and then gored her through the stomach. Antonio, who accompanied her in the medical van transporting her to the hospital, cried, "Look at you, bruised like a Christ! Do you finally understand how impossible this is?" He admonished himself for not having taken the bull by the horns when she was young by confiscating her $1,000 sword and her $2,000 *traje de luces* (suit of lights), ending the madness. Post recovery, Sánchez could not wait to get back into action, "To be in front of the bull is a feeling so great that it can't be described. Outside the ring I am a normal, shy girl. But in the ring, I am transformed. I'm not a girl anymore. I am a bullfighter."

At age twenty-one, in the historic city of Toledo, Sánchez made history in 1993 by becoming the first woman to fight and kill six bulls in succession in a single *corrida*. Because of her prowess, the crowd carried her on their shoulders amid thunderous applause. In her resplendent attire, her hair wound in a pigtail, she had knelt defiantly in front of one bull, thrown aside the *muleta*, and run her finger along the horn of another. Away from the blood-drenched sand, Cristina transformed into a down-to-earth woman in T-shirt, tight jeans, and Dr. Scholl sandals. *Paris Match* photographed her in a Christian Dior gown and asked her if she wasn't afraid of scaring off suitors. She responded to such questions by clarifying that the only boyfriends she had time for were *los toros*.

Sánchez also had a ready response when asked about the morality of her profession. She became extremely distressed (though not as distressed as the hundreds of bulls she dispatched to the great meadow in the sky) when detractors called her a bloody executioner. She claimed, "I regard bullfighting as an art form. In Spain it is part of our culture, our heritage, like flamenco." She adds the fight carries sexual innuendo, "The matador must penetrate the animal, until you become one being. For me, it is the moment of supreme happiness. I am content." For some, bullfighting does indeed serve as an aphrodisiac. By the time Luis Dominguin died at the age of seventy, he had bedded a reported four thousand females. (His death was, unsurprisingly, due to heart failure.) One of his bevy of beauties was Ava Gardner, with whom he had a torrid affair; and when he later married Italian actress Lucia Bose, his rejected lover, Mexican film star Miroslova Stern, committed suicide.

While Don Quixote jostled at windmills, Sánchez jousted at the *alternativa*—the august ceremony where a bullfighter first kills a full-grown bull in public and is formally recognized as a matador—or in her case, a *matadora*. In a ceremony in Nimes, France, Sánchez became the first woman in Europe to storm the macho world of bullfighting at the master level. At the close of the historic event, veteran bullfighter Curro Romero handed her his sword and cape with the words, "I am old, Cristina, and have acted in several *alternativas*, but no other has moved me as much as this one."

Her new status was an incredible accomplishment for a woman in a country where female bullfighting was thought as far-fetched as being a female pope. A 1908 law had banned "the weaker sex" from the ring on the grounds of "decency and public morality." The restriction ended when Spain became a republic in the 1930s but was reinstituted by the Fascist dictator Francisco Franco in 1940, though he did allow females to participate as *rejoneadores*—those who perform from the safety of a horse. The ban was ultimately laid to rest by the Spanish Supreme Court, but the court of public opinion lagged behind. Sánchez's achievement was also a victory for Spanish feminism; after all, if a woman could become

a full-fledged matador, there was no wall they could
not scale. Her win was all the more wondrous as at the
time, the country's feminist movement was only twenty
years old. Until Franco's death in 1975, a woman could
not open her own bank account or travel without her
husband's permission. Legally, she was a man's property.
In 1976, two thousand women demonstrated for the first
time, and as they marched along Goya Street, they did
so to shouts of "Putas!" ("Whores!") After her crowning
achievement, Sánchez had seventy engagements
in Spain, France, Mexico, and South America with a
paycheck of $1.6 million for one season. Not too shabby
for a former hairdresser from working-class Parla.

What proved sharper than a bull's horn was the
entrenched machismo of her native land. Her countrymen
regarded a female bullfighter as a contradiction in
terms. Jesulin de Ubrique, a strutting superstar matador,
refused to appear on the same bill as Sánchez. Historian
Muriel Feiner explained, "To appear inferior to a woman
would have been tantamount to a loss of manhood. No
one would risk it." The ladies who dared had not only to
face an enraged bull but also jeers from the audience.
As Cristina performed in the Las Ventas Plaza in Madrid,
comments and sniggers flowed from the stands,
"Cristina, where are your balls?" "A woman and a frying
pan belong in the kitchen!"

In 1999, Spain's only full-fledged female matador
revealed that after a decade, she was hanging up her
cape. She attributed her departure to her colleagues'

machismo. Her swan song was in Madrid's Las Ventas bullring, dubbed "the cathedral of bullfighting." She stated of her last *olé*, "I've never traded on the fact that I am a woman; I've never used it to get ahead, but I've certainly suffered because of it. Bulls are associated with courage and virility, and some men cannot forgive a woman for being able to hold her own in that environment. I realized prejudice had won when I wasn't accepted in any of the top festivals this year, and I refuse to accept a life trailing around second-rate rings fighting dud bulls." At a farewell press conference, fans greeted her with applause and shouts of *torero!*

Senorita Sánchez's bulges may have been ill-distributed for a bullfighter—as a journalist once remarked, but she had *cojones*, and in Spain, having balls is what counts. Unfortunately, due to years of systematic sexism, Cristina well understood the bullfighter's adage, "*Mas cornadas da la vida*," which means, "Life inflicts the worst gorings."

Chapter 28

That Special Place (1997)

President John Adams outlined the requisite qualities for a Secretary of State, "He ought to be a Man of universal Reading in Laws, Governments, History." Madeleine Albright fulfilled these requirements—except for the words "he ought to be a man"—as America's first female Secretary of State.

The woman who put the preface "extra" before the word "ordinary" was Marie Jana, the daughter of the diplomat Josef Korbelova and his wife, Mandula. In 1939, the family fled Prague after the Nazi invasion and took refuge in England. They survived the Blitz and returned to their homeland after Germany's defeat. Three years later, the family escaped once more in the wake of the Communist coup that snuffed out Czechoslovak democracy. They sought asylum in the United States, which became their permanent residence. Josef obtained a position as the Dean of the University of Denver's school of international studies; one of his students was Condoleeza Rice. Eager to assimilate, Josef shorted their name to Korbel; Marie Jana went by the name Madeleine. She attended Wellesley College and majored in political science even though in the 1950s, few opportunities were available for girls aspiring to a career in this field.

What lessened the sting was Prince Disarming—Joseph Medill Patterson Albright—the possessor of three surnames and a stratospheric family fortune; both he and Madeleine had summer jobs at *The Denver Post*. He was a scion of media royalty; his great-aunt Cissy Patterson had been the owner of the *Washington Times-Herald*. Although Madeleine had a difficult time winning over his parents, he proposed six weeks later, and they married after her graduation. In the vein of Henry IV—for whom Paris was worth a mass—Madeleine traded her Roman Catholic religion for the Albrights' Episcopalian church. The romance, she said, made her feel like Cinderella. Although anxious for a career, she had also had her eye on the prize of wedlock and had wanted to get married "as soon as possible to a perfect partner." The couple's residences were a well-appointed Georgetown home and a quail-hunting estate in Georgia, the latter bequeathed to Joseph by his aunt Alicia Patterson.

The publishing prince whisked Madeleine away to a rarified zip code where she gave birth to premature twins, Alice and Anne, who struggled for life but survived.

Six months into her second pregnancy, Madeleine contracted German measles, and her doctor warned her the baby was most likely brain damaged. A late-term abortion was not an option, and the infant died at birth. Her last pregnancy resulted in a healthy daughter, Katherine. Madeleine reminisced, "A portrait of the Albright family in the mid-seventies would have shown a happily married couple, with three smart and beautiful daughters." Madeleine studied for a PhD in public law and government at Columbia University; the only way she was able to write her thesis as the mother of three (despite hired help) was rising every morning at 4:30 for three years. While Joseph forged his career as a journalist, she followed him from city to city, finally settling in Washington. As her girls grew older, Madeleine worked as a Democrat fundraiser and eventually found a position in the White House under the tutelage of her former professor, Zbigniew Brzezinski, President Carter's national security advisor. When Ronald Reagan won the next election, Madeleine lost her position and found herself in the political periphery.

At this juncture, Joseph, her husband of twenty-three years, dropped what she called a thunderbolt on their gilded life. While sitting in their living room having coffee, Joe informed Madeleine that their marriage was dead; he had fallen for someone younger and more attractive. The P.S. to the conversation was he was moving to Atlanta, where the woman he loved was a reporter. Madeleine wrote in her biography that she did not know what had upset her most: that Joe had presented her with a done deal, that he had said she had become too old looking, or that he could not see why she was so upset. Joseph left that afternoon but developed misgivings about his decision and kept calling his wife to inform her of his daily feelings; "I love you 60 percent and her 40 percent." Then the next day, "I love her 70 percent and you 30 percent."

The Albrights attempted a reconciliation with a ski trip to Aspen where Joseph complimented Madeleine on her weight loss, a result of the Diet Center plus the specter of divorce. She recalled she skied better than at any other time, "perhaps because I didn't particularly care if I broke my neck." Any hope of a reunion soon vanished. The Pulitzer Prize was looming—an award Joseph had long coveted—and he offered the proposition that if he won, he would stay, as he would not want a marital scandal to tarnish his achievement. The woman who would one day tell Fidel Castro that he had no *cojones* rolled over and took it.

The Albright marriage would have survived had the Pulitzer committee made a different decision. When Joseph went AWOL, what was a middle-aged matron to do? (1) Take a piece of priceless bric-a-brac to the family jewels, thus ending the other woman's appeal; (2) book an appointment with Dr. Kevorkian; (3) become a contemporary Miss Havisham. She stated of her abyss, "I had tried the glass slipper, and it had fit. In the fairytale, that is where the story ends. In life, it is merely the beginning of a new chapter." The wife scorned had to navigate unchartered territory as she figured out her new romantic life, a difficult feat as she had not looked at a man other than her husband since she had been twenty. Moreover, she had no self-confidence—compliments of Joe's parting comments about her looks. She said she had no idea of how to deal with the dating arena and felt like a forty-five-year-old virgin. Pulling herself up by the proverbial boot-straps, Madeleine decided her best course of action was to fill her time and to move quickly because the ice under her was so thin. Succor came—not in the arms of another man, but rather by leaning on female friends, developing self-reliance, and receiving an extremely generous settlement. Eventually, she "no longer felt like an egg without a shell."

In a nod to there being life after loss, Madeleine found an outlet as a professor at Georgetown University and pursued a further foray into politics. From there, she went into foreign policy and fundraising, finding that as she rose through the ranks, male colleagues regarded the female interloper with suspicion. She soon transformed herself into a leading authority on international diplomacy and rose to prominence as the US ambassador to the United Nations. Despite her lofty title, the predominantly male press corps deemed her not in the same league as her testosterone-charged predecessors. A reporter wrote that women are just too emotional to do the job, and a running joke was their referring to Albright as Half-Bright. Despite the slights, Madeleine soldiered on. During her ambassadorship, she famously celebrated Bill Clinton's election victory by swinging her hips and clutching her buttocks in the Security Council chamber to the tune of "La Macarena."

A dozen years after her divorce, Madeleine became the most powerful female official to that date in American history when at age sixty, President Clinton appointed her the 64th Secretary of State, a fact that shattered a 208-year reign of men. The aforementioned reporter, her personal Lex Luthor, dismissed her appointment nomination as leftwing political correctness, arguing she had only received the post because of her sex, "Window dressing for the Clinton administration." At least former Secretary of State Henry Kissinger was polite when he learned a woman was walking in his old shoes. "Welcome to the fraternity," to which she shot back, "Henry, I hate to tell you, but it's not a fraternity anymore." In her autobiography, *Madame Secretary*, published at age sixty-six, she wrote that despite meetings with kings and presidents and overseeing treaties, she could not separate gender from her job. Case in point, a to-do list: (1) Call Senator Helms. (2) Call King Hussein. (3) Call Foreign Minister Moussa.(4) Congressional calls. (5) Prepare for China meeting. (6) Buy nonfat yogurt. Her book provides a feminist perspective into foreign affairs, explaining, "If women leaders had acted the way Arafat and Barak did during Camp David, they would have been dismissed as menopausal."

For all her success, both politically and as a feminist, the most telling moment of *Madame Secretary* is her questioning of whether a married woman with full domestic responsibilities could ever be the player she had been on the world stage if she remained a wife. "When I became the Secretary of State, I realized that I would never have climbed that high had I still been married. Yet I am deeply saddened to have been divorced. I know that at the time, I would have given up any thought of a career if it would have made Joe change his mind." She ruminated that after a private dinner with Hillary Clinton and the recently widowed Queen Noor of Jordan, Albright calculated the impact of their marriages on each woman. "In different ways we had each been left to explore the boundaries of our own inner strength by a husband who had deceived, deserted, or died."

Just as President Reagan was known for his jar of omnipresent jelly beans on his Oval Office desk, Madeleine Albright was known for her brooches. Her collection of three-dimensional emojis bear messages. In 1990, she learned the Russians had bugged a conference room near her State Department office, and at her next meeting with Russian diplomats, she sported a huge insect pin. They got the message. When the Iraqi media compared her to an "unparalleled serpent," she displayed a snake pin. An exhibition and book entitled *Read My Pins*—an allusion to the first President Bush's "Read My Lips"—are dedicated to her unique array.

Despite her event-filled life as the Secretary of State, it hit Madeleine on a visceral level when *The Washington Post* revealed the Korbels had not been Catholic Czechs. Rather, they had been Jews, and three of her grandparents had perished in Nazi death camps. Critics implied that her gobsmacked response was voluntary amnesia and that it had been something she had knowingly concealed. When asked if she would revert to Judaism, she replied, "I was raised a Christian. Now that I'm sixty-six, why would I suddenly change who I am?"

Today, life is anything but quiet for the octogenarian. The New York Stock Exchange elected her as a member, she launched an investment firm, and she is the chairperson of the Hague Institute for Global Justice. Albright is far too busy to nurse regrets, except the one that has no expiration date—the loss of her husband. Still single, she told her daughters her only dating deal breaker, "I can't go out with a Republican."

Madeleine Albright, the refugee who rose to the highest ranks, has as many memorable quotations as she does brooches. Perhaps the greatest of these was her pronouncement, "There's a special place in Hell for women who don't help each other." As Madeleine shattered the Secretary of State glass ceiling, she paved the way for Condoleezza Rice (the first African American woman to attain the position) and Hillary Clinton, so she need not fear that special place.

Chapter 29

Moment of a Lifetime (2010)

And the Oscar for Best Director goes to Victor Fleming for *Gone with the Wind*; and the Oscar for Best Director goes to John Ford for *The Grapes of Wrath*; and the Oscar for Best Director goes to Steven Spielberg for *Schindler's List*." The fact that the Academy of Motion Pictures Arts and Sciences has always gifted the coveted statue to men makes one wonder if there is—to borrow the title of Elia Kazan's film for which he won best director—a Gentleman's Agreement. If institutionalized sexism is indeed the norm, the Academy breached it after eight decades when Kathryn Bigelow made a rip in Hollywood's seemingly shatterproof celluloid ceiling by winning the Academy Award for Best Director.

In a *Vanity Fair* issue, photographer Annie Leibovitz created a classic image of a film director. George

Clooney posed with shirt ripped open, trousers tucked into boots, an amalgam of a youthful Orson Welles and Michelangelo's vision of God. His crew consisted of female models in flesh-colored lingerie, looking adoringly on.

In response to the Hollywood testosterone, the Guerrilla Girls—feminist activists with zero tolerance for intuitional sexism, whose trademark is gorilla masks—erected a 2003 billboard featuring the "anatomically Correct Oscar" which was white and male—"just like the guys who win!" The following year, their new billboard featured the "Trent L'Ottscar," a nod to the fact that "even the US Senate is more progressive than Hollywood." Fourteen percent of the Senate is female, while only 4 percent of the past year's one hundred top-grossing films had women directors.

The chauvinistic paradigm took its first step in becoming 'gone with the wind' thanks to Kathryn Bigelow, who was born in 1951 in suburban San Carlos, a town situated twenty-five miles south of San Francisco; she was the only child of Gertrude Kathryn, an English teacher, and Ronald, a manager in a paint factory. His aspiration was to become a cartoonist, but he never could figure out how to escape his day job. He entertained his daughter by drawing himself in caricatures, emphasizing what he considered his homely features. His hobby sparked Kathryn's creativity, and she began painting from the age of six. She recalls being a gawky and solitary child whose height (she is just under six feet tall and extremely thin) made her painfully self-conscious. Even now, Kathryn wears sociability like an uncomfortable garment and keeps personal details close. At age fourteen, she was interested in the Old Masters; she took segments of their replicas and painted them on twelve-by-fourteen-foot canvasses. She explained, "I don't know why I was interested in magnification—maybe because I'm large, the Big People Syndrome."

Having learned the cost of settling from her father, the teenaged Kathryn followed passion rather than practicality and enrolled in the Art Institute of San Francisco. Two years later she won a scholarship to the Whitney Museum's Independent Study Program where her mentor was Susan Sontag and photographer Robert Mapplethorpe was an upstairs neighbor. Kathryn embodied the stereotype of the starving artist; her student digs were in a condemned structure without heat or electricity, three stories below ground level in an off-track betting building. She reminisced about freezing, huddled in a sleeping bag, lulled to sleep by the sound of gunshots. She joined a conceptual art group and acted in the feminist movie *Born in Flames*. During this time, she had a conversation with a friend by the name of Andy Warhol that impacted her life: he suggested she trade her paintbrush for a camera. Accordingly, Kathryn produced *The Set-Up*; filmmaker Milos Forman was so impressed he arranged a scholarship to Columbia where she earned her master's degree. At the end of the decade, she directed *The Loveless*, a film about sexy bikers in which William Dafoe made his debut. The project led to a development offer at Universal that took Bigelow to

Los Angeles. The studio deal did not pan out, but Bigelow eventually secured financing for *Near Dark* (1987), which relocated the vampire myth to the American desert, followed by *Blue Steel* (1990) starring Jamie Lee Curtis as a rookie cop.

At age thirty-eight, Ms. Bigelow had quite the curriculum vitae under her belt: she had directed several movies, obtained a master's degree from Columbia, modeled for Gap, and climbed Mount Kilimanjaro in sub-zero temperature. On the romantic front, in 1989, Bigelow married Canadian director James Cameron, producer of *The Terminator*, a low-budget, high-earning sci-fi thriller whose male lead would go on to govern California. The high-powered couple shared an estate in the mansion-dotted mountains between Beverly Hills and Studio City, a stone's throw from homes owned by Jack Nicholson and Warren Beatty, a far cry from the condemned building of her earlier years. Although her union with Hollywood royalty came with professional and personal perks, Cameron was high maintenance. He became so enraged when crew members' phones rang on the *Avatar* set, he nail-gunned the phones to the wall—the phones, not the crew members, though it probably could have gone either way. During the shooting of *The Abyss*, the crew took to wearing T-shirts with the inscription: "You can't scare me. I work for James Cameron." The marriage terminated when Cameron told Bigelow *hasta la vista, baby*, as he left her for Linda Hamilton, the lead actress in *The Terminator*. Although Bigelow kept the mansion, currently listed for $12.9 million, the divorce papers showed the settlement was remarkably slanted in ex-hubby's favor. He paid the cost of her lawyers and gave her half a million dollars with the stipulation she sign away future spousal support, including any claim on a share of his multimillion earnings from *Terminator* 2. The fact Bigelow came away with the short end of the stick became apparent when Cameron fell for *Titanic* actress Susan Amis and Hamilton waltzed off with $50 million.

Metaphorically clad in a T-shirt that said, "You can't scare me. I married James Cameron," Bigelow, rather than bemoaning her status as a newly single forty-year-old, poured her energies into her career. In 2010, the Academy announced Kathryn was up for Best Director for *The Hurt Locker*; the fact sent out shock ripples as women had been notoriously underrepresented in this category. Moreover, Bigelow's film was not the stereotypical chick flick, but rather a guy's movie about soldiers, focusing on the gory details never mentioned in letters home to mom. Her closest rival was none other than her ex, who had received the same Oscar nod for *Avatar*; both films had earned nine Oscar nods making their race to the finish line the most buzzed about rivalry in Hollywood. Bigelow was only the fourth woman in history to secure the best director nomination. The other ladies who had lost out on the big prize were: Lina Wertmuller for *Seven Beauties* (1976), Jane Campion for *The Piano* (1993), and Sophia Coppola for *Lost in Translation* (2003).

The odds did not look good for Ms. Bigelow: not only was her gender a Hollywood handicap, the Academy tends to favor financially successful films; and while Cameron's baby brought in $42 billion, making it the highest grossing film of all time, Bigelow's baby only earned a meager $16 million. In addition, Cameron was already a directorial blue blood; his *Titanic* had sunk the competition at the 1998 ceremony. Countering these drawbacks was Cameron's biblically inspired level of hubris, and many were chomping at the bit for his comeuppance. In his acceptance speech for the epic *Titanic*, Cameron had raised his trophy over his head and shouted, "I'm the king of the world!"—an echo from his movie's signature scene, in which Leonardo DiCaprio's Jack had jubilantly hollered the selfsame words from the bow of the doomed ship. Not rooting for Cameron—no shoe-in for Mr. Congeniality—were the four members of his ex-wives club, as well as actors who were miffed by their having been replaced by animated blue pixels. La-La Land held its collective breath: had the Academy determined that calling out "Action!" and "Cut!" was indeed within the purview of possessors of estrogen?

In the almost century of the Academy Awards, there have been memorable Oscar firsts, such as the first color movie to win a Best Picture Oscar: *Gone with the Wind* in 1940; the first black artist to win an Oscar: Hattie McDaniel, in the same film and year; and the first animated film to earn a best picture nomination: *Beauty and the Beast* (1991). And there was one that occurred in 2010. The presenter for that year's ceremony, Barbra Streisand, the director of *Yentl* and *The Prince of Tides*, announced, "The time has come. The winner is Kathryn

Bigelow." James, sitting directly behind his ex, put his hands around Kathryn's neck and mock strangled her; however, her muscular arms showed she could well have bested her attacker without mussing her perfect hair and then gone off to defuse a bomb. Stunning in a pewter colored Marchesa gown with a brocaded top, Kathryn ascended the stage to hold her eight-pound Oscar, giving hope to women who make movies and women who watch them.

Females, of course, have been extravagantly praised as actresses and have provided the glamorous media faces of the ceremony, the red-carpet icons, and the fashion queens. But never before had a woman been distinguished for being at a movie's helm. The newly crowned Bigelow, who must surely have felt that night she was the queen of the world, received a standing ovation from the star-studded audience. She brought tears to their eyes when she dedicated her award to "the people who risk their lives on a daily basis in Iraq and Afghanistan...may they come home safe." The magic moment felt like a potential game-changer for every female who had ever smacked her head into the glass ceiling of male-dominated Hollywood.

Afterward, she spoke about her historic win, the first the Academy had given a female director in its eighty-two-year history. She said, "First of all, I hope I'm the first of many. But I'm ever grateful if I can inspire some young, intrepid, tenacious male or female filmmakers and have them feel that the impossible is possible and never give up on your dream." She floated off the stage while the orchestra played Helen Reddy's 1970s feminist anthem "I Am Woman." She returned to the podium shortly after *The Hurt Locker* won best film. The movie garnered six Oscars including best original screenplay, making it the undisputed winner in the publicized battle against *Avatar,* which picked up three Oscars for visual effects, art direction, and cinematography. In interviews after the ceremony, when reporters encouraged her to gloat over Cameron, Bigelow showed her personality encompassed the first three letters of her surname when she refused to turn the screws on her ex, saying only, "I think he is an extraordinary filmmaker."

Unfortunately, to date, Kathryn's singular first has not been repeated. Stories of misogyny in Hollywood have been so disturbing the Equal Employment Opportunity Commission launched an investigation into sexism against female directors in 2016. However, as Hollywood is the very stuff that dreams are made of, one day the term "female director" will be as obsolete as the terms "female doctor," "female lawyer," and "female artist." Until this more egalitarian future arrives, countering the disturbing statistic that of the ninety-one Academy Awards for Best Director, only one woman has held such an Oscar, there are Kathryn Bigelow's words, a nod to hope following her win, "There's no other way to describe it. It's the moment of a lifetime."

Chapter 30

I Will What I Want
(2015)

Dance Moms, a Lifetime Network Channel television show, features stage moms on steroids endlessly exhorting their rhinestone-clad daughters to lift the *barre* on their competitors. In contrast to the dancing divas is Misty Copeland, the first African American woman to be named a principal dancer at the prestigious American Ballet Theatre (ABT).

A common adage holds that little girls are made of sugar and spice; while that stance is subjective, what does hold true is that most of them are enamored with the world of dance. Because of this connection, jewelry boxes come with pirouetting tulle-clad figurines, birthday cakes bear pink beribboned slippers, and Christmas viewings of *The Nutcracker* are de rigueur. Unsurprisingly, mothers enroll their mini-mes in dance classes following first steps. In contrast, the life of a future prima ballerina followed a different path.

Misty Danielle was born in 1982 in Dorothy country—Kansas, the daughter of Sylvia DelaCerna, a former Kansas City Chief cheerleader. Sylvia had married Mike immediately after high school; tragically, a stray bullet had ended his life in Oakland. His best friend, Douglas Copeland, helped her through her mourning, and Misty was a product of Sylvia and Douglas' marriage. While Dorothy left Kansas via a tornado that deposited her in the Emerald City, Misty departed Kansas on a Greyhound bus and ended up in Bellflower, a working-class suburb of Los Angeles. Sylvia wanted a new life after her divorce from Douglas, and the two-year-old Misty would not set eyes on her father until twenty years later. In Copeland's 2014 memoir, *Life in Motion: An Unlikely Ballerina*, she wrote, "When my mom squeezed our lives onto a bus heading west, our family began a pattern that would define my siblings' and my childhood: packing, scrambling, leaving—often barely surviving." Sylvia wed third husband, Harold, a loving step-father and a dedicated alcoholic. When Misty was seven, the family—sans Harold—left for San Pedro, California, where Sylvia wed fourth husband Robert; this union also came with an expiration date due to his propensity for violence. Sylvia and her six children from various daddies fled to downtown Los Angeles. The neighborhood was considered the turf of the Crips, one of the city's most notorious gangs, and one evening a bloodied stranger lay outside their door, a casualty of a drive-by shooting.

Their next residence was with Sylvia's boyfriend; though the couple was big on PDA, they were short on cash and the family subsisted on Top Ramen noodles, potato chips, and sodas. Post PDA, Sylvia moved her brood into the Sunset Inn motel, one that did not even remotely resemble its poetic name.

The trajectory of Misty's life changed at age thirteen when her history teacher, Elizabeth Cantine, suggested she take a ballet class taught by her friend Cindy Bradley at the Boys and Girls Club. Though the makeshift studio was a basketball court, it became Misty's refuge. After Cindy saw Misty's moves, she knew the teen was a star waiting to be born and used the word prodigy, a term Misty did not understand. Within a couple of weeks, Bradley offered Misty a full scholarship to train at her studio, the San Pedro Dance Center. Bradley was an anomaly of her time; the prevalent zeitgeist of the era was the belief Giselle and Odette were best performed by girls whose skin tones matched the hue of the pastel pink leotards. The problem was the long commute between motel and studio, and one afternoon, after missing her bus, Misty had to walk thirteen miles home. Sylvia told Misty she would have to give up her class; but when Cindy offered to let Misty live with her family, Misty's mother agreed.

For the next two years, Copeland lived with Bradley, her husband, and the couple's young son, Wolf; she also went with them to synagogue. Their home near the beach held paintings, sculptures, and tranquility. Tensions arose when Misty visited her family and complained about the canned string beans, saying she preferred the Bradley family's dinners of shrimp scampi. In the belief Cindy was trying to steal her daughter, Sylvia demanded Misty return home. In response, the Bradleys hired a lawyer with the intention of making Misty an emancipated minor. For her part, mother DelaCerna filed a restraining order, and at one bitter point, police officers picked Misty up to take her back to her family. Famed attorney Gloria Allred decided to represent Sylvia, lured by the catnip of Misty's celebrity status; she had become a media darling as a child prodigy. In her memoir, Copeland wrote, "Hiring Gloria Allred was like posting the details of your life in neon on the Sunset Strip." The shy Misty cringed at the crush of reporters that hovered outside the Torrance Courthouse and the entrance of the Sunset Inn and at the fact her classmates were privy to her family's drama. The courts sided with her mother, and for the next decade, Ms. Copeland had scarcely any contact with her benefactor.

At age seventeen, the California teen departed for New York City to try out for ABT's summer intensive session; by its conclusion, they had invited her to join their venerated company despite her unconventional appearance. Traditionally, the ideal person for the profession was tall and white, and Misty, at five foot two, was neither. Despite her ecstasy at having her dream come true, she hit an emotional road bump. As Copeland wrote, "We don't know in history that black women, from the beginning of time in ballet, have been told to lighten their skin, and to shade their nose in a certain way to look white. A big part of my youth at American Ballet Theater [where she was the only black among eighty dancers] was hearing those words." Unwilling to downplay her race—both for her own sake and for those who wanted to follow in her pink-shod footsteps—she refused to try to appear more Caucasian.

Growing up in inner cities in California, Misty had never felt her skin color was a liability, but color blindness was not the state of the dance world's inner sanctum. At one point, someone told her that she could not participate in the second act of *Swan Lake*, first performed in late nineteenth-century Russia, because of her ethnicity. She recalled the whispers that she should not even be in the production at all. Philanthropist Susan Fales-Hill once wrote, "Most ballet companies look like an Alabama country club in 1952." Separated from family and friends, feeling like an outsider, Misty turned to food for comfort. Krispy Kreme donuts made deliveries if the order was large enough, and after practice, Misty would sit in her apartment and consume two dozen. In response, her company told her to "lengthen"—ballet-speak for "lose weight."

In addition to prejudice, a few months later, Misty discovered she had a lower-vertebrae fracture, a result of putting her body through painful gyrations that appeared as effortless moves on stage. She had to wear a brace twenty-three hours a day, and was unable to appear on stage for a year. A doctor also attributed her condition to weakness of the bones and prescribed medication, and a short time later, her body, which at the time of her acceptance in the corps de ballet had been considered perfect for her art—she was said to have the "Balanchine body"—was no longer the ideal. Before the injury, she had been slated to star as Clara in *The Nutcracker*, but the ABT withdrew their offer. However, holding fast to the courage of her convictions worked; in 2015, Misty became the first African American female principal dancer at the American Ballet Theater. The promotion caused seismic results, and in the same year, she was named to the Time 100, *Time* magazine's annual list of the world's most influential people.

Copeland made her debut at the Kennedy Center in the role of Odette, the tragically fated princess-turned-swan, marking a historic moment: a dancer from one of the world's most prestigious companies had finally plausibly proved that one can be black and dance the role of the white swan. The production is the ballet equivalent of playing Hamlet for the Royal Shakespeare Company; the drama spins the tale of Prince Siegfried, who is poised to kill the majestic creature when he witnesses her transformation into a beautiful woman—a storyline that can serve as a metaphor for Copeland's life. In a nod to life imitating art, the girl who had scavenged under couch pillows for change to buy dinner at 7/11 underwent a similar metamorphosis. Not since Mikhail Baryshnikov defected from the Soviet Union in the midst of the Cold War had a dancer so captivated the public. Misty had her acting debut in Disney's *The Nutcracker*, endorsed Estee Lauder cosmetics, and amassed an Instagram following of over 1.6 million. Copeland danced atop a grand piano during Prince's 2010 "Welcome 2 America" tour and starred in commercials for Diet Dr. Pepper and Dannon. Misty also appeared in a commercial for the athletic wear brand Under Armour; within a week of the ad's release, it had racked up more than four million YouTube views. In the ad, a voice-over reads a rejection letter detailing why "the candidate" is not a good fit for ballet while Copeland, wearing a sports bra and underwear, slowly rises onto pointe. The campaign's appeal was showcasing a woman doing more than looking sexy serving as a star of ESPN. Ballet product endorsement, though a rarity, had a precedent: Anna Pavlova was the face of Pond's Vanishing Cream.

With all the acclaim, Copeland was the subject of the documentary, *A Ballerina's Tale*, garnered a segment on *60 Minutes*, and judged contestants on Fox's *So You Think You Can Dance*. Barbara Walters named Ms. Copeland as one of the 10 Most Fascinating People of 2015. The ballerina pirouetted over the wave of fame and penned *Firebird*, an inspirational children's story of the rewards of persistence, as well as her memoir and "Ballerina's Body," a health and fitness guide intended for girls that encouraged them to embrace their physiques, whatever their builds. Misty stated of her annus mirabilis, "I'm not trying to dilute the ballet world, but for a long time I wanted to be at the forefront of pop culture." Her niche was secured in 2016 when Mattel released a Barbie doll in Copeland's image. Misty insisted that her plastic likeness not come with a lightened skin tone and that its nose was not shaded to appear more Caucasian. She stated, "It's so empowering for young girls to grow up with a brown Barbie that's a ballerina." To further help those navigating her own thorn-strewn path, she helped start Project Plié, a nonprofit that offers training to children from economically disadvantaged backgrounds. President Obama selected Copeland to serve on his Turnaround Arts program, one that employs the arts to interest students in school. One of the stops on her crowded itinerary was Rwanda, Africa, to help the organization Mindleaps start a dance program.

The ballerina became a bride in 2016 when Misty married her decade-long love, attorney Olu Evans, who gifted her with a serious sparkler. The couple wed in a seaside ceremony at the Montage Hotel in Laguna Beach, California, amid a hundred guests and a backdrop of pink hydrangeas and white roses. The bride wore an Inbal Dror gown and Christian Louboutin shoes; the consensus: she looked like an "ethereal goddess."

Misty Copeland's remarkable rise in the ABT's seventy-five-year history has been as dramatic as the plots of a classic ballet. Her tale can be encapsulated in the Under Armour tagline, "I Will What I Want."

Chapter 31

The Dark Mirror
(2018)

The British National Anthem begins with the words, "God save our gracious queen, long live our noble queen, long may she reign." As part of her reign, Queen Elizabeth II dominated Canadian currency; however, while her likeness appeared as a result of sovereignty, in 2018, Viola Desmond represented the sisterhood as the first non-royal woman to appear alone on Canada's ten-dollar banknote.

As with many cherished beliefs, Canada's historic treatment of its black population is one that does not bear too much scrutiny. The popular misconception is when the Moses of the Underground Railroad, Harriet Tubman, delivered her passengers to the North, they had entered the land of milk and honey. The biography of a woman from its eastern province sadly places this belief into the realm of urban myth.

In *Twelfth Night,* Shakespeare wrote, "Some men are born great, some achieve greatness, and some have greatness thrust upon them;" the latter was the case with Viola, born in 1914 in Halifax, one of fifteen children of James and Gwendolyn Davis. Her mother was a housewife; her father was a barber, one of the few livelihoods available to black men as most white barbers refused to cut African American hair. The members of the family were descendants of former slaves who had settled in the province of Nova Scotia at the close of the American Revolutionary War. During the first half of the twentieth century, because of sexism and racism, most African-Canadian women were housewives or maids. After graduating from Bloomfield High School, Viola bypassed the domestic-worker avenue and set her sights on teaching. Although Canada did not have Jim Crow laws, it did have policies that enforced segregation, though they were couched in terms that masked racist intent. Viola could not attend the provincial college in Truro and could only work at racially segregated schools.

Her career focus changed after reading an article about Madam C. J. Walker, an entrepreneur, civil rights advocate, and the first American woman of any race to become a self-made millionaire, a feat she accomplished by catering to black beauty needs. Viola wanted to follow in Walker's footsteps; barred from schools in Halifax, at age twenty, she received a diploma from Apex College of Beauty Culture and Hairdressing in Atlantic City.

Before her departure, Viola had begun dating Jack Desmond, the owner of Jack's Barber Shop on Gottingen's commercial strip in the black district of the city. Jack traveled by train to visit Viola, and in 1936, a Baptist minister sealed their wedding vows. Mrs. Desmond founded the first hairdresser salon for black women in Halifax, sharing commercial space with Jack's barbershop. Vi's Studio of Beauty Culture attracted a clientele that included community activist Carrie M. Best, opera singer Portia White, and one of the first black nurses in Nova Scotia, Gwen Jenkins. In the early 1940s, Viola established the Desmond School of Beauty Culture, where she resumed teaching, except this time, she taught those who wanted to learn about the cosmetic industry. The school had an excellent reputation and attracted women from Nova Scotia, New Brunswick, and Quebec. The graduates went on to sell Desmond cosmetics.

In 1945, Viola bought a 1940 Dodge for business purposes; the purchase was remarkable as most women of her era did not even possess a driver's license. As fate transpired, the vehicle was to have a huge impact on her life, making her the Canadian Rosa Parks.

A year later, during a business trip to Sydney, Nova Scotia, her car broke down in New Glasgow, and rather than wait at the garage, she decided to see a murder mystery starring Olivia de Havilland, her favorite actress, at the Roseland Theater. She was excited at the prospect because as a workaholic, she rarely took time out for entertainment. As she was in a new city, she was unaware of its segregation policy restricting black customers to the balcony; Viola requested a ground floor seat, something that was important to her as she was near-sighted. The cashier, without explaining the situation, sold her a ticket for the balcony. Once inside, an usher told her she had to move, and she returned to the cashier and asked to exchange her ticket for a ground floor seat, explaining she would gladly pay the extra ten cents. In response, the girl explained, "I'm not permitted to sell downstairs tickets to you people."

Livid, Viola returned to her original seat, which resulted in the manager, Henry MacNeil, calling the police. When the officer arrived, he grabbed one of Viola's arms and the manager took her other; they dragged her out of the theater. Viola resisted arrest, and in the scuffle, she lost purse, one shoe, and injured her hip. The thirty-two-year-old Ms. Desmond spent twelve hours behind bars, where she was never told of her legal right to a lawyer or to seek bail. Throughout the night, she sat with her back ramrod straight, her way of dealing with an upside down world. She kept her spotless white gloves on; although she was behind bars, she could remain a lady. To add insult to injury, a few local drunks joined her and made obscene sexual comments.

The incident was not the only traumatic one she had endured. In 1917, when she was three years old, the *Imo*, a Norwegian supply ship, and the *Mont-Blanc*, a

French cargo ship carrying munitions, collided at the mouth of Halifax Harbor. The resulting explosion caused two thousand deaths and devastated the city's North End, home to the city's black residents. Viola was living on Gottingen Street and was in her high chair when the blast shook her rental home and shattered the kitchen window, showering her with broken glass. The window blind fell on her, and her father thought she had been killed.

The charge against Ms. Desmond was tax evasion, trying to defraud the provincial government of one cent; the cost of an amusement tax. In the trial, the theater owner acted as the prosecutor; Viola did not have an attorney. The judge sentenced her to a $26 fine and to either pay $6 in court costs or serve thirty days in jail. Initially, Viola wanted to take the prison sentence to draw attention to her cause, but she reconsidered as she felt her students needed her.

To fight the conviction, Viola hired an attorney, Frederick William Bissett, who asked the Supreme Court of Nova Scotia to overturn the lower court's decision, but the effort proved futile. Rather than arguing that the theater was using a racially neutral tax law to enforce segregation, her attorney tried to get the decision overturned on a technicality. Despite the court's decision, one of the judges questioned, "if the manager who laid the complaint was so zealous because of a *bona fide* belief that there had been an attempt to defraud the province of Nova Scotia of the sum of one cent, or was it a surreptitious endeavor to enforce a Jim Crow-style rule by misuse of a public statute." The recent World War had ended Hitler's reign of Aryan supremacy, but racial intolerance continued in the home country.

Nevertheless, the little woman had lit a huge spark, one that helped ignite Canada's civil rights movement and ushered in Nova Scotia's legal end to segregation in 1954. Her refusal to give up her seat occurred nine years before Rosa Parks did the same on a Montgomery, Alabama, bus, but while the American became an icon, Desmond became a forgotten footnote.

Viola suffered personal and professional repercussions for her act of resistance, and her notoriety contributed to the dissolution of her marriage. She shut down her beauty shop and relocated, first to Montreal and then to New York City, where she worked for a time as a cigarette girl at Small's Paradise Club in Harlem. Viola died alone from a gastrointestinal hemorrhage in 1965 at the age of fifty. Her interment was in Camp Hill Cemetery, Halifax.

The feminist—well before the term was coined—would have been forgotten had it not been for an act of serendipity. Wanda Robson, who had put her education on hold to raise her children, enrolled in a course on race relations at University College of Cape Breton in Nova Scotia at age seventy-three. When her professor, Graham Reynolds, delivered a lecture regarding the 1946 incident where Viola Desmond first took a seat and then refused to relinquish it, and held up a picture of the activist, Wanda raised her hand and said that was her sister. The moment provided a life-changing moment for both the teacher, the student, and the country.

At age seventy-seven, Wanda received her Bachelor of Arts diploma, and after graduation, she launched a campaign to educate the public about her older sister. She gave numerous media interviews and presentations in schools; as a result, the government of Nova Scotia granted Ms. Desmond a posthumous pardon in 2010. Mayann Francis, the lieutenant governor, signed it into law with the remark, "Here I am, sixty-four years later—a black woman giving freedom to another black woman. I believe she has to know that she is now free." Because of the renewed interest in the miscarriage of justice, Viola emerged from the shadows and became a national civil rights icon.

In 2016, Prime Minister Justin Trudeau, who describes himself as a feminist and whose government requires departments to examine their programs to ensure gender equality, stated Canada would, for the first time, introduce the image of a woman who was not reigning royalty to grace the front of its ten-dollar banknotes. In a break with tradition, the Bank of Canada asked the public for nominations, and more than 26,000 suggestions poured in. A panel of experts from a variety of fields pared the list to 461 names.

Viola Desmond—fifty-three years after her death—was the winning candidate, and her likeness replaced that of Sir John A. Macdonald, Canada's first Prime Minister. The bill is the first vertical banknote and displays Viola's image; behind her portrait is a stretch of Gottingen Street, the black community where she was born and started her beauty salon. Ms. Desmond became the first black person—and the first woman other than a British queen—to appear alone on Canadian currency. One of the wonderful aspects of the new currency is it honors a Canadian heroine; it also lifts a curtain on the country's unsavory past, something that should not be swept under a historic carpet.

Ninety-year-old Wanda was present at the bill's unveiling at the Canadian Museum for Human Rights, and she stated, "It's unbelievable to think that my sister—a black woman—is on the $10 bill. The Queen is in good company." Other tributes showered on Ms. Desmond included a commemorative stamp and a Google Doodle on what would have been her 104th birthday. The name of the movie that made Viola a historic first can serve as a microcosm of her era: *The Dark Mirror.*

Chapter 32

A Beautiful Mind
(2019)

In a former, less tolerant clime, a woman mathematician was considered an oxymoron. The paradigm that the sciences were the realm of men was deeply entrenched; the arts were the realm of women. The gender stereotype received a kidney punch when Karen Uhlenbeck became the first (and only) female recipient of the mathematics' Nobel Prize, the Abel Award.

One woman who ingrained the stereotype that math was not a feminist pursuit was blonde bombshell Barbie. She promoted the trends that pink was the de rigueur hue, that feet were made for stilettoes, that success meant designer duds. In 1993, feminists saw red when Mattel released Teen Talk Barbie. The plastic princess came with pre-programmed phrases such as, "Math class is tough;" the Association of University Women demanded a recall.

Equally outraged, a group of East Village performance artists formed the Barbie Liberation Organization (BLO); they argued the curvaceous cutie taught girls that looks triumphed over intellect. They infiltrated Toys 'R' Us in New York City and California and switched out Barbie's voice box with that of GI Joe. When the girls opened their presents, the bodacious blonde cried, "Eat lead, Cobra!" while the macho soldier cooed, "Let's plan our dream wedding." Hopefully, the children received the requisite therapy.

Karen Uhlenbeck, who helped topple the paradigm that math is for men, was born in 1942 in Cleveland, Ohio, to mother Carolyn, a schoolteacher and artist, and father Arnold Keskulla, an MIT graduate and engineer. When Karen was in third grade, the family relocated to the whistle-stop country town of West Millington, in New Jersey. She was the eldest of four children (three girls and a boy), and stated having siblings was the hardest thing she ever had to deal with. Hence, she desired a career that did not entail working with other people.

Contrary to popular belief, mathematicians are not holed up in rooms studying numbers. Karen's parents instilled in her their love of the outdoors, and like them, she enjoys sports such as mountain climbing, backpacking, and canoeing. At age forty, she took up surfing. She claims she is most at home in nature, and when unable to be in the wilderness, Karen is often in her garden. Another interest she cultivated as a child was reading books on science, and she pored over them into the night. At school, she placed the books under her desk and surreptitiously continued her evening pursuit. Rather than take pride in her hobby, her father was more concerned with his son having a scientific career.

When it came time for college, there was no question of remaining in her home state as Rutgers and Princeton were all male. She had set her sights on MIT and Cornell, but the tuition was too steep, and Ivy League schools were not forthcoming with scholarships for females. As a freshman at the University of Michigan, she took classes in physics and astronomy; in 1960, in the wake of Sputnik, the curriculum added honors calculus classes. Her eureka moment occurred when she realized math was her destiny as its intellectual challenge was what excited her. A year abroad was spent studying in Munich, where she learned to speak German and developed an appreciation for theater and opera.

Post-graduation, Karen spent a year at New York University's Courant Institute, where she met biochemist Olke Cornelis Uhlenbeck, whom she married in 1963. Her husband's parents were older intellectuals from Holland; her father-in-law was the renowned physicist, George Uhlenbeck. She stated, "I don't think I would have survived at that stage of my career without the encouragement from my husband's family." When Olke transferred to Harvard, Karen, aware of the misogynist culture in academia, avoided applying to prestigious schools where the competition would be fierce. Instead, she enrolled at Brandeis University, where she earned her PhD in 1968. Karen recalled of those days, "We were told that we couldn't do math because we were women. So, if anything, there was a tendency to not be friendly with other women. There was a lot of blatant, overt discouragement, but there was also subtle encouragement. There were a lot of people who appreciated good students, male or female, and I was a very good student. I liked doing what I wasn't supposed to do. It was a sort of legitimate rebellion." Karen dreaded being relegated to being a mere faculty wife, especially as many of the wives were disapproving of female students.

After graduate school, Karen held two temporary positions; she taught for a year at MIT while her husband was working on his doctorate and then left for the University of California at Berkeley, a time she recalls as one of the momentous years of her life. Berkeley in the 1960s was a hotbed of activism, and she recalled the Vietnam War demonstrations—the tear gas, the speeches, the classes cancelled in the wake of the Kent State shootings. She added, "And oh, there was a lot of fuss about women, too, at that time." The "fuss about women" referred to was that concurrently with the burgeoning feminist movement, females were entering graduate school and academic positions. On the other hand, "A lot of people didn't think that women were suitable, and lots of things were said and lots of improper things done." Karen explained for those younger than the baby boomers what the gender imbalance was like, "The women who had jobs during World War Two were fired. Men came home from the war, and women sat at home.

And it was only because of the women's movement and books like Betty Friedman's *The Feminist Mystique* that the consciousness came up that women could actually do other things. I figured if I'd been five years older, I could not have become a mathematician, because the disapproval would have been so strong."

As she searched for employment after her two university positions, people warned her that employers did not hire female mathematicians, since the current zeitgeist was that little ladies were supposed to be home having babies. Thus, the places interested in hiring Olke—MIT, Stanford, and Princeton—were not interested in her. The schools insisted their disinterest did not stem from sexism, but rather from the need to avoid charges of nepotism due to having a husband and wife on the same faculty.

Dr. Uhlenbeck ended up at the University of Illinois, Champaign-Urbana, because they offered her a position. In solidarity, her husband followed her as she had done in the past for him. Although Karen was very appreciative of him sacrificing the Ivy League schools on her behalf, and although she adored his parents, her marriage was not working out with the precision of a mathematical equation. They divorced in 1976. Her second husband, Robert F. Williams, a professor at Northwestern University, is also a mathematician. She explained, "Lots of women mathematicians are married to male mathematicians, and maybe more male mathematicians would be married to more women mathematicians if there were more women mathematicians. But the answer is: other mathematicians understand completely. They know that you're abstract and your mind is off somewhere and you're really not paying attention..."

Despite obstacles, Karen persevered, and in her late thirties, she began publishing important work; however, the prestigious Field Medal, awarded every four years to mathematicians forty years of age or younger, proved elusive. In 1983, she received a MacArthur Fellowship that brought with it the hefty sum of $204,000. Seven years later, Karen became the second woman to speak at the International Congress of Mathematicians. (Emmy Noether, a prominent German mathematician, had been the first in 1932.)

Alfred Nobel, when creating his eponymous prize, had not designated a math category. To rectify the omission, in 2003, the Norwegian Academy of Science and Letters created the Abel Prize—named after Norwegian mathematician Niels Abel, and created on the two-hundreth anniversary of his birth—to provide a correspondingly prestigious award. At age 76, Dr. Uhlenbeck, who had retired from her post as an emeritus professor at the University of Texas at Austin, shattered the glass ceiling of mathematics when she became the first woman to receive the eminent distinction. Karen learned of the honor as she was leaving the Unitarian Universalist Church in Princeton, New Jersey, and saw a text message on her phone from Princeton colleague Alice Chang saying she should accept a call from

Norway. Karen understood the implication and was so overwhelmed she said she had to sit down. What the message entailed was that in the near future, she would be jetting off to Norway, meeting its King, and receiving 6 million kroner, equivalent to $700,000. Whatever prayer she may have made at church that morning must have been quite persuasive. Dr. Uhlenbeck, a visiting associate at the Institute for Advanced Study in Princeton, told the press she had not decided what to do with her windfall. She said she has a few project ideas—and a lot more women for whom she intends to set an example before she's done.

In Norway, the Abel Prize week kicked off with the Laureate laying a wreath at the statue of Niels Henrik Abel in the Palace Park. The woman of the hour also met with King Harald V at his palace. While the royal was dressed in an elegant black suit and blue silk tie, Karen's attire showed that you can take the hippie out of Berkeley but can't take Berkeley out of the hippie. Her wavy, gray hair was at its customary shoulder length; her black slacks were short enough to reveal Birkenstock sandals. His Majesty the King presented the prestigious Abel Prize to Dr. Karen Keskulla Uhlenbeck in a ceremony in the Aula of the University of Oslo, whose walls showcase murals by Edvard Munch, painter of *The Scream*. She was the honored recipient "for her pioneering achievements in geometric partial differential equations, gauge theory and integrable systems..." In layman lingo, for the past fifty years, her research had assisted in the development of computers and artificial intelligence. In her acceptance speech, the Abel Laureate stressed the importance of gender equality in academia. In her address, Dr. Uhlenbeck affirmed, "All in all, I have found great delight and pleasure in the pursuit of mathematics. I have been saved from boredom, dourness, and self-absorption. One cannot ask for more." Following the ceremony, a reception was held at Norway's National Theater with performances by the Norwegian Soloists' Choir and Camilla Spidsoe of the Norwegian National Ballet. In the evening, there was a banquet at Oslo's historic Akershus Fortress and Castle.

Karen revealed that her childhood idol was famed chef Julia Child. "She was six feet, two inches, a big woman with this immense presence. It wasn't her cooking but her personality, that she was smart, funny, and not perfect." Uhlenbeck recalled the story of Ms. Child dropping a turkey on her television show *French Chef* and carried on unfazed. "The feeling was if Julia Child could do it, maybe you could too."

Of the previous nineteen Abel laureates, one was John F. Nash, Jr. who suffered from schizophrenia. The title of the movie about Nash can serve to evoke Dr. Uhlenbeck's encapsulated biography: *A Beautiful Mind*.

Epilogue

On Their Shoulders We Stand

While writing a biography entails research, writing the epilogue entails reflection. Stepping back, what did I learn from the trailblazers whose lives were a race to be the first of their sex to reach the finish line, a marathon run that involved jumping hurdles of entrenched sexism? While each woman had a different endgame, they shared the commonality of possessing grit that led to greatness. Although their paths were perilous, the end results were worth the struggle: Junko Tabei standing on the summit of Mt. Everest, Sandra Day O'Connor presiding over America's highest bench, Sally Ride soaring among the stars.

What adds to their legacies is they paved the way for their sisters; once individuals have made the impossible possible, the fight of their successors is far less. Marie Curie showed that a female could grasp a Nobel Prize; Kathryn Bigelow showed that a female could excel behind the camera; Dr. Karen Uhlenbeck showed that mathematics is not just the realm of men.

There were other fabulous female firsts who did not receive a chapter even though they deserve well-merited praise. In 1977, Janet Guthrie shattered the stereotype of women drivers when she became the first female to compete in the Indianapolis 500. In 2006, at the age of ninety-eight, Keiko Fekuda earned the honorific title of sensei (master) when she became the first female to earn the tenth-degree black belt rank. (She was the last remaining student of the founder of judo, Kano Jigoro.) When Christine Lagarde became the first woman to head the International Monetary Fund in 2011, and when Jane Yellen became the first woman to serve as the head of the Federal Reserve in 2014, they proved the ladies could do more with money than spend it. What would J. Edgar Hoover have said upon the 2018 appointment of Gina Haspel when she became the first female head of the CIA?

Men have governed Vatican City since its establishment as an independent state in 1929. In 2016, Barbara Jatta became an unwitting feminist symbol when Pope Francis appointed her as the first female director of the Vatican Museum. For Jatta, overseeing priceless artifacts—from the Stone Age to the Space Age—as well as the world's most famous frescoed ceiling, the Sistine Chapel, is all in a day's work. The view from her office is none too shabby: her window provides a vista of the dome of St. Peter's Basilica, designed in 1547 by Michelangelo.

The world of media—which reflects the mores of society— illustrates gender-leveling progression. Leonardo,

Donatello, Michelangelo, and Raphael, the four martial arts experts with the DNA of turtles, welcomed to their ranks Venus de Milo. If a female of the species can be a reptilian ninja, what can she not be? Rumor has it that the most charming misogynist, James Bond, is retiring, and that movie-goers will see—in a popcorn dropping moment—the replacement of 007: actress Lashana Lynch. Marvel Studios revealed that their forthcoming film will showcase Natalie Portman wielding the hammer as a female Thor. The US Treasury is negotiating the creation of a twenty-dollar banknote bearing the image of Harriet Tubman, the intrepid abolitionist; it would be the first bill depicting an African-American. She would replace President Andrew Jackson, a slave-owner. The name NFL, with its exclusive testosterone, could be an acronym for Not For Women. Estrogen entered with Sarah Thomas, the first female to officiate a playoff game. Fans cheered, and of their number was tennis great Billie Jean King, who tweeted, "You have to see it to be it, and little girls everywhere are watching. Way to go, Sarah Thomas!"

Alas, there is the other side of the proverbial coin: arenas where women have not yet entered. Never has there been a female American president or vice president. There has yet to be a woman head of the United Nations. A woman has never been a member of the Catholic clergy, let alone a pope; in the Catholic Church, only males can receive the sacrament of Holy Orders through which they become bishops or priests. (Nuns must make do with serving as the brides of Christ.) When Neil Armstrong stepped on the moon, he deemed it, "One small step for a man." The eleven moonwalkers (and Michael Jackson) have all been male. Fifty years later, there still has not been a "small step for a woman."

In the 1900s, a young British baroness, Lady Violet Bonham Carter, asked her governess how she would spend her life. The reply was, "Until you are eighteen, you will do lessons. And afterwards—you will do nothing." The ladies profiled in *Fabulous Female Firsts* were cut from a different cloth. They balked against the current zeitgeists of their times that told them their sole functions were motherhood and marriage. They did so armed with the knowledge that for their "unnatural behavior," namely, following pursuits best left to men, they would find themselves ostracized. In addition, they were often not considered matrimonial material. Spinsterhood—as was the case with financial wizard Muriel Siebert and iron-fisted Attorney General Janet Reno—was the price paid for success and for being considered by men as too clever for their own good. In 1920, Crystal Eastman, a nineteenth-century lawyer and co-founder of the American Civil Liberties Union, elegantly stated that the problem was, "how to arrange the world so that women can be human beings with a chance to exercise their infinitely varied gifts in infinitely varied ways..." Although progress has been made, we still await the answer.

The message of each of the indefatigable ladies is dreams do not just have to be for sleeping. Putting one's hands over ears to block out the naysayers, placing blinders beside one's eyes to keep the eyes on the prize, led them to be the first in their fields, thereby proving the old adage that what is good for the goose is good for the gander.

Culture holds up a mirror to society, and it has not always reflected the most ideal of images. Picasso's canvasses depicted vivisected women; art imitated life as his significant others, after becoming insignificant (with one exception) fell into the abyss of madness or suicide. Blue Period, indeed.

In the 1996 musical, *My Fair Lady*, master linguist Dr. Henry Higgins is perplexed when, after enduring months of his put-downs, his protégée/human guinea pig, Eliza Doolittle, finally rebels. The good doctor's response was, "Why can't a woman be more like a man?"

Pop music has portrayed women in a condescending light. In 1964, William "Mickey" Stevenson sang, "Devil with a Blue Dress On," whose lyrics contained tidbits such as, "Not too skinny not too fat / Real humdinger." Two years later, Bob Dylan made a scathing attack on females who, "Takes just like a woman, yes, she does / She makes love just like a woman, yes, she does / And she aches just like a woman / But she breaks just like a little girl." Sadly, a woman's principal activities are lyrically narrowed down to taking, making love, aching, and breaking. The same year, James Brown released a recording with a redundant title, "It's a Man's Man's Man's World;" *Rolling Stone* deemed it, "biblically chauvinistic." In his ode to a milieu before women, he attributed the cornerstones of civilization to men: cars, trains, electric lights, and boats ("like Noah made the Ark"). However, he added all these Herculean accomplishments would mean nothing without the little lady patiently waiting back home—in Penelope fashion—for the conquering hero. (No wonder they granted us the vote.) If these lyrics were not enough to launch the burning of countless bras, in 1967, in the song "Pussycat," Tom Jones crooned, "So go and make up your big little pussycat eyes." Five years later, in "Chantilly Lace," Jiles Perry, The Big Bopper, sang of the girl with the ponytail, "Make me act so funny / Make me spend my money..." With the respective nods to Satan, female fragility, Man as Superman, the anthropomorphic quality of felines, and a Lolita, no wonder twentieth-century feminists were on high alert.

The women of *Fabulous Female Firsts* were incarnations of Rosie the Riveter, the ladies who "manned" the factories until Johnny came marching home again and then were once more consigned to home and hearth. They maintained, "We can do it!"—and they did. And it is on their shoulders we stand.

Acknowledgments

Winners of the world's most prestigious awards are confronted with the daunting task of thanking those who helped them along their paths and have to squeeze their tributes into a few words—a daunting task. Now it is my time to acknowledge those who made *Fabulous Female Firsts* transition from a twinkle in my eye to its journey into the world.

Roger Williams and I have birthed five books together, and I am indebted to him for his steadfast support. Everything a writer could hope for in a literary agent I have found in him. Brenda Knight, my editor, despite her innumerable hats, is never too busy to offer invaluable help.

A serendipitous result of publishing is it allows writers to interact with individuals who would never otherwise have crossed their paths. If I were to list them all, this Acknowledgements page would resemble a phone book, but I do have to mention a very special woman. Jamie Lovett emailed me many years ago in reference to my first book, *Once Again to Zelda*; she has become not only my first reader but also my dearest friend.

My late mother, Gilda Wagman, has my everlasting appreciation. She always believed in my writing, even in the years when publishing was in the realm of the *Man of La Macha's* "To dream the impossible dream." No one was ever more in my corner. What I would give to see her holding my book. A nod to my dear daughter, Jordanna Geller, first in my heart.

A heartfelt hug to my readers who have been kind enough to attend my readings, leave Amazon and Goodread reviews, and post my covers on their Facebook. You know who you are and know the depth of my gratitude.

Writing, especially in the context of my job as a high school teacher, is daunting. Having back-to-back jobs means watching television, attending movies, and going out for lunch are pastimes of yesteryear. Those who have shown solidarity have made my path less thorny.

And, lastly, a shout-out to the ladies of *Fabulous Female Firsts* who have taught us lessons on the power of persistence, who have delivered the message to forge ahead despite impediments, who have shown that the only failure is fear to follow one's dreams.

Marlene Wagman-Geller

San Diego, California, 2019

It Couldn't Be Done

By Edgar Albert Guest (1919)

Somebody said that it couldn't be done
But he with a chuckle replied
That "maybe it couldn't," but he would be one
Who wouldn't say so till he'd tried.
So he buckled right in with the trace of a grin
On his face. If he worried he hid it.
He started to sing as he tackled the thing
That couldn't be done, and he did it!

Somebody scoffed: "Oh, you'll never do that;
At least no one ever has done it;"
But he took off his coat and he took off his hat
And the first thing we knew he'd begun it.
With a lift of his chin and a bit of a grin,
Without any doubting or quiddit,
He started to sing as he tackled the thing
That couldn't be done, and he did it.

There are thousands to tell you it cannot be done,
There are thousands to prophesy failure,
There are thousands to point out to you one by one,
The dangers that wait to assail you.
But just buckle in with a bit of a grin,
Just take off your coat and go to it;
Just start in to sing as you tackle the thing
That "cannot be done," and you'll do it.

*Feel free to interchange the pronoun "she" for "he."

Bibliography

Chapter 1 – Dr. Mary Edward Walker

Blakemore, Erin. "How a Woman Won the Medal of Honor 150 Years Before She Could Serve in Combat." *Time*, March 1, 2016. https://time.com/4235358/mary-edwards-walker/.

Lineberry, Cate. "'I Wear My Own Clothes'." *The New York Times*, December 2, 2013. https://opinionator.blogs.nytimes.com/2013/12/02/i-wear-my-own-clothes/.

"The Case of Dr. Walker, Only Woman To Win (and Lose) the Medal of Honor." *The New York Times*, June 4, 1977. https://www.nytimes.com/1977/06/04/archives/the-case-of-dr-walker-only-woman-to-win-and-lose-the-medal-of-honor.html.

Chapter 2 – Victoria Woodhull.

Bell, Millicent. "Victoria's Secrets." *The New York Review of Books*, May 14, 1998. https://www.nybooks.com/articles/1998/05/14/victorias-secrets/.

Crouse, Russel. "The First Woman to Run for President." *The New Yorker*, February 1, 2019. https://www.newyorker.com/magazine/1928/10/27/that-was-new-york.

Hess, Amanda. "The Dream - and the Myth - of the 'Women's Vote'." *The New York Times*, November 15, 2016. https://www.nytimes.com/2016/11/15/magazine/the-dream-and-the-myth-of-the-womens-vote.html.

Horne, Eileen. "Notorious Victoria: the First Woman to Run for President." *The Guardian*, July 20, 2016. https://www.theguardian.com/us-news/2016/jul/20/notorious-victoria-first-woman-run-for-us-president.

McShane, Julianne. "These 'Rebel Women' Sought Equality in 19th-Century New York." *The New York Times*, July 25, 2018. https://www.nytimes.com/2018/07/25/arts/design/rebel-women-museum-of-the-city-of-new-york.html.

Wright, Jennifer. "Meet 'Mrs. Satan,' AKA America's First Female Presidential Candidate." *Marie Claire*, October 11, 2017. https://www.marieclaire.com/politics/a23781/victoria-woodhull-first-female-presidential-candidate/.

Yaeger, Lynn. "Move Over, Hillary! Victoria Woodhull Was the First Woman to Run for U.S. President." *Vogue*, February 1, 2017. https://www.vogue.com/article/victoria-woodhull-first-woman-to-run-for-president.

Chapter 3 – Marie Curie

Gillis, Anna Maria. "Meet Marie Curie." *The Washington Post*, July 9, 1997. https://www.washingtonpost.com/archive/1997/07/09/meet-marie-curie/501299d5-e13f-4a46-87bc-1acc38248147/?utm_term=.ebc4e5fa8b30.

Maddox, Brenda. "'Obsessive Genius': Too Hot to Handle." *The New York Times*, November 28, 2004. https://www.nytimes.com/2004/11/28/books/review/obsessive-genius-too-hot-to-handle.html.

McKie, Robin. "Marie, Marie, Quite Contrary." *The Guardian*, February 6, 2005. https://www.theguardian.com/books/2005/feb/06/biography.scienceandnature.

Press, The Associated. "Marie Curie Enshrined in Pantheon." *The New York Times*, April 21, 1995. https://www.nytimes.com/1995/04/21/world/marie-curie-enshrined-in-pantheon.html.

Wilkie, Tom. "The Secret Sex Life of Marie Curie." *The Independent*, October 23, 2011. https://www.independent.co.uk/news/science/the-secret-sex-life-of-marie-curie-1586244.html.

Chapter 4 – Elsie de Wolfe

"Design Notebook—The Decorative Life of Elsie de Wolfe." *The New York Times*, May 20, 1982. https://

www.nytimes.com/1982/05/20/garden/design-notebook.html.

Flanner, Janet. "Handsprings Across the Sea." *The New Yorker*, January 7, 1938. https://www.newyorker.com/magazine/1938/01/15/handsprings-across-the-sea.

Munhall, Edgar. "Design Legends: Elsie De Wolfe." *Architectural Digest*, June 30, 2016. https://www.architecturaldigest.com/story/dewolfe-article-012000.

Owens, Mitchell. "At Long Last Love." *The New York Times*, April 29, 2001. https://www.nytimes.com/2001/04/29/magazine/at-long-last-love.html.

Chapter 5 – Gertrude Ederle

Bernstein, Adam. "Gertrude Ederle." *The Washington Post*, December 3, 2003. https://www.washingtonpost.com/archive/local/2003/12/03/gertrude-ederle/b731b02e-d167-4a70-ad5f-720166dcb7d8/.

Denman, Elliott. "A Pioneer Looks Back on Her Unforgettable Feat." *The New York Times*, April 30, 2001. https://www.nytimes.com/2001/04/30/sports/swimming-a-pioneer-looks-back-on-her-unforgettable-feat.html.

Gillies, Midge. "In 1926, Gertrude Ederle Became the First Woman to Swim the Channel, Trouncing All Male Records." *The Guardian*, October 15, 2006.

https://www.theguardian.com/world/2006/oct/16/gender.uk.

Mortimer, Gavin. "When Gertrude Ederle Turned the Tide." *The Telegraph*, April 27, 2008. https://www.telegraph.co.uk/culture/donotmigrate/3672954/When-Gertrude-Ederle-turned-the-tide.html.

Severo, Richard. "Gertrude Ederle, the First Woman to Swim Across the English Channel, Dies at 98." *The New York Times*, December 1, 2003. https://www.nytimes.com/2003/12/01/sports/gertrude-ederle-the-first-woman-to-swim-across-the-english-channel-dies-at-98.html.

Chapter 6 – Hattie McDaniel

Agard, Chancellor. "The Mystery of Hattie McDaniel's Missing Oscar—and the Incredible Life of the First African-American Oscar Winner." *People*, February 27, 2016. http://people.com/awards/oscars-2016-6-things-to-know-about-hattie-mcdaniel/.

Als, Hilton. "Mammmy for the Masses." *The New Yorker*, June 20, 2017. http://www.newyorker.com/magazine/2005/09/26/mammmy-for-the-masses.

Curtis, Mary C. "SAG Awards: From Hattie McDaniel to Viola Davis, Still Winning for Playing 'The Help'." *The Washington Post*, January 30, 2012. https://www.washingtonpost.com/blogs/she-the-people/post/

from-hattie-mcdaniel-to-viola-davis-still-winning-
for-playing-the-help/2012/01/30/gIQAT3WTcQ_
blog.html.

"Hattie McDaniel Loved Her Role as 'Mammy' in 'Gone
With the Wind'." *World News*, March 23, 2014. https://
article.wn.com/view/2014/03/23/Hattie_McDaniel_
loved_her_role_as_Mammy_in_Gone_With_the_Win/.

Witheridge, Annette. "How the FIRST Black Oscar
Winner Hattie McDaniel Dealt with Being Segregated."
Daily Mail, February 25, 2016. http://www.dailymail.
co.uk/news/article-3462821/I-d-make-700-week-
playing-maid-working-one-Hattie-McDaniel-black-
Oscar-winner-Mammy-Gone-Wind-segregated-Clark-
Gable-white-actors-Acade.

Chapter 7 – Bette Davis

Basinger, Jeanine. "The Real Margo Channing's
Fasten-Your-Seatbelts Life." *The New York Times*,
November 12, 2007. https://www.nytimes.
com/2007/11/12/books/12basi.html.

Bianco, Marcie, and Merryn Johns. "How Bette Davis
Became a Hollywood Icon By Refusing to Conform
at Every Turn." *Vanity Fair*, April 6, 2016. https://
www.vanityfair.com/hollywood/2016/04/bette-
davis-birthday.

Darrach, Brad. "Grand Dame, Grande Dame." *People,* October 23, 1989. https://people.com/archive/cover-story-grand-dame-grande-dame-vol-32-no-17/.

Davies, Hugh. "From the Archives: Bette Davis Dies in Paris at 81." *Los Angeles Times*, October 8, 1989. https://www.latimes.com/local/obituaries/la-me-bette-davis-19891008-story.html.

———. "The World through Bette Davis Eyes." *The Telegraph*, February 11, 2006. https://www.telegraph.co.uk/news/worldnews/northamerica/usa/1510230/The-world-through-Bette-Davis-eyes.html.

French, Philip. "Philip French's Screen Legends: Bette Davis." *The Guardian*, March 23, 2008. https://www.theguardian.com/film/2008/mar/23/bettedavis.

Johnston, Sheila. "Bette Davis Centenary." *The Telegraph*, March 22, 2008. https://www.telegraph.co.uk/culture/film/starsandstories/3671990/Bette-Davis-centenary.html.

Krebs, Albin. "Bette Davis, a Queen of Hollywood, Dies at 81." *The New York Times*, October 8, 1989. https://www.nytimes.com/1989/10/08/obituaries/bette-davis-a-queen-of-hollywood-dies-at-81.html.

Chapter 8 – Susan Travers

Riding, Alan. "A Legionnaire, She Was Never Timid In Amour or War." *The New York Times*, April 21, 2001. https://www.nytimes.com/2001/04/21/books/a-legionnaire-she-was-never-timid-in-amour-or-war.html.

"Susan Travers." *The Telegraph*, December 23, 2003. https://www.telegraph.co.uk/news/obituaries/1450081/Susan-Travers.html.

"Susan Travers." *The Guardian*, December 7, 2000. https://www.theguardian.com/Columnists/Column/0,,407808,00.html.

"The Only Woman in the French Foreign Legion." *BBC News*, September 24, 2009. http://news.bbc.co.uk/2/hi/uk_news/magazine/8271773.stm.

Travers, Susan, and Wendy Holden. *Tomorrow to Be Brave: A Memoir of the Only Woman Ever to Serve in the French Foreign Legion*. New York: Free Press, 2007.

Chapter 9 – Alice Coachman

Alexander, Ella. "Alice Coachman Davis Dead: First Black Woman to Win Olympic Gold Medal." *The Independent*, July 15, 2014. https://www.independent.co.uk/news/people/alice-coachman-davis-dead-first-black-woman-to-win-olympic-gold-medal-dies-aged-90-9607462.html.

"Alice Coachman - Obituary." *The Telegraph*, July 15, 2014. https://www.telegraph.co.uk/news/obituaries/10968896/Alice-Coachman-obituary.html.

Goldstein, Richard. "Alice Coachman, 90, Dies; First Black Woman to Win Olympic Gold." *The New York Times*, July 15, 2014. https://www.nytimes.com/2014/07/15/sports/alice-coachman-90-dies-groundbreaking-medalist.html.

"'Hitler Was There. But Jesse Had Gone to Fulfil a Dream'." *The Independent*, October 23, 2011. https://www.independent.co.uk/sport/general/athletics/hitler-was-there-but-jesse-had-gone-to-fulfil-a-dream-1770303.html.

Langer, Emily. "Alice Coachman, First Black Woman to Win an Olympic Gold Medal, Dies at 91." *The Washington Post*, July 15, 2014. https://www.washingtonpost.com/sports/alice-coachman-first-black-woman-to-win-an-olympic-gold-medal-dies-at-91/2014/07/15/f48251d0-0c2e-11e4-b8e5-d0de80767fc2_story.html.

"Obituary: Alice Coachman / First Black Woman to Win Olympic Gold." *Gazette*, July 16, 2014. https://www.post-gazette.com/news/obituaries/2014/07/17/Obituary-Alice-Coachman-First-black-woman-to-win-Olympic-gold/stories/201901010050.

Chapter 10 – Emma Gatewood

Montgomery, Ben. *Grandma Gatewood's Walk: The Inspiring Story of the Woman Who Saved the Appalachian Trail.* Chicago: Chicago Review Press, Incorporated, 2014.

Reese, Diana. "Grandma Gatewood Survived Domestic Violence to Walk the Appalachian Trail Alone at 67." *The Washington Post*, April 5, 2019. https://www.washingtonpost.com/blogs/she-the-people/wp/2015/01/05/grandma-gatewood-survived-domestic-violence-to-walk-the-appalachian-trail-alone-at-67/.

Seelye, Katharine Q. "Overlooked No More: Emma Gatewood, First Woman to Conquer the Appalachian Trail Alone." *The New York Times*, June 27, 2018. https://www.nytimes.com/2018/06/27/obituaries/grandma-emma-gatewood-overlooked.html.

Chapter 11 – Angela Buxton and Althea Gibson

Carlson, Michael. "Obituary: Althea Gibson." *The Guardian*, September 30, 2003. https://www.theguardian.com/news/2003/sep/30/guardianobituaries.tennis.

Henderson, Jon. "Triumphing over Prejudice." *The Guardian*, July 8, 2001. https://www.theguardian.com/sport/2001/jul/08/features.sport.

Jacobs, Sally H. "Althea Gibson, Tennis Star Ahead of Her Time, Gets Her Due at Last." *The New York Times*, August 26, 2019. https://www.nytimes.com/2019/08/26/sports/tennis/althea-gibson-statue-us-open.html.

Jones, Sally. "Angela Buxton and Althea Gibson's Friendship Was No Ordinary Bond, but Their Outsider Statuses Brought Them Together." *The Telegraph*, June 20, 2019. https://www.telegraph.co.uk/tennis/2019/06/20/angela-buxton-althea-gibsons-friendship-no-ordinary-bond-outsider/.

Schoenfeld, Bruce. *The Match: Althea Gibson and Angela Buxton: How Two Outsiders—One Black, the Other Jewish—Forged a Friendship and Made Sports History*. New York: Amistad, 2004.

Vecsey, George. "Sports of The Times; Gibson Deserved A Better Old Age." The *New York Times*, September 29, 2003. https://www.nytimes.com/2003/09/29/sports/sports-of-the-times-gibson-deserved-a-better-old-age.html.

Chapter 12 – Kathrine Switzer

Doward, Jamie. "Woman Who Blazed a Trail for Equality in Marathons Hits London's Starting Line." *The Guardian*, April 21, 2018. https://www.theguardian.com/sport/2018/apr/21/kathrine-switzer-boston-london-marathon-gender-equality.

Gorman, Michele. "The Boston Marathon and How Kathrine Switzer's Number 261 Became a Symbol for Women in Sports." *Newsweek*, July 7, 2017. https://www.newsweek.com/boston-marathon-kathrine-switzer-261-fearless-symbol-women-running-584645.

Switzer, Kathrine. *Marathon Woman: Running the Race to Revolutionize Women's Sports.* Philadelphia: Da Capo Press, 2017.

Chapter 13 – Muriel Siebert

Alden, William. "Remembering Muriel Siebert, an 'Icon' for Women." *The New York Times*, August 26, 2013. https://dealbook.nytimes.com/2013/08/26/remembering-muriel-siebert-an-icon-for-women-2/.

Langer, Emily. "Muriel Siebert, First Woman to Join the New York Stock Exchange, Dies at 84." *The Washington Post*, August 27, 2013. https://www.washingtonpost.com/business/muriel-siebert-first-woman-to-join-the-new-york-stock-exchange-dies-at-84/2013/08/27/85cc1eea-0f24-11e3-8cdd-bcdc09410972_story.html.

Nemy, Enid. "Muriel Siebert, a Determined Trailblazer for Women on Wall Street, Dies at 84." *The New York Times*, August 25, 2013. https://www.nytimes.com/2013/08/26/business/muriel-siebert-first-woman-to-own-a-seat-on-wall-st-dies-at-80.html.

Siebert, Muriel, and Aimee Lee Ball. *Changing the Rules: Adventures of a Wall Street Maverick.* New York: Free Press, 2002.

Chapter 14 – Nichelle Nichols

Hattenstone, Simon. "Star Trek's Nichelle Nichols: 'Martin Luther King was a Trekker.'" *The Guardian*, October 18, 2016. https://www.theguardian.com/tv-and-radio/2016/oct/18/star-trek-nichelle-nichols-martin-luther-king-trekker.

Lloyd, Robert. "Television Review: 'Pioneers of Television'." *Los Angeles Times,* January 18, 2011. http://articles.latimes.com/2011/jan/18/entertainment/la-et-tv-pioneers-20110118.

Nichols, Nichelle. *Beyond Uhura: Star Trek and Other Memories.* New York: Boxtree, 1996.

Chapter 15 – Golda Meir

Herrmann, Dorothy. "Irresistible Golda." *Chicago Tribune*, September 3, 2018. http://articles.chicagotribune.com/1988-12-11/entertainment/8802240220_1_golda-meir-arab-attacks-minister.

Peres, Shimon. "Theater; Always a Lioness, Protecting Her Beloved Israel." *The New York Times*, March 16,

2003. http://www.nytimes.com/2003/03/16/theater/theater-always-a-lioness-protecting-her-beloved-israel.html.

Shlaim, Avi. "Review: *Golda Meir: The Iron Lady of the Middle East* by Elinor Burkett." *The Guardian*, August 15, 2008. https://www.theguardian.com/books/2008/aug/16/biography.politics.

Chapter 16 – General Anna Hays

"Anna Mae Hays." *The Times*, January 17, 2018. https://www.thetimes.co.uk/article/anna-mae-hays-obituary-057s5jg05.

Begley, Sarah. "This Woman Was the First Female General in the U.S. Armed Forces." *Time*, June 11, 2015. https://time.com/3916073/anna-mae-hays-female-general/.

Keller, Jared. "Anna Mae Hays, the US Military's First Female General, Has Died." *Business Insider*, January 10, 2018. https://www.businessinsider.com/anna-mae-hays-us-military-first-female-general-dies-2018-1.

Manson, Katrina. "Anna Mae Hays, the First Female US General, 1920-2018." *Financial Times*, January 19, 2018. https://www.ft.com/content/83e57eb0-fcf9-11e7-a492-2c9be7f3120a.

Roberts, Sam. "Anna Mae Hays, 97, U.S. Military's First Female General, Dies." *The New York Times*, January

10, 2018. https://www.nytimes.com/2018/01/10/
obituaries/anna-mae-hays-97-us-militarys-first-
female-general-dies.html.

Smith, Harrison. "Anna Mae Hays, Nurse Who Became
U.S. Military's First Female General, Dies at 97."
The Washington Post, January 8, 2018. https://www.
washingtonpost.com/local/obituaries/anna-mae-
hays-nurse-who-became-us-militarys-first-female-
general-dies-at-97/2018/01/08/276de52e-f48d-
11e7-b34a-b85626af34ef_story.html.

———. "Anna Mae Hays, at Age 97, Army's First
Female General - The Boston Globe." *The Boston Globe*,
January 12, 2018. https://www.bostonglobe.com/
metro/obituaries/2018/01/11/anna-mae-hays-
nurse-who-became-military-first-female-general-dies/
CRR6hM3MlZI2zf0FYRPosM/story.html.

Venditta, David. "Allentonian Anna Mae Hays, First
Female General in U.S. Armed Forces, Dies at 97."
The Morning Call, January 8, 2018. https://www.mcall.
com/news/breaking/mc-nws-anna-mae-hayes-dies-
20180107-story.html.

Chapter 17 – Diane Crump

"Diane Crump Gets to Winner's Circle, but Not in
Kentucky Derby." *The New York Times*, May 3, 1970.
https://www.nytimes.com/1970/05/03/archives/

diane-crump-gets-to-winners-circle-but-not-in-kentucky-derby.html.

Mark, Simon. "Crump, First Female Jockey, Reflects on Trail She Blazed." DRF, June 20, 2013. https://www.drf.com/news/crump-first-female-jockey-reflects-trail-she-blazed.

McKenzie, Sheena. "Jockey Who Refused to Stay in the Kitchen." Cable News Network, October 2, 2012. https://www.cnn.com/2012/09/26/sport/diane-crump-first-female-jockey/index.html.

Moss, Josh. "Meet the First Woman to Ride in the Derby." *Louisville Magazine*, April 12, 2018. https://www.louisville.com/content/portrait-diane-crump.

Chapter 18 – Carol Channing

Bergan, Ronald. "Carol Channing Obituary." *The Guardian*, January 15, 2019. https://www.theguardian.com/stage/2019/jan/15/carol-channing-obituary.

Carpenter, Les. "Carol Channing at the Super Bowl: 'It Was like an Opening Night on Broadway'." *The Guardian*, February 6, 2016. https://www.theguardian.com/sport/2016/feb/06/carol-channing-super-bowl-broadway.

Nemy, Enid. "Carol Channing Dies at 97; a Larger-Than-Life Broadway Star." *The New York Times*, January

15, 2019. https://www.nytimes.com/2019/01/15/obituaries/carol-channing-dead.html.

Obituaries, Telegraph. "Carol Channing, Sparkling Comedienne and Star of Broadway Shows Such as 'Hello, Dolly!' and 'Gentlemen Prefer Blondes' – Obituary." *The Telegraph*, January 15, 2019. https://www.telegraph.co.uk/obituaries/2019/01/15/carol-channing-sparkling-comedienne-star-broadway-shows-hello/.

Teeman, Tim. "R.I.P. Carol Channing: How The 'Hello, Dolly!' Star Became The Queen of Broadway." *The Daily Beast*, January 15, 2019. https://www.thedailybeast.com/rip-carol-channing-how-the-hello-dolly-star-became-the-queen-of-broadway.

Wiegand, Chris. "Carol Channing, Star of Hello, Dolly! on Broadway, Dies Aged 97." *The Guardian*, January 15, 2019. https://www.theguardian.com/stage/2019/jan/15/carol-channing-star-of-hello-dolly-on-broadway-dies-aged-97.

Chapter 19 – Junko Tabei

Bumiller, Elisabeth. "AT THE PEAK OF HER PROFESSION." *The Washington Post*, April 8, 1991. https://www.washingtonpost.com/archive/lifestyle/1991/04/08/at-the-peak-of-her-profession/ffa414fb-fd52-455b-b582-850dfa3c9bc9/.

Douglas, Ed. "Junko Tabei Obituary." *The Guardian*,
November 10, 2016. https://www.theguardian.com/
world/2016/nov/10/junko-tabei-obituary.

Hornyak, Tim. "Mountain High: Junko Tabei's
Adventures at the Top of the World." *The Japan Times*,
October 13, 2018. https://www.japantimes.co.jp/
culture/2018/10/13/books/mountain-high-junko-
tabeis-adventures-top-world/.

"Junko Tabei, First Woman to Conquer Everest—
Obituary." *The Telegraph*, October 28, 2016. https://
www.telegraph.co.uk/obituaries/2016/10/28/junko-
tabei-first-woman-to-conquer-everest--obituary/.

Roberts, Sam. "Junko Tabei, First Woman to Conquer
Everest, Dies at 77." *The New York Times*, October 26,
2016. https://www.nytimes.com/2016/10/27/world/
asia/junko-tabei-dead.html.

Verducci, Tom, Robert H. Boyle, Bill Colson, Richard
Deutsch, Robinson Holloway, Tim Rosaforte, Jack
McCallum, et al. "No Mountain Too High for Her Junko
Tabei Defied Japanese Views of Women to Become an
Expert Climber." *Vault*, April 29, 1996. https://www.
si.com/vault/1996/04/29/212374/no-mountain-
too-high-for-her-junko-tabei-defied-japanese-views-of-
women-to-become-an-expert-climber.

Chapter 20 – Pauli Murray

Bell-Scott, Patricia. *The Firebrand and the First Lady: Portrait of a Friendship: Pauli Murray, Eleanor Roosevelt, and the Struggle for Social Justice.* New York: First Vintage Books, 2017.

"Dr. Pauli Murray, Episcopal Priest." *The New York Times*, July 4, 1985. https://www.nytimes.com/1985/07/04/us/dr-pauli-murray-episcopal-priest.html.

Malveaux, Julianne. "The Little-Known Black Activist Who Captured a First Lady's Attention." *The Washington Post*, March 11, 2016. https://www.washingtonpost.com/opinions/the-little-known-black-activist-who-captured-a-first-ladys-attention/2016/03/10/fd995f12-d738-11e5-be55-2cc3c1e4b76b_story.html.

Schulz, Kathryn. "The Civil-Rights Luminary You've Never Heard Of." *The New Yorker*, July 9, 2019. https://www.newyorker.com/magazine/2017/04/17/the-many-lives-of-pauli-murray.

Yardley, Jonathan. "FAITH AND TRUE GRIT THE LIFE OF PAULI MURRAY." *The Washington Post*, April 5, 1987. https://www.washingtonpost.com/archive/entertainment/books/1987/04/05/faith-and-true-grit-the-life-of-pauli-murray/d09e326c-c19c-4256-85b1-d10c4f4e45c8/.

Chapter 21 – Sandra Day O'Connor

Greenhouse, Linda. "When Sandra Day O'Connor Broke Into the Men's Club." *The New York Times*, August 4, 2016. https://www.nytimes.com/2016/08/04/opinion/when-sandra-day-oconnor-broke-into-the-mens-club.html.

Haag, Matthew. "Sandra Day O'Connor, First Woman on Supreme Court, Reveals Dementia Diagnosis." *The New York Times*, October 23, 2018. https://www.nytimes.com/2018/10/23/us/politics/sandra-day-oconnor-dementia-alzheimers.html.

Liptak, Adam. "Battling Dementia, Sandra Day O'Connor Leaves Public Life With Plea for Bipartisanship." *The New York Times*, October 23, 2018. https://www.nytimes.com/2018/10/23/us/politics/dementia-sandra-day-supreme-court.html.

Lowe, Rebecca. "Supremely Confident: the Legacy of Sandra Day O'Connor | Rebecca Lowe." *The Guardian*, August 30, 2011. https://www.theguardian.com/law/2011/aug/30/us-supreme-court-george-bush.

Thomas, Evan. *First: Sandra Day O'Connor*. New York: Random House Large Print, 2019.

Toobin, Jeffrey. "An Intimate Portrait of Sandra Day O'Connor, First Woman on the Supreme Court." *The New York Times*, March 18, 2019. https://www.nytimes.com/2019/03/18/books/review/evan-thomas-first-sandra-day-oconnor.html.

Chapter 22 – Sally Ride

Borenstein, Seth and Alicia Chang. "Sally Ride, First US Woman in Space, Dies at 61." *The Boston Globe*, July 23, 2012. http://archive.boston.com/news/nation/articles/2012/07/23/sally_ride_first_us_woman_in_space_dies_at_61/.

Grady, Denise. "American Woman Who Shattered Space Ceiling." *The New York Times*, July 23, 2012. https://www.nytimes.com/2012/07/24/science/space/sally-ride-trailblazing-astronaut-dies-at-61.html.

Kluger, Jeffrey. "Tribute: Sally Ride, First American Woman in Space." *Time*, July 23, 2012. http://content.time.com/time/health/article/0,8599,2120274,00.html.

Majors, Dan. "Obituary: Sally Ride / Astronaut's Mission—Inspiring Women." *Pittsburgh Post-Gazette*, July 23, 2012. https://www.post-gazette.com/news/obituaries/2012/07/24/Obituary-Sally-Ride-Astronaut-s-mission-inspiring-women/stories/201207240183.

Ryan, Michael. "A Ride in Space." *People*, June 20, 1983. https://people.com/archive/cover-story-a-ride-in-space-vol-19-no-24/.

Sherr, Lynn. "Sally Ride's Secret: Why the First American Woman in Space Stayed in the Closet." Slate Magazine, May 30, 2014. https://slate.com/human-

interest/2014/05/sally-ride-lesbian-why-did-the-first-
american-woman-in-space-stay-in-the-closet.html

Sorkin, Amy Davidson. "The Astronaut Bride." *The New
Yorker*, June 19, 2017. https://www.newyorker.com/
news/daily-comment/the-astronaut-bride.

Turnill, Reginald. "Sally Ride Obituary." *The Guardian*,
July 24, 2012. https://www.theguardian.com/
science/2012/jul/24/sally-ride.

Chapter 23 – Wilma Mankiller

Biema, David Van. "Activist Wilma Mankiller Is Set
to Become the First Female Chief of the Cherokee
Nation." *People*, December 2, 1985. https://people.
com/archive/activist-wilma-mankiller-is-set-to-
become-the-first-female-chief-of-the-cherokee-nation-
vol-24-no-23/.

"Heart of a Nation: As Chief of the Cherokees, Wilma
Mankiller Meshes Traditional and Modern Indian
Issues. The Tribe's Strength, She Says, Lies in Self-
Determination." *Los Angeles Times*, November 1, 1993.
https://www.latimes.com/archives/la-xpm-1993-11-
01-vw-52033-story.html.

Hines, Rochelle, and Murray Evans. "Former Cherokee
Chief Dies" *Native American Times*, April 10, 2010.
https://nativetimes.com/current-news/49-life/
people/3322-former-cherokee-chief-dies.

Mankiller, Wilma, and Michael Wallis. *Mankiller: A Chief and Her People.* New York: St. Martin's Griffin, 1999.

Reinhold, Robert. "Cherokees Install First Woman As Chief Of Major American Indian Tribe." *The New York Times*, December 15, 1985. https://www.nytimes. com/1985/12/15/us/cherokees-install-first-woman- as-chief-of-major-american-indian-tribe.html.

Verhovek, Sam Howe. "At Work With: Chief Wilma Mankiller; The Name's the Most and Least of Her." *The New York Times*, November 4, 1993. https://www. nytimes.com/by/sam-howe-verhovek.

———. "Wilma Mankiller, Cherokee Chief and First Woman to Lead Major Tribe, Is Dead at 64." *The New York Times*, April 7, 2010. https://www.nytimes. com/2010/04/07/us/07mankiller.html.

Weinraub, Judith. "Mankiller." *The Washington Post*, December 10, 1993. https://www. washingtonpost.com/archive/lifestyle/1993/12/10/ mankiller/3d557ae0-2ea0-4638-b071-c3efcd24593d/.

Chapter 24 – Aretha Franklin

"Aretha Franklin: The Artist We Knew, and the Woman We Didn't." *The New York Times*, August 17, 2018. https://www.nytimes.com/2018/08/17/arts/music/ popcast-aretha-franklin.html.

"Aretha Franklin | Music." *The Guardian*, September 2009. https://www.theguardian.com/music/aretha-franklin.

Brown, DeNeen L. "How Aretha Franklin's 'Respect' Became an Anthem for Civil Rights and Feminism." *The Washington Post*, April 1, 2019. https://www.washingtonpost.com/news/retropolis/wp/2018/08/14/how-aretha-franklins-respect-became-an-anthem-for-civil-rights-and-feminism/.

Lac, J. Freedom du. "Aretha Franklin, Music's 'Queen of Soul,' Dies at 76." *The Washington Post*, August 16, 2018. https://www.washingtonpost.com/local/obituaries/aretha-franklin-musics-queen-of-soul-dies-at-76/2018/08/16/c35de4b8-9e9f-11e8-83d2-70203b8d7b44_story.html.

Pareles, Jon. "Aretha Franklin, Indomitable 'Queen of Soul,' Dies at 76." *The New York Times*, August 16, 2018. https://www.nytimes.com/2018/08/16/obituaries/aretha-franklin-dead.html.

"Pin on Inspirational People." Pinterest. Accessed September 26, 2019. https://www.pinterest.com/pin/550635491936626477/?lp=true.

Ritz, David. *Respect: The Life of Aretha Franklin*. New York: Little, Brown & Company, 2014.

Snapes, Laura, and Ben Beaumont-Thomas. "Aretha Franklin, 'the Queen of Soul', Dies Aged 76." *The Guardian*, August 16, 2018. https://www.theguardian.

com/music/2018/aug/16/aretha-franklin-queen-
of-soul-dies.

Watson, Elwood. "Aretha Franklin, Feminist and
Activist." *The Washington Post*, August 19, 2018.
https://www.washingtonpost.com/news/made-by-
history/wp/2018/08/19/aretha-franklin-feminist-
and-activist/.

Chapter 25 – Zsuzsa Polgár

Flora, Carlin. "The Grandmaster Experiment."
Psychology Today, July 1,2005. https://www.
psychologytoday.com/us/articles/200507/the-
grandmaster-experiment.

James, Oliver. "How to Raise a Brilliant Child without
Screwing Them Up." *The Guardian*, February 27, 2016.
https://www.theguardian.com/lifeandstyle/2016/
feb/27/how-to-raise-a-brilliant-child-without-
screwing-them-up.

"Susan Polgár (Polgár Zsuzsa) Was Inducted into U.S.
Chess Hall of Fame." *Hungarian Free Press*, April 2,
2019. https://hungarianfreepress.com/2019/04/02/
susan-polgar-polgar-zsuzsa-was-inducted-into-u-s-
chess-hall-of-fame/.

"Susan Polgár." Accessed September 26, 2019.
https://www.jewishvirtuallibrary.org/susan-polgar.

Chapter 26 – Janet Reno

Campo-Flores, Arian. "Janet Reno, First Female U.S. Attorney General, Dies at 78." *The Wall Street Journal*, November 8, 2016. https://www.wsj.com/articles/former-u-s-attorney-general-janet-reno-dies-at-78-1478510932.

Carlson, Michael. "Janet Reno Obituary." *The Guardian*, November 7, 2016. https://www.theguardian.com/us-news/2016/nov/07/janet-reno-obituary.

Drehle, David Von. "Why Janet Reno Mattered." *Time*, November 7, 2016. https://time.com/4561331/janet-reno-remembrance/.

Hulse, Carl. "Janet Reno, First Woman to Serve as U.S. Attorney General, Dies at 78." *The New York Times*, November 7, 2016. https://www.nytimes.com/2016/11/08/us/janet-reno-dead.html.

Newsdesk, Irish Independent. "Obituary: Janet Reno." *Irish Independent,* October 7, 2019. https://www.independent.ie/world-news/north-america/obituary-janet-reno-35210789.html.

People Staff. "Janet Reno." *People*, December 27, 1993. https://people.com/archive/janet-reno/.

Zorthian, Julia. "Janet Reno Remembered: How She Got Her Start." *Time,* November 7, 2016. https://time.com/4560767/janet-reno-early-history/.

Chapter 27 – Cristina Sánchez

"Cristina Sánchez." The Women of Action Network. Accessed September 26, 2019. http://www.woa.tv/articles/at_sanchezc.html.

Gooch, Adela. "Bullfighter Gored by Male Rivals." *The Guardian*, May 21, 1999. https://www.theguardian.com/world/1999/may/22/1.

Nash, Elizabeth. "Does Machismo Face Death in the Bullring?" *The Independent*, October 23, 2011. https://www.independent.co.uk/voices/does-machismo-face-death-in-the-bullring-1349576.html.

Philip, Robert. "Spanish See Red over Bullfight Ban." *The Telegraph*, September 4, 2007. https://www.telegraph.co.uk/sport/othersports/2320511/Spanish-see-red-over-bullfight-ban.html.

Staff, Newsweek. "A 'Sacrilege'—Or Just Bull?" *Newsweek*, November 8, 1992. https://www.newsweek.com/sacrilege-or-just-bull-196854.

Steinbreder, John, Albert Kim, Glen Craney, Leo W. Banks, E.M. Swift, Curry Kirkpatrick, Merrell Noden, et al. "A Female Bullfighter Tries to Break into a Male-Dominated Sport." *Vault*, March 9, 1992. https://www.si.com/vault/1992/03/09/126115/a-womans-place-novice-bullfighter-cristina-sanchez-intends-to-show-spains-male-matadors-that-the-bullring-is-not-their-exclusive-domain.

Vrazo, Fawn. "Female Matador Has Lots To Dodge."
Seattle Times Newspaper, September 22, 1996.
http://community.seattletimes.nwsource.com/
archive/?date=19960922&slug=2350458.

Chapter 28 – Madeleine Albright

Brockes, Emma. "I Love What I Did." *The Guardian*,
October 30, 2003. https://www.theguardian.com/
world/2003/oct/30/usa.emmabrockes.

Davies, Caroline. "Joe Just Said: 'This Marriage Is
Dead and I Am in Love with Someone Younger and
Beautiful'." *The Telegraph*, September 17, 2003.
https://www.telegraph.co.uk/news/worldnews/
northamerica/usa/1441700/Joe-just-said-This-
marriage-is-dead-and-I-am-in-love-with-someone-
younger-and-beautiful.html.

Dobbs, Michael. "Becoming Madeleine
Albright." *The Washington Post*, May 2, 1999.
https://www.washingtonpost.com/archive/
lifestyle/magazine/1999/05/02/becoming-
madeleine-albright/00193605-9959-442a-9f80-
a6a8fd55a8bf/?utm_term=.427720fbbb50.

Krum, Sharon. "Women: Madeleine Albright's New
Memoirs." *The Guardian*, September 18, 2003.
https://www.theguardian.com/world/2003/sep/18/
gender.uk.

Sciolino, Elaine. "Prepare for China Meeting. Buy Nonfat Yogurt." *The New York Times*, October 12, 2003. https://www.nytimes.com/2003/10/12/books/ prepare-for-china-meeting-buy-nonfat-yogurt.html.

Shelden, Michael. "Divorce Drove Me to the White House." *The Telegraph*, October 15, 2003. https://www. telegraph.co.uk/culture/books/3604635/Divorce-drove-me-to-the-White-House.html.

Chapter 29 – Kathryn Bigelow

Bamigboye, Baz. "James Cameron Won the Divorce... but Kathryn Bigelow Got the Oscars." Daily Mail Online, March 9, 2010. https://www.dailymail.co.uk/ tvshowbiz/article-1256505/James-Cameron-won-divorce--Kathryn-Bigelow-got-Oscars.html.

Blakeley, Kiri. "Kathryn Bigelow Vs. James Cameron: An Oscar-Themed Battle Of The Exes." *Forbes Magazine*, July 11, 2012. https://www.forbes.com/2010/02/02/ james-cameron-avatar-kathryn-bigelow-hurt-locker-forbes-woman-time-oscar-nominations.html.

Dargis, Manohla. "Action!" *The New York Times*, June 19, 2009. https://www.nytimes.com/2009/06/21/ movies/21darg.html.

Chapter 30 – Misty Copeland

Copeland, Misty. *Life in Motion: An Unlikely Ballerina*. New York: Touchstone, 2014.

Cunningham, Lillian, and Drew Harwell. "Misty Copeland Makes History as First Black Female Principal Dancer with American Ballet Theatre." *The Washington Post*, June 30, 2015. https://www.washingtonpost.com/news/on-leadership/wp/2015/06/30/misty-copeland-makes-history-as-first-african-american-to-become-principal-dancer-with-american-ballet-theatre/.

Forbes, Moira. "Misty Copeland On Shattering Stereotypes And Redefining The Future Of Ballet." *Forbes Magazine*, November 15, 2018. https://www.forbes.com/sites/moiraforbes/2018/11/15/how-misty-copeland-is-shattering-stereotypes-and-redefining-the-future-of-ballet/.

Galchen, Rivka. "An Unlikely Ballerina." *The New Yorker*, July 9, 2019. https://www.newyorker.com/magazine/2014/09/22/unlikely-ballerina.

Gregory, Sean. "How Ballet Dancer Misty Copeland Shattered Barriers." *Time Magazine*, September 21, 2018. http://time.com/5401055/how-ballet-dancer-misty-copeland-shattered-barriers/.

Kaufman, Sarah L. "Misty Copeland's New Book Offers Advice—and Perhaps False Hope." *The Washington Post*, March 23, 2017. https://www.washingtonpost.com/

entertainment/books/misty-copelands-new-book-
offers-advice--and-perhaps-false-hope/2017/03/22/
b0aa5366-0e3f-11e7-9d5a-a83e627dc120_story.html.

Keating, Caitlin. "Misty Copeland Opens Up About
the Dance Teacher Who Changed Her Life: 'She Took
a Huge Leap'." *People*, November 10, 2018. https://
people.com/human-interest/misty-copeland-teacher-
changed-life/.

La Ferla, Ruth. "The Rise and Rise of Misty Copeland."
The New York Times, December 18, 2015. https://www.
nytimes.com/2015/12/20/fashion/the-rise-and-rise-
of-misty-copeland.html.

Chapter 31 – Viola Desmond

"A Viola Desmond Primer: Who's the Woman on
Today's New Canadian $10 Bill?" *The Globe and Mail*,
November 19, 2018. https://www.theglobeandmail.
com/canada/article-viola-desmond-10-bill-explainer/.

Austen, Ian. "A Black Woman Who Defied Segregation
in Canada Will Appear on Its Currency." *The New
York Times*, March 13, 2018. https://www.nytimes.
com/2018/03/12/world/canada/viola-desmond-
currency.html.

Kassam, Ashifa. "Civil Rights Pioneer Viola Desmond
Is First Canadian Woman on Currency." *The Guardian*,
March 9, 2018. https://www.theguardian.com/

world/2018/mar/09/civil-rights-pioneer-viola-desmond-is-first-woman-on-canadian-currency.

Reynolds, Graham, and Wanda Robson. *Viola Desmond: Her Life and Times.* Blackpoint: Roseway Publishing, 2018.

Chapter 32 – Dr. Karen Uhlenbeck

"A Personal Profile of Karen K. Uhlenbeck." Department of Mathematics, University of Texas at Austin. Accessed September 27, 2019. https://web.ma.utexas.edu/users/uhlen/vita/pers.html.

Chang, Kenneth. "Karen Uhlenbeck Is First Woman to Win Abel Prize for Mathematics." *The New York Times,* March 19, 2019. https://www.nytimes.com/2019/03/19/science/karen-uhlenbeck-abel-prize.html.

Chotiner, Isaac. "A Groundbreaking Mathematician on the Gender Politics of Her Field." *The New Yorker*, March 29, 2019. https://www.newyorker.com/news/q-and-a/groundbreaking-mathematician-karen-uhlenbeck-on-the-politics-of-her-field.

Jackson, Allyn. "Celebratio Mathematica: Interview with Karen Uhlenbeck." 2018. https://celebratio.org/Uhlenbeck_K/article/634/.

O'Connor, JJ, and EF Robertson. "Karen Keskulla Uhlenbeck." September 2009. https://www-history.

mcs.st-andrews.ac.uk/Biographies/Uhlenbeck_
Karen.html.

Solly, Meilan. "Karen Uhlenbeck Is the First Woman to Win Math's Top Prize." *Smithsonian Institution*, March 20, 2019. https://www.smithsonianmag.com/smart-news/karen-uhlenbeck-first-woman-win-maths-top-prize-180971758/.

"The 2019 Abel Prize." The Royal House of Norway, May 21, 2019. https://www.royalcourt.no/nyhet.html?tid=169828&sek=27262.

About the Author

Marlene Wagman-Geller received her Bachelor of Arts from York University and her teaching credentials from the University of Toronto and San Diego State University. Currently, she teaches high school English in National City, California, and shares her San Diego home with her husband, Joel, daughter, Jordanna, cat, Moe, and dog, Harley. Reviews of her books have appeared in *The New York Times* and dozens of other newspapers such as *The Washington Post*, *The Chicago Tribune*, and *The Huffington Post*.

Please feel free to contact Marlene at :

marlenewagmangeller.com
https://www.facebook.com/marlene.wagman.5
wagmangeller@hotmail.com

Mango Publishing, established in 2014, publishes an eclectic list of books by diverse authors—both new and established voices—on topics ranging from business, personal growth, women's empowerment, LGBTQ studies, health, and spirituality to history, popular culture, time management, decluttering, lifestyle, mental wellness, aging, and sustainable living. We were recently named 2019's #1 fastest growing independent publisher by *Publishers Weekly*. Our success is driven by our main goal, which is to publish high quality books that will entertain readers as well as make a positive difference in their lives.

Our readers are our most important resource; we value your input, suggestions, and ideas. We'd love to hear from you—after all, we are publishing books for you!

Please stay in touch with us and follow us at:

Facebook: Mango Publishing
Twitter: @MangoPublishing
Instagram: @MangoPublishing
LinkedIn: Mango Publishing
Pinterest: Mango Publishing

Sign up for our newsletter at www.mango.bz and receive a free book!

Join us on Mango's journey to reinvent publishing, one book at a time.